Anderson County
Tennessee

WILLS AND
SETTLEMENTS
1830–1842

WPA RECORDS

Heritage Books
2024

HERITAGE BOOKS

AN IMPRINT OF HERITAGE BOOKS, INC.

Books, CDs, and more—Worldwide

For our listing of thousands of titles see our website
at
www.HeritageBooks.com

A Facsimile Reprint
Published 2024 by
HERITAGE BOOKS, INC.
Publishing Division
5810 Ruatan Street
Berwyn Heights, MD 20740

International Standard Book Number
Paperbound: 978-0-7884-8646-3

ANDERSON COUNTY, TENNESSEE

Matthew Rhea's Map - 1830s

RECORDS OF ANDERSON COUNTY

TENNESSEE

WILLS AND SETTLEMENTS

1830-1842

COPYING HISTORICAL RECORDS PROJECTS

WORKS PROGRESS ADMINISTRATION

Official Project No. 165-44-6999

MRS. JOHN TROTWOOD MOORE

STATE LIBRIAN & ARCHIVIST SPONSOR

MRS. ELIZABETH D. COPPEDGE

STATE DIRECTOR OF WOMEN'S & PROFESSIONAL PROJECTS

MRS. PENELOPE JOHNSON ALLEN

STATE SUPERVISOR

MRS. MARGARET HELMS RICHARDSON

PROJECT SUPERVISOR

WORKERS:

MRS. MINNIE WEBSTER

MRS. ETHEL MEREDITH

TYPISTS:

MRS. DELLA CONNER MOSER

MISS LILLIE MAY JENNINGS

Knox County

Reprinted
2012
MOUNTAIN PRESS
Post Office Box 400
Signal Mountain, Tennessee 37377-0400
423-886-6369 - office   423-886-5312- fax
www.mountainpress.com

WILLS & SETTLEMENTS

William Hogshead Will

    I William Hogshead of the County of Anderson and S tate of Tennessee do This Twenty Ninth day of January in the year of Our Lord One
Thousand Eight hundred and twenty eight Make and publish This my last
will and Testament in the following Names (to wit) I ucommend andresine
My Soul to the God of Heaven who gave it and that my body beread in
adecent Christian like way. Manner   as to all my Estate or Worldly Substance it is my Will and desire that it be disposed off in the way and
Manner herein after directed first I love and bequeath to my Daughter
Annie Hogshead all that track of land beging on Clinch river whereon
George Severs Now lives which is bounded as follows begining on the
West Camp of said river in the upper line of left # in Henderson. J.P.
Grant Thence along said Line North 4° 5 West to James Kirkpatrick Corner Thence South 4° 5 West to the line that divides said left Thence
with said division line South 4° 5 East to the Corner of Wm Seviers land
Thence with Severs line to the river Clinch Thence up the River to the
begining   I love and bequeath to My Daughter Elizabeht Hogshead all the
track of land on Clinch River by the Island ford place bounded by James
Kirkpatrick land on the South by John Scruggs on the East and Clinch river are the North as the deed to the Same will Show   it is Also My Will
and desire that my beloved wife Anne
(Pg.2) Hogshead who I do Order Counstudute and appointed hir Executor
of this My last Will and Testament Save full power and authority of all
the rusidue of my E state both real and personal to sell the Whole or in
parts and Convey the Same by deed or Otherwise and the money airising
from Such Sales to divide as Equally as preluce may direct between my
Children (to wit) John Hogshead Patience Hogshead Peggy Hogshead
William Hogshead Alexander Hogshead and Jane Hogshead or Next said
Meny in Other lands or property as in hir Description she May think last
and that property to be Divided among at last Mintioned Children a
equal as it Convenietly be done   it is my will that My beloved wife
Executrix Anne Hogshead retain out of any part of My Estate Such porton as she deem Sufficient for hir Support support during hir lifetime
provided it dose amount to More one fourth of my whole Estate which
last Mentioned property I allow at the decease of My said wife to be
equally divided amongst My Children that may then be living   as to
my legal representatizes generally it is my will and desire that my
said wife and Executrix take Care of and provide what will be a reasonable and Comfortable leaving for my Daughter Polly Hogshead during
            the lifetime of the said Polly   it is also My Wish that My
Children May be supported with there part of My Estate as soon as it
Can be Conveniently done are they may need it is also my will that
as soon as it Can be done Consistently all my Just debt
(Pg.3) be paid and those due to me Collected itis also my will and
Testament No Security Shall be required of My said Executrix for hir
faithful Executior of this my last will and testament in witness whereof I have hereunto set my hand and affixed My Seal the day and year also
written Signed and Sealed in presents of
Arthur Kirkpatrick   )
Thom Gennings   )
    Mark   )
)   Wm Hogshead   (seal)
John McAdoo   )
John McAdoo Junr.   )

John Sharp Last Will

State of Tennessee   )   January 2ond 1830
Anderson County   )
in the name of God amen I John Joseph Senoir being of said Sound and perfect mind and memory to this day and year above written make and publish
this my last will and Testament in the following manner that is today
first I give and bequeath my Soul to Almight God who gave it and my
body to the earth to be berried in a Christian like manner Secondly I
wish all my Just debts to be paid out of my Estate Thirdly I give and
bequeath to my wife Phillis Sharp hir maintanance out of the plantation
on which I now live during hir natural life the dwelling house and
guarden with such of the house hold funture as the my said wife may wish
to keep at my death for hir use during hir life with a sufficently for
hir support untill the year provisear
shall come again also one horse beast and one cow and calf choice of each
and one third part of the orchard three of my choice hogs at my Death
fourthly I give and bequeath to my Daughter Sally Norman my chest and all
the dresser ware. and one oven and larg Pot iron at the death of my said
wife and all my moveable property at my death to be equally divided amongst
my seven children to Wit. William, Johm, George, David and Nichalos Sharp
and Mary Ridenour and Sally Norman either to be sold or divided majarity
of them snall think proper except as devised before to my will and desire
that my wife and Daughter it is more over my will and desire that my
son John Sharp move and reside on the plantation on which I now live
immedately after my death that he shall take care of his Mother during hir
life that he shall pay to his brothers and Sisters thim equal proportion
of the value of the land in Six years. from the day of my death and my
said son John shall fail to pay to his said brothers and sisters their
equal proportions of the value of the land. Then the land to be equally
divided amongst them my son John being entilled to aqual part with the
rest of my children inf the division as value of the land I intend that
my son John's paying to his brothers and sisters four hundred dollars in
the above named time of six years from the day of my death that the land
shall belong to him and also that he shall maintain
his mother during hir life as a condition that the land belong to him
and that he shall he shall not pay rent during the above time and more
over I do hereby appoint John Whitson and my son John Sharp to be my
Execution of this my last will and Testament with full power and authority
to carry the same into full affect in Witness when of I the said John
Sharp seen have hereunto set my hand and seal to this my last will and
Testament the day and year above written.   )
Signed Sealed and publishedin presence of us)
Loyd Rutherford   )   John Sharp
William Weaver   )   his mark
                                                          (seal)

John Tennessee Estate
Settlement with Jesse Worthington Adm. Recorded in M. B. P. 208 Oct. 1829

Elizabeth Worthington Divided in part recorded in M. B. P. 216 Apr. 1829
Another part in M. B. P. 240 July 1829

Sherwood Bowman Estate Settlement with CY. Oliver & A. Crozier administrator of said Estate recorded in M. B. P. 230 July 1829.

Mary Haskins Estate Settlement with Geo. Haskins Adm. recorded in M. B. P
231 July 1829.

6   Inventory
            of Ann Coles Estate deceased per envoices receipt my possission
two Feather beds four Counterpaines one Piller Three bed steads 8 Cards
one Cotton wheel one table two dutch ovens 8 one llid one pair of pots
hooks one dozen puter Plates four dish Plates one dish one coffee pot
one Shovel plough two Hoes one axe Six tin cups two Pales one tub one
Churn one Keeler, two Chairs one Sifter one black bottle one Jug two
tin pans four tea cups & Saucers one pepper box one pint cup one tin
bucket one candlesticks one Candle Mould one Bible Then tawels wearing
appual one flash fork one Iron ladle one Sad Iron two Slays and harness
Strainer one Check real one bread tray one mans Saddle one table Cloth
four Kinves and forks, a bread waiter four books one pair of Spictacles
one dresser one bead tick two meal tubs one cow & calf & one yearling
one hose a fenall stock of hogs.
            July 11th 1827   J. M. Lamar
                                             Administrator

Account Current of the sale of the property Ann Cole deceased August 11th
182 7. Adkins Elijah Hars $38. 1 bread and tin ware 75 cents
Bowling Abraham 1 plough 68¼ cents 1 Pale & 1 Pint cup 50 cents 1 Check
runs 18¾ 1 pair cards 18¼ Counterpains $2.25 cents

Page 7   43cts.

Bowling Larking H 24 head hogs	6.62½
Oelph ware	1.00
1 Saddle	2.75
1 Slay	.50
Evans Carnelius 1 Sad Iron	1.06¼
Harman Powell tin wair	.62¼
Johnson William 1 arm Chair from	.18¼
Kirkpatrick James 2 towels	.37½
one bedstead & Card	2. 83¾
Kenny William 1 Cattle	.25
1 Jug	.43¾
Miller Cely 6 puter plates	1.75
Miller Jacob 6 puter plates	2.00
Miller George 1 bedstead & card	2.06¼
1 Counterpaine	3.00
Mc Ghee John 1 Bed	3.13½
1 Counterpaine	2.06¼
1 Bed Tick	1.18¾
Mc Ghee James C. 2 books	1.06¼
Praesnice Sampson 1 bed stead	
Card & tick	1. 87½
Wooden wair	.25
1 pair of gears	.25
1 bed tick	.62¼
1 tub	.25
1 Churn	.50

Philips John 1 pair of Wool Cards	12½
Miller Daniel 1 Cotton Wheel	3.00
Reynolds Delilah Tin wair	.50
3 Tubs	.50
Spesard O. John 1 Heifer	3.00
Roberts William 1 towel	.18¾
Webb George 3 hoes	.56¼
Williams Samuel 1 Oven & hooks	1.50
Wilson James H. 1 Tin Bucket	.18¾
1 Table	1.75
1 Chair	.25
1 Pillar	.12½
Wilson Abram 1 pair Spectacles	1.50
1 Song hoe	.25
Webb William 3 books	.06¼
Webb John 1 cow & calf	12.25
White John 1 Slay	.75
Warman Joseph 1 Bed	3.25
Wilson Clinton 1 pale	.25
Vandegriff William 1 ov en & led	3.00
Vandegriff John 1 axe	1.00
1 Pickle Pot	.06¼
1 Dresser	1.00
1 pair gears	1.00
Daw Wallace 35 bushels corn	5.03½

Total one hundred twenty one dollars 10¾ cents

        J. M. Lamar   121.10¾
        Administrator

Erras Excepted

A Statement of property Sold of the Estate of Powell Hugh deceased and

amount three of Coheb Butler a man's saddle	15.25
1 Sauel Horse	80.75
Jacob Butler one Broad Axe	1.00
100 Bushels Corn	25.00
1 Stack fodder	4.77
Henry Butler one Cow	6.00
Thomas Butler one stack of Rye	6.25
George Craw one tanned beast skin	2.00
Elijah Cross Machine to make Shingles	1.60
Hugh Crozier 16 Lbs. Bacon	1.33¼
2 pails	.47¼
Alexander Davidson one Axe	.50
1 Do	1.06½
1 pair gears	2.50
1 pair Harness & Collar	1.56½
1 Squar & Compass	.25
1 Bucket & Pan	.50
1 Gun	1.50
1 Black Cow & Calf	6.00
1 Prindle Bull	1.50
1 fire Shovel	.50
1 bay mare	60.00

1 Negro gire Mariah	292.20
1 Grind Stone	1.00
	368.87½
Thomas Dickey 1 Large Pot	1.62½
Samuel Dickey 1 Bedstead	.62½
Isaac Freel plains	2.50
Nancy Hughs 1 Young Cow	4.25
68 Lbs. Bacon 19cts.	6.12
Thomas Hunter 4 Hogs	1.50
2 Slays	1.62½
Alvira Hughs Bed & furniture	5.00
1 Bed	3.00
1 Cotton Wheel	1.00
1Chest	3.00
John Hughs 50 bushels corn	12.50
Peter Johnson 1 waggon	69.13
John W. Kington 2 plains	2.50
John Mc Kamey 1 Small pot	1.25
1 Blind Bridle	2.50
1 Heifer	2.10
Douglass Oliver 1 Tenant Saw	1.68¾
Richard Oliver 1 Box alensils (?)	1.25
1 Cow	6.87½
1 Calf	1.00
3 hogs	2.00
Ezra Russell 1 Brace & bits	2.75
3 Chisels	.87½
1 Jug	.13 {775½
Hary Russell 1 plain & bits	4.00
David M. Roberts 1 Shot Gun	7.56¼
William M. Roberts 2 Stacks fodder	8.01¼
Lewis Rector 75 bushels Corn	18.62½
Samuel Taylor 3 plains	2.00
1 Jointer	1.40
1 Plain & Bits	.25
Willis Syens 1 table	1.00
William Scott 3 Hogs	3.75
Joseph Vance 1 frying Pan	1.12½
5 head of Hogs	2.37½
1 Stack of Oats	4.06¼
Luther White 3 Hogs	4.56¼
James Wilson 1 Young Mare	30.31¼
Jesse Prince 27 bushels corn	5.13
David M. Roberts 1 bridle	2.12½
William A. Butler 37 Lbs. bacon	3.33
Pnicent Bennett 1 Win. Sill	1.00
	750.63

the above Statement and Calalation of the Sale of the estate of Powell
Hugh Deceased are herewith Submitted to the worshipful Court Errars
Excepted Richard Oliver administrator the above being the amount of the
Sale of the Estate of Powell Hughs deceased.(to Wit)   750.63
To cash collected from Thom. Harris Cash Collected from Jonathan Bailey

and Thom. Walker from him for waggon $5.00 To cash due and hands.
Richard Oliver $761.63
Administrator

An Inventory of the personal Estate of Moses Farmer deceased Two Negroes 4 head of Horses 13 head of Cattle 7 or 8 head of Sheep 18 head of Hogs 4 feather Beds & Furniture 1 Cupboard & Furniture 2 tables 1 Chest 1 Loom 2 wheels 1 Reel 1 Sythe 3 ploughs 3 Hoes 4 axes 2 pair of gears 1 Matack half a sat of Smith tools 1 Rifle Gun 2 Saddles 3 Bridles 2 Pots 4 ovens 2 Skillets pair of fire dogs 1 Plate iron 1 fire Shewel 1 pair of sheys Shears one case and a half
11 of Knives and forks 1 looking Glass 3 pails 3 Crocks 1 Sugar Canester 1 Honney Pot 2 Jugs 2 beegums 7 Chairs 4 Tubs 4 bedSteads 1 pot trommel with the crop that is now standing.

The demands againist the Estate of William Worthington that are property outher licated(?), (to Wit)

William Dickerson	2.33½
William Lamar	4.07½
Douglass Oliver	7.12½
John Murray	2.33¼
12 Obediah Ashlock	75
John Tovera	416¼
Soloman Allred	10
William Tunnell	600
John Ashlock	325
James Noel	425
Dennis Vann	412
John Cross	175

Schedule of the personal property directed to be sold by the last will & testament of John Sharp deceased 4 head horses to wit 3 mares & one colt 13 head Hogs, 10 head Sheep, 10 head Cattle, 2 Barr Shear ploughs, 2 Shovel ploughs 1 Bull tongue 3 hoes 3 pair traces 2 horse Collars 2 pair harness 2 back bands 2 grind Stones 1 mans Saddle 1 Still & tubs 1 Still Cutting Knife & Box 1 Dutch Scythe 1 Cross Cut Saw 1 hand Saw 2 Swingle trees 1 Shot Gun & Shot bag Powder horn & 4 Keggs 3 augers 2 Chissels 2 tumblets 1 draw Knife 2 bush Stands 2 Choppin axes 1 iron wedge 1 blough line 3 Bridles 3 Clivies

Jno. Whitson & John Sharp
Executor

Inventory of the property Sold of the Estate Aron Jenkins deceased Rebecca Jenkins part and also the purchases name s artickles prices three of June 28th 1828

Austin Jenkins 4 Hogs	631¼
13 Austin Jenkins 4 Hogs	4.25
Austin Jenkins 4 Hogs	.62½
Austin Jenkins 4 pigs	.62½
Saml. Ross 1 cow & Calf	9.00
Austin Jenkins 6 Sheep	6.50
Austin Jenkins 5 Sheep	5.00
A. Jenkins 9 Geese	2.18¾

A Jenkins 1 Steer	7.06¼
A Jenkins 1 Steer	4.93¼
J. R. Edmundson 1 Colt	27.10
A Jenkins 1 Scythe & Cradle	3.00
A Jenkins 30 pounds of Bacon	2.10
James Childress 7 lbs. of Lard	.42
Austin Jenkins 4 bushell	1.48
Caty Jenkins & furniture	22.70
Caty Jenkins looking glass	.16

The above Inventory Correct) J. R. Edmundson
) Stephen Marshall

A list of the amount of sale of the Estate of Elijah Black deceast 1828

Joseph Keeny to one Shovel plough Clevis Sueintrees	1.25
Joseph Keeny to one Bull tongue	37½
Samuel Moore one pair of tree chains	1.30
John Harrill 2 Swingtrees	.50
Richard Adkins to one Pot	.18½
George Webb double tree	.62½
Joseph C. Moore one oven & lid	.12½
George Miller one Skillet	.62½
Tobitha Bratcher to one dish & bacon	32
James Kirkpatrick to plates	87½
Aron Slaver to two Hamr	50
Tobitha Bratcher to one axe	18¼
Banister Vowell to one Colt	6.50
Aron Slover to one Pot rack	1.06¼
Tobitha Bratcher to one table	1.63¼
George Miller to one Chest	2.67¼
Joseph C. Moore to one bed	2.25
Tobitha Brather to one dish	1.00
Tobitha Brather to one dresser	51
Aron Slover to one proe(?)	40
Samuel Moore to one wedge	40
John Harrell to one bason	41
James Kirpatrick to one Shingles	1.37½
Samuel Moore to one Bee Stand	31¼
James Kirpatrick to one Sheep	1.12½
Joseph C. Moore Heifer	4.43
James Kirpatrick to one Cow & Bull	8.75
John Leach to one cow	6.00
William Webb to one cow	7.81
William Webb to one cow	8.00
Joseph C. Moore to one Steer	4.00
George Webb to one yearling	215
Joseph C. Moore firs lot of Hogs	10.00
Tobitha Bratcher 2 lot of Hogs	8.12
Tobitha Bratcher 3 lot of Hogs	2.6¼
Tobitha Bratcher to one side Saddle	4.25
Aron Slover to one Auger	12½

J. C. Moore & James Kirkpatrick
Administrator of Elijah Beach deceased

8   **ANDERSON COUNTY, TENNESSEE - Wills and Settlements - 1830 - 1842**

****

15   The Executor of the last will & Testment of John Sharp deceased beg leave
to make the following return of the personal property which was sold
aqueally which was sold to the directions in the said last will & testment
to the honorable the County Court of Anderson at thire July term 1830

Articls Sold

one pair drawing chains	75¢
1 do do	65
1 do do	2.00
1 Lock Chain	75
2 Augers	68¾
2 do	46¼
2 Chissels	37½
1 Hammer & Stake	33¼
3 Clevises	50
1 Chopping Axe	87½
1 do do	50
1 do & Branding iron	80
1 froe & draw knife	20
2 Saw plats & iron wedge	40
1 hoe & Sundries	25
1 Bull tonge	25
1 Shovel Mould	25
1 dutch Scythe	1.50
3 Collars & 2 back bands	57¼
2 Swingle trees	1.00
1 Barr Shear plough	1.00 ⊃ B
2 Briddles	12½
3 Bridles	26
1 Bell	20
1 do	50
1 Cutting Knife & Box	75
1 Sang hoe	12½
1 man's Saddle	1.25
1 Loom	2.75
1 Kag	36
1 do	52
1 do	38
1 do	.50
1 do	65
1 do	68¾
1 Barrel	50
1 Shot Gun	3.75
1 pair of Still yards	2.75
1 Still Cap & worm	5.50
1 Still tub	25
1 do	38¼
1 do	50
1 do	50
3 tubs & 1 water pump	37½
1 Bee Stand	1.25
1 do do	1.48¾
1 do do	1.75
15 Hogs	7.00

	15 Hogs	7.00
16	4 Sheep	2.88¾
	4 do	2.52
	4 do	2.56
	1 yearling Calf	1.56¼
	1 Cow	5.18¾
	1 Heifer	5.25
	1 do	4.56
	1 yearling	1.93¾
	1 do	2.12½
	1 cow & calf	5.56¼
	1 Heifer	3.50
	1 yearling	2.00
	1 Bull	8.06¼
	1 Mare	21.18¾
	1 Mare & Colt	40.00
	3 Still tubs 27-25-06¼	.58¼
		165.69 1/5

The above amount is secured by bond and good Security payable in twelve months from the 13th day of May 1830 the Executor would further State to the Honarable Court thire is yet to be sold a small balance of the personal property which will be done in the due time (to Wit) one mare and a few small articles which were not found on the day of sale with the other property John Whitson

John Sharp
Executor

Dr. Abner Farmer and Ninian Roberts Adms. Account Current with the Estate Moses Farmer deceased to amount sals as per Clerks certificator $22,46/06
To the amount collected from John Foster in part of his nots given to the deceased   30.00
To balance of Fosters nots an collection   64.62
To amount collected from Benjamin P. Heakney an a
note givin to the deceased   8.12 1/5

Amt. of Debt		13,48.80½
17	By Cash paid Samuel C. Young for Servias as Clerk at the Sale	$2.50
	By Dr. James King for attending the deceased	18.00
	By Cash paid Clerk County Court	4.12½
	By Cash paid J. R. Edmundson Ink. at Sale	2.50
	By Services and Expenses allowed Abner Farmer for attending to business of said Estate	21.00
	By Cash pd. Clerk Commissioner for Settlement	5.00
	By Cash pd. Clerk of Knox County for recording Deed for Conveyance	.45
	By Balance of John Foster Notes in the hands an officer for Collection	62.64
	Amt. of Credits	134.19½
		13,48.80½

By amount the hands of the administrater a
    appears an Settlement   1214.61
given under an hand this 10th day April 1830

                    Saml. Dunn   )
                    John Chiles   )   Commission
                    Michall Clardy   )

Clerk fee for recording the above Sixty two and a half cents.
                    J. Harding D. Clk.

18   An Pursuance to an order from the worshipful Court of pleas and Quarter
        Sessions for Anderson County Tennessee was undersigned Commissioners have
        proveded to Settle with Jesse Wothington & William Tunnell the Executor
        of the last will and Testament of William Worthington deceased which is
        following to Wit.

        Jesse Worthington & William Tennell Executor of the Estate of William
        Worthington deceased Dr per Statement from the Clerk of said Court
                                                  $ 182.20½

        To discharge the above demand the Executoes tender the following vouchers
        (to Wit) ft one proven account of William Lemar for 2) recept R. M.
        Anderson 500.00 3) one proven ak of A. B. Ashlock for. 75
        4th one proven ak of Dennis Vann   4.62½
        5th one do do of Buck Johnson   1.43 3/7
        6th one do do of Dickson Jarnagin   2.33¼
        7 one Do ak of William C. Griffith   2.00
        8 one do Bill to John Cross with Interist   2.00
        9th an proven ak of John Ashlock   3.25
        10th one due Bill to Solomallred with enterst   10.95
        11th one proven of Solom Allred   1.00
        12th one due Bill to D. Oliver   7.00
        13th Receipt for D. Oliver   .12½
        14th one proven ak of Charles Price   1.25
        15th one do ak of John Taverea   4.16 2/3
        16th one proven ok of John Maury   2.33 1/3
        17th one do ok of Wm. Tennell   6.00
19   18th by Clerk Receipt   2.50
        19th one proven ok of James Noel   4.62½
        20th by Note on Betsey Worthington   68.42
            Widow and Guardian   13.50
        21th by note Betsy Worthington the Guardian & Isaac
            Sartain   30.80
        22th by note on Susannah Underwood
                    William Tunnell   5.50
        23 bym note on John Tandulds on Titus England   2.75
                                                   _____

                    Balance due   120.97

The amount as per Settlement of the Clerk as aforesaid

182.20½

Cr. by amount vouchers   120.97

brought down which leaves a balance remaining in   61.23½
          the hands of the Executor   61.23½
All of which are respectfully submitted 10th July 1830
                              Richard Oliver   )   Commissioner
                              John Chiles   )

Will of William Scarbrough Sen. in the name of God I William Scarbrough
Senior of the County of Anderson in the State of Tennessee being weak in
body but of Sound memery do make and ordain thir my last will and
Testament hereby revoking all farm wells in the first place I recommend
my Soul to the Allmighty God and my body to be dicently committed to the
earth.   Secondly it is my wish and command that all deeds of land heretofore made by me to my respective children together with all personable
property whats over which I have from time to given to them be hereby
confirmed to them never hereafter to be recanclled by law or otherwise
in the next place all the property that I am now prossessed with I require
may be sold reasanable credit and the proceeds thereof to be equally
divided thereof to be equally divided amongst my children in Witness
where of I have hereunto set my hand and seal this 4th day of June in the
year of our Lord one thousand eight hundred and thirty
      Signed Sealed and delivered in person of Geo. Gordon   )
                              Henry Peters Senr.) Wm. Scarbrough
                              Thomas Peters   )   his mark
                                                   (Seal)

I moreover appoint as an appendage to the within mentioned will Charles
Y. Oliver and Aurthur Crozier Esq. Executors of this my last will &
Testament witness my hand & Seal this fourth day of June 4th 1830.
in person of Geo. Gordon   )
          Henry Peters Senr.)   William Scarbrough
          Thomas Peters   )   his Mark
                                     (seal)

Anderson County July Sessions 1830. I certify that the within
I desire that my mother be supported during her life.

Will was duly proven in open Court by two of the Subscribing Witnesses
thireto and ordered to be recorded.
                              Hn. Barton Clk.
                              by his Depety
                              J. Harding

Additional Inventory of Ann Coles property Deceased 35 bushels of Corn.
                         J. M. Lamar
                         Administrator

Tobias Peters Will in the name of God Amen
      Tobias Peters of the County of Anderson an State of Tennessee being
Sick and weak of body but of Sound mind and disposing memory for which

I think God and calling to mind the uncertainly of human life and being
dangerous to dispose of all Such worldy Substance as it has pleased God
to help me with I give and bequath the same in manner and form following
that is to say I give and bequath to my Rachel that part of my land which
lies on the South Side of the Creek for hir Support but not granding hir
the liberty of Selling the same I desire also my children which have not
received any part of the Estate shall have in proportion with those that
have received I desire the ballance of the Estate be sold and Equal
division made amongst the heirs. and lastly I do constitute and appoint
my two sons James Peters & John Peters Executres of this my last will
and Testament and also Guardian for my Daughter Rachael in Testemony
where of I have hereunto set my hand & Seal this 25th of January 1831
Signed and acknowledged in the presents of us Robert Galbreath , Samuel
Tunnell.

Tobiah Peters
his mark
(Seal)

22   Inventory of the estate of William Lamor Deceased

James Moore 1 bare Shear Plow	1.56¼
Eli Rhea 1 Plow	.50
Charles Lullen 1 Plow	2.06¼
Richard Taylor 1 Plow	.65¼
John Rhea 1 cuttin knife & Box	1.43¾
Polly Lamor 1 flat Break	.50
James Lamor 1 plow	1.56¼
Polly Lamor 1 plow	1.56¼
James Lamor 1 Mattack	1.12½
Polly Lamor 1 Mattack	.87½
Polly Lamor 1 hoe	.25
Polly Lamor 1 hoe	.25
James Lamor 1 hoe	.12½
Moses Overton 1 hoe	.12½
Polly Lamor 1 Axe	.12½
William Dale 1 Axe	.18 1/3
Elijah Adkins 1 Shovel	.50
William Dale 1 Shovel & Single tree	.41¼
John M. Lamor 1 broad axe	3.00
Polly Lamor 1 Axe	1.06 1/3
Polly Lamor 1 Axe	.93¾
Polly Lamor 1 Axe	1.06¼
James Lamor 1 Axe	1.12½
William Dale 1 Axe	.50
Alijah Adkins 1 Spade	.56¼
Polly Lamor 2 Single trees	.62½
James Overton 2 Single trees	.57¼
Charles Luallen 1 double tree	.41
23 Samuel Moore 1 Axe	1.25
	————————
	24.83¼
Moses Moore 1 Plow	.56¼
Polla Lamor 1 Plow	.68¾

****

Polly Lamor 1 Plow	.63
William Mc Adoo 1 Plow	1.12½
William Severs Sen. 1 Sythe & cradle	.37½
Isaac Foster 1 Sythe	.75
Polly Lamor 1 grind Stone	.57
Charles Lamor 1 pr Stillgrads	3.37½
Polly Lamor 1 small pr Stillgards	2.06¼
George Moore 1 pr gears	3.12½
Elijah Adkins 1 Set bridle Leathing	1.12½
George Moore 2 Neck Chains	1.18¾
Mastin Hill 1 Neck Chain	.81¼
Henry Mc Coy 1 Neck Chain	1.25
Polly Lamor 1 pr. gurs	4.06¼
Polly Lamor 1 pr gurs	3.12½
James Lamor 1 Cow & Calf	8.00
Polly Lamor 1 Cow & Calf	6.56½
Richard Taylor 1 Cow & Calf	8.06¼
William Sivers Sen. 1 Cow & Calf	7.25
Sib Baley 1 Cow & Calf	5.50
Thomas Dikes 1 Cow & Calf	8.31¼
Charles Lamor 1 Cow & Calf	8.25
Polly Lamor 1 Cow	6.00
Polly Larmor 1 Cow & Calf	7.06¼
Thomas Dikey 1 Cow & Calf	9.06¼
Polly Lamor 1 Cow	4.50
Samuel Moore 1 Cow	5.62½
James Lamor 1 Cow	5.55
Polly Lamor 1 Cow	5.06¼
Polly Lamor 2 Steers	11.00
	112.96

24	Amt. prot forward	112.99
	James Larmor 1 Steer	5.50
	William Roysden 1 Heifer	4.12½
	Samuel Moore 1 Steer	3.37½
	Samuel Moor 1 Heifer	2.31¼
	Sib Baley 1 Heifer	1.78
	Polly Lamor 1 Heifer	1.25
	Sib Baley 1 Heifer	2.00
	James Moore 1 Heifer	1.50
	James Moore 1 Heifer	1.50
	Sib Baley 1 Heifer	.81
	Polly Lamor 1 Heifer	1.06¼
	John Severs 1 Steer	3.56¼
	John Severs 1 Steer	1.87½
	Mastin Hill 1 Heifer	1.00
	Moses Overton 2 Steers	3.62½
	Lawson Fawler 2 Steers	3.50
	Sib Baley 1 Steer	.88
	Martin Hill 1 Bull	1.50

Richard Scruggs 1 Steer	2.00
Martin Hill 1 Heifer	1.89
Samuel Edminson 1 pecee(?) leather	.90
James Lamor 1 pr leather	2.00
John Childress 1 pr Leather	3.06¼
Polly Lamor 1 pr Leather	2.18¾
Samuel Edminson Leather	2.07½
Samuel Edminson Leather	1.06
John Rains 1 Earrsole & harness	68.00
George Moore 109 lbs. bacon	10.90
James Lamor 108 lbs. bacon	10.80
James Lamor 109Lbs. bacon	11.23½
James Lamor 95 Lbs. bacon	10.45
	$ 331.87

25	Amt. brot forward	331.87
	Samuel Moore 1 Sugar	.81¼
	James Lamor 1 Mare	46.47½
	Ann Wheeler 1 Sorrel Mare	40.00
	Polly Lamor 1 Mare	30.50
	Polly Lamor 1 horse	60.12½
	Wallace Dew 1 horse	62.00
	Wallace Dew 1 horse	29.50
	Wallace Dew 1 horse	28.00
	John M. Lamor 1 Mare	25.25
	Polly Lamor 1 Mare	26.00
	John Dew 1 Colt	10.00
	Hugh B. Lamor 1 Colt	10.00
	John Taylor 5 Sheep	3.00
	Caleb Moore 4 Sheep	2.26
	Richard Scruggs 1½ bushel	.18¾
	James Moore 1 double tree	.12
	James Lamor 1 bed & furnature	3.00
	Polly Lamor 1 Water Pail	.13
	Wm. Smith 1 Iron Wedge	.61
	Polly Lamor 3 Vessels	.57
	Richard Scruggs 1 Wedge	.41¼
	Polly Lamor 2 Vessells	.14
	James Lamor 1 Leather Line	.75
	Hugh B. Lamor case Razors	1.25
	Wm. Mc Cormack 1 Coffee pot	.62½
	Polly Lamor 1 Coffee Pot	.25
	Polly Lamor 1 Un bucket	.25
	Polly Lamor 1 Tea Kettle	1.00
	Elijah Adkins 1 Pot Rack	1.75
	Polly Lamor 1 Pot Rack	1.08½
	Polly Lamor 1 oven & led	.85
	Polly Lamor 1 oven & led	1.12½
		689.73½
	Amt. brot forward	689.73½

26   Amt. brought forward $689.73½

      Polly Lamor 1 kettle & lid   .62½
      Polly Lamor 1 Skillet & lid   1.00
      William Dale 1 washing tub   .49
      John R. Edmondson 1 pot & hook   1.50
      William Seivers Junr. 2 wash tubs   .33½
      William Dale 1 sad iron   .56¼
      Isaac Foster 1 pr pot hooks   .32½
      Richard Quallen 1 pot & hooks   1.12½
      Richard Taylor 1 bee Stand   1.80
      William Mc Adoo 1 book   1.50
      George Smith 1 book   1.75
      Elijah Adkins 1 book   1.56½
      Absolum Bowling 1 book   .50
      Henry Mc Coy 1 book   .50
      Polly Lamor 6 book   .50
      Polly Lamor 1 book   .12½
      Ausberry R. Moore 3 book   .26
      Jefferson Smith 1 book   1.50
      Polly Lamor 2 books   .25
      Polly Lamor 1 cupboard & furniture   4.25
      Polly Lamor 1 chest   5.12½
      Polly Lamor 1 bed & furniture   10.00
      Polly Lamor 1 chest   1.50
      Polly Lamor 1 bed & furniture   6.12½
      Polly Lamor 1 bed & furniture   12.25
      James Moore 1 bed & furniture   5.50
      Charles Lamor 1 cross cut saw   1.00
      Polly Lamor 1 cotton wheel   1.00
      Polly Lamor 1 flax wheel   1.00
      James Lamor 1 flax wheel   2.81½
      William Ervin 1 cotton wheel   1.12½
                                                              $766.39½
27   Polly Lamor 1 cotton Wheel   1.43 3/3
      James Larmor 1 set of B. Smith tools   31.56½
      George Moore 1 Jack Saw   3.87½
      Caswell Mayberry 1 iron tooth harrow   3.50
      Polly Lamor 1 kettle & hooks   2.63½
      Polly Lamor 1 oven   .63
      Polly Lamor 1 washing tub   .25
      Charles Lamor 1 log chain   2.56½
      Polly Lamor 1 pot & hook   .50
      Isaac Foster 1 small kettle   .62½
      Joseph Overton 1 hide   2.32¼
      Charles Quallen 89 bu. corn 31¢   27.84½
      Richard Quallen 50 bu. corn 35¢   17.50
      William M. Cormac 50 bu. corn 31¢   15.62½
      James Lamor 50 bu corn 36¢   18.00
      Polly Lamor 1 wagon   30.06 1/3
      Wallace Due 1 wagon   105.00
      Richard Scruggs 1 Hay fork   .50
      Elijah Adkins 1 Hay fork   .50

Ansbern R. Moore 1 Yoke Steers		30.38½
John M. Lamor 1 Bee Stand		1.00
Anderson Landrum 2 Bee Gums		.25
Isaac Foster 2 tubs & saddle		1.06¼
Isaac Foster 1 hand Saw		.75
William Smith 1 hand Saw		.76
William Severs Junr. 1 inch Anger		.50
Sib Bailey 1 draw Knife		.57
James Lamor 1 hammer		1.25
Joseph Overton 1 parcel Iron		.50
28	John Severs Iron	.81¼

```
                                              1090.15
Amt. brot forward                             1090.15
```

Charles Lamor 1 lot of Hogs	12.06¼
Samuel Moore 1 lot of Hogs	15.75
Polly Lamor 1 lot of Hogs	12.37½
Charles Lamor 1 lot of hogs	17.06¼
George Moore 1 lot of hogs	23.75
Elijah Adkins 2 tubs	1.00
William Dale 1 hoe	.13
Elijah Adkins 2 tubs	.56¼
William Dale 1 ½ bushel	.32¼
Abraham Bowling 1 bu (?) 37½¢	3.75
John Severs 1 beef hide	5.75
Samuel Edmonson 1 pr dog Iron	2. 19 1/3
John Childress 1 Shovel	.68 1/3
Polly Lamor 2 Ladles & fork	.25
Polly Lamor 2 candle sticks & Pan	.20
John Childress 1 pr dog Iron	.56½
Polly Lamor 1 Puter Bason	1.75
Polly Lamor 1 Puter Bason	1.88½
George Moore 1 puter Bason	2.12½
Samuel Edminson 1 pr Mattres Saddle	.37½
James Lamor 1 lock & Key	.54
Polly Lamor 2 Crocks & Strainer	. 12½
Polly Lamor 1 Churn	.12½
Elijah Adkins 1 Whiskey Lard(?)	.25
Soloman Webber 1 tin Pot	.37½
James Still 1 Still 66 Mash tubs	37.50
Charles Lamor 1 Still 6 Mash tubs	25.00
Charles Lamor 1½ gallon measure	.12½
John Dew 28 Lb. Iron 5¼¢	1.47½
John Cox 1 Sythe Anvil	.31
John Ray 2 Sythes	.26
Samuel Moore 1 Skillet lid 8 wash bowl	.36
	1258.99¾

29	John Ray 1 Set of Spools	.27
	John Cox 1 Chisel	.40
	Caswell Maberry 1 Soap Iron	.50

Polly Lamor 1 Shovel Maul	.54
Samuel Moore 1 bell	.50
John R. Edmonson 1 bell	1.25½
William Severs Sen. 1 Mans Saddel	3.06¼
John M Lamor 1 Keag	.50
Wallace Dew 1 Tub of Tar	.12½
Hugh B. Lamor 1 reap Hook	.26
Thomas Lamor 1 reap hock	.12
John Rhea 2 reap hooks	.12½
John Rhea 2 reap hooks	.19¾
William Severs 2 meal bags	.25
John Rhea 2 meal bags	1.00
Polly Lamor 2 Slays 1 pr gurs	.25
James Lamor 1 Armid Chair	.58
Polly Lamor 8 Chair fraims	.75
John M. Lamor 1 howe	1.12½
John Cox 1 hip Strap	.61¼
Polly Lamor 9 Chairs	1.00
William Severs 1 Box	.12½
John Taylor 1 Bull	8.50
Wallace Dew 1 waggon Standard	.06½
James Moore 1 Cake Tallow	2.18¾
James Moore 1 Cake Tallow	1.23½
William Severs 1 double tree & band	.50
William Severs Junr. 1 Meal bag	.37
Charles Lamor 6 pr. Gurs	1.50
	1287.50
Amt. brot forward	1287.50
Wallace Dew 18 pr Gars	$ 3.00
John Dew Balland of Gars	.37
Hugh B. Lamor 3 bridle	.25
John M. Lamor 1 Cradle Simpson	.50
George Moore Rqeat 33¢ pr.	
John M Lamor 2 tubs	.50
Polly Lamor 1 Meal bag	.50
Polly Lamor 1 Shelf	.12½
Polly Lamor 1 Table	m1.00
Richard Taylor Parcel leather	2.25
Polly Larmor 3 tubs	.50
Polly Lamor 2 Meal bags	1.00
Polly Lamor 2 tubs & bunch wheat	.25
William Senr. Severs 1 looking glass	.32
Polly Lamor 1 table Cloth	2.00
Polly Lamor 2 table Cloth	1.00
Polly Lamor 1 Loom & bars	1.00
Polly Lamor 1 table cloth	.25
William Severs Junr. 1 hammer	.51
Cawell Maberry 1 box Scraps	.31
Sib Bailey 1 Bell	.31
James Moore 1 Bill	.15
	1302.89¾

30

Total amount not added   54
                J· M. Lamer
                Administrator

                Polly Lamer
                Administrative
April 11th 1831
                                            _____
                                            $1303.60

31   Inventory of property brough the Sale of John Spessard Dec'd. on the 29
        8:30 of October 1830
                    Elizabeth Spessard

        2 Bells & Collars   . 44
        2 pr haims Chains & Collars   1.93¾
        1 Blind Bridle   .25
        1 Kettle   1.00
        1 Axe   .62½
        1 Old Axe & Streachers   1.18¾
        1 fifth Chain   .81¼
        1 Bee hive & Wheel Barrow   1.00.
        1 Cow   4.00
        1 horse   20.00
        1 horse   31.00
        1 drawing Knife 2 Angers hand axe
         2 Chisels & hammer   3.25
        Puter Knife forks & Spoons   4.00
        1 pair Stell gards   1.25½
        1 washing tub & some others   .06¼
        2 Small tin trunks   .25
        1 German bible & Six other G Books   .06¼
        1 flax wheel & Cotton Wheel   1.50
        1 L Saddle   4.00
        1 Small Pot and Oven   .58
        1 Small Skillet and Oven   .25
        1 Camp Kettle   .50
        1 tea Kettle 2 leads   .56¼
        1 Coffee Mill and Candle Stick & whip Clamp .50.
        2 flat hackles   2.00
32   Cotton in the seed   3.67
        bed and furnature & Stead   4.75
        1 do do   2.00
        1 do do   3.18¼
                                                _____
                                                102.66¾

        Absolum Bowling
        2 Coulters   .43¾
        1 Pot and bails   .87½

        Joseph Stout
        1 Sythe & Cradle   .25

Joseph L. C. Moore
1 Anger Chesil & $ .06¼
2 hoes   .37½
1 Cow   6.56½
1 hand Saw   1.26
fire dogs   .06¼
George Winton
2 Plows Shovels & 1 Mattock   1.00
1 Still 4 tubs Kigs   32.50
Samuel Robbins
1 Stone hammer   .43¾
                                                    3.18¾

1 Cupboard
James Ross
1 Sprouting hoe   .25
1 Waggon   20.18¾
George Webb
1 Mattock haims   .18¾
2 Small Heifers   3.75
Samuel Moore 1 Sickle   .06¼
John Severs
1 Cotton line hains Chain   .87½
33   1 grind Stone   .56¼
1 Copper Gallon & fund.   .49
1 Plow tree & Clevis   1.26
2 barrels to hoes   1.01
Same Iron padlock   1.12½
1 Chair Seissors looking glass & Book   .46
fork brand Iron & Bails   .40
Saddle and breachere   .15
Fredrick Shenliver
1 Sythe & Anville   .12½
1 Cockle Sifter   1.25
Mastin Hill
1 hoe & dung fork   .37½
John Hogshead
1 Single Tree   .25
1 W Whip   .76
1 Jointer   .13½
1 Plaine   .25
1 Broad Axe   2.81½
1 Iron Squar   .41
Samuel Dunn
1 grind. Stone & Crank   .62½
1 pr breach bands   8.31¼ - 8.93 2/4
Williams Stephens
1 hog Clamp   .05
Michael Spessard
1 log Chains   4.00
2 tubs & some leather   .18¾
                                                   -4.18¾

William Mc Kamey
1 Carring Knife   .12½
Jacob Vandegriff
1 Heifer & 1 Steer 4.75   4.77

	Adovijoh Thomas		
	1 Heifer	1.06¼	
	8 head of Sheep	6.06¼	
		7.12½	
34	John Miller 1 Cow	6.00	
	2 Calves	2.73½	
	1 Small Heifer	.61½	
	1 horse	17.12½	
	1 Table	.12½	
	Cups & Saucers	.56¼	
	1 table pale & Cup	.12½	
	7 Chairs Book & State	.62½	
	1 Bead furnature & Sted	6.00	
	1 Shest	3.27	
	33 head Geese	6.00	
	Some Oats	51.45	15½
			75
	John Milikin and axe		
	John Vandegriff		
	2 wedges & faules Coulter	1.00	
	1 Mare	13.31¼	
			14.31¼
	Charles Luallen		
	1 - 65 Gal. Still	25.25	
	Sterling Smith	12.91	
	John Dew	1.81¼	
	William Lynard	.50	
	William Webb	1.06¼	
	John Luallen	.68¾	
	M. Smith	1.18¾	
	John Payne	1.25	
	John Lynard	6¼	
	William Mc Kamly	.25	
	Hugh Melican	6.97¾	
	Jacob Clodfetler	.12½	
	Larkin Bowling	4.32	
	William Melican	4.12½	
35	John Johnson	2.14	
	Polly Miller	1.06¾	
	Aggregate		
		$ 336.27¾	
	The above Sum is the amount of property sold on the 29th , 30th day October 1830.		
	John Severs	5.04	
	Larkin H. Bowling	9.98¾	
	Elizabeth Spessard	3.50	
		354.82¾	
	Amt. of sale		
	Amt. due on the Estate by Notes	17.00	
		371.82¾	

Samuel Dunn
    Administrator

An account of the sale of the personal property of the Estate of John
Sampson decd.

Martha Tompson	$491.69½
Jesse Noel	37.40
Thomas Wilson	.74
Samuel Galbreath	.18¾
John Tompson	471.86¾
Willis W. Talley	3.20
John Parks	.77
Andrew Tompson	145.01½
Joseph Black	85.12½
David Rector b	4.50
Arthur Crozier	34.43
Nancy Thompson	78.00
Martha Thompson	32.25
Margaret Thompson	80.51¼
George Winton	58.96½
William T. Gevers	13.07¼
	————
	1537.72¼

36   Amount brough over 1537 - 72

Austin Jenkins	3.17
Benjamin Graves	5.25
Neucon Roberts	5.06½
Richard Oliver	8.78¾
Elias Butler	1.06¼
John Childress	1.00
John Cox	.63
Waller Vann	3.25
Samuel Frost	1.90
Sarah Thompson	1.91½
John Nickle	1.57
James Black	1 0.00
William B. Carnes	1.25
Harvey Russell	.18½
Lazarus Moore	.41
John Oneel	.70¼
Hannah Thompson	8.00
Eli Norman	.82
Douglass Oliver	.17
Jacob Rector	2 0.00
Moses Roberts	4.70
Jacob Rector	50.17
William Scott	2.01
William M. Rector	29.00
William M. Rankins	1.06½
James Brown	.06¼
James H. Black	5.06¼

Dennis Vann
George Winton

25.80
$ 1732.95¼

Alexander Davidson aquartely if ways
    the mumber no know at 15 pr. cent
    William Griffith and stock of way
    15 pr. Bu.

37   Peter Elrod Dr. by acpt. 6.78¾
        Hardy Marshall do   8.81¼
        William Gorsough & John White by note 3.55
        William Gorsough by account 24.00
        Henry Edwards by acpt.   1.75¾
        James Edwards do   4.50
        The Estate of William Thompson do 143.62½
        John Merry do   2.80¾
        Robert & Samuel Mc Campbell by note 50.00
        Elijah Morse do   13.33
        Thomas Gardner do   17.00
        Abner Farmer & Benj. Hackney do 60.00
        Benjamin P. Hackney & Abraham Sinclair 10.64
        George Graves do   60.00
        Thomas Mouston Senr. & Junr.   91.68
        John Bradshaw do   .75
        Coleman Pare do   2.00
        Philip Mulky .   3.25
        Abraham & James Sinclair 37.00
        Jacob Buttler   18.00
        Joseph Parks   43.00
        Elijah Frost   1.00
        John Cross   2.00
        William Henderson &
        William Morton   41.00
        Chesley Pendleson   1.00
        John Glass   63.00
        John & Isaac & Jas. Glass 25.00
        Robert Dickson   7.00
        Daniel Yarnall 2 Notes 150.00
        John Campbell & Stephen
          Marshall & J. Chiles 100.00

                                ─────────
                                1117.49

38   Amount brough over $ 1117.49
        Hardy F. Marshall &
        Stephen Marshall   100.00
        Hardy F. & Richard
          Marshall   100.00
        Hardy F. Marshall   59.58
        Benjamin Duret forfuting 800.00
          a pnalbox
        Amount of Money on hand 1282.62
        Alexander Davidson Acpt. 29.95
          the amt. brot from   1117.49
              36th page $47o7.13

The last Will & Testament of Daniel Teller in the name of God I Daniel
Teller of Anderson County & State of Tennessee being weak in body but
in perfect mind & Memory pleased be Almighty God do this Nineteenth
day of July 1830 make and establish this my last will and Testament
in maner and from as follows ftrst it is my desire that all my Just debts
be paid Secondly it is my will that my Daughter Elizabeth Teller have
my Sorrel horse & one cow & calf it is my will that the ballance of my
property both real & personal shall be & remain in the hands of my beloved
wife Rebecca Teller so long as she lives or remain a widow and at hir
death or marrage the property all to be equally divided amongst four of
my children Thomas H. Teller, Elizabeth H. C. Teller, Lewis C. Teller &
Stephen T. Teller & my son Daniel Teller wish to receive five dollars which
will make a full shear with what he has alread received also the heirs

39   of my daughter Nancy to receive five dollars & lastly I appoint my two
sons Thomas H. Teller & Stephen T. Teller my executors to this my last
will & Testament I witness where of I have here unto set my Seal this 19th
day of July 1830.
William Tennell   Daniel Teller
Jesse Noel   his X mark
Thomas Peters   (Seal)

John Mc Adoo will in the name of God Amen I John Mc Adoo Senior of the
County of Anderson and State of Tennessee being of sound mind & memery
being in advanced years & feeling from the cause of nature that I cannot
live very long and feeling deserous to regulate my temporal affairs do
hereby make ordain & constitute this my last will and Testament teraking
all others by me heretofore made first it is my wish that all my Just
debts be paid living my wife Martha a Childs part of all my real and
personal Estate unless she should feel better satisfied to but hir part
with mine in the hands and popepion of our son William Mc Adoo & in that
event he my said son William to find hir deacent Support during hir
natural life it would be most agreeable to my wishes that she would embrace
the latter she being old and verry enfirm so my son John Mc Adoo Jun.
Myra Fench my Daughter & wife of Aron Finch & Eliza Mc Adoo my youngest
Daughter I leave five dollars each to be paid out of my

40   Estate to my Son William Mc Adoo
I leave & bequath all my personal Estate of very Kind description that
I may die possessed of togather with all the outstanding debts I may leave
behind meat my death I also leave him all the money I my have at my death
I do further bequath to my said son William all my real Estate (toWit) the
home farm containing one hundred & fifty four acres also and other farm
adjoining containing forty acres in persuance of this my last will I do
herdly require my said son William to support his mother & his sister
Eliza during thire natural life are to have it done without any expence
trouble to any of my other children I do here by constitute & appoint
my said son William Mc Adoo my sale executor to this my last will &
Testament in order to the conveying into effect & true meaning as here
enserted in all respects what ever and it is distinction to be under
stood that having the most confidence in my said son William I do not
wish that Security may be required from him for the faithful performance
of the matters & things here in contaned in Testemony where of I have sat
my hand & seal this 18th day of August 1829.

Arthur Crozier   )
Wm. Dickson   )   John Mc Adoo
                          (Seal)

Arthur Crozier

41   John Tovera S.   Will
         in the name of God Amen I John Tovera of the County of Anderson State
of Tennessee being sick and weak of body but sound of mind & dispsing
memory (for which I think God) and calling to mind the uncertainly of
human life & living diservous to dispose of all such wordlyy Substance
as it has pleased God to bless me with I give & bequath the same in
manner following that is to say I give unto my wife Mary Tovera the
plantation that I now live and togather with my Gray horse side Saddle
bridle my yoke of oxens & wagon all my farming utenteals house hold and
kitchen furnature my stock of cattle & out hgs & fifteen sheep of the
Choise of my flock for hir support during hir natural life then to be
disposed as here after disceted & also allow my wife Mary to have four
of the largest hogs now in the pen & the corn in the Barn & Crib for hir
sepport family ensuing year I then 1st give and bequath unto my son
John Tovera my plantation in Anderson County adjoining the widow England
dower forever togather one boy horse colt Item 2nd I give & bequath
unto my Daughter Rachel Tovera one young bay mare togather with bead
& bed furnature & five head of sheep: I then 3rd I give & bequath unto
my Daughter Charlotia Hail forty six dollars that is now in the hands of
John Weeks in the State of Kentuckey (?) 4th after the decease of my
Mary I give and bequath unto my son Bartly Tovera the plantation that I
now live and to be enjoyed by him & his hears forever

42   togeather with my new Saddle at my death (?) I desire all my debts be
collected emmedeately after my decease & that my Executors hereafter
namer sell the remander of my pro. Lable property & out of the moneys
arising thire from & debts oweing pay all my Just debts which are but few
& distrebut the remander as follous to my son John ten dollars to buy
him a saddle to my Daughter Rachel twenty dollars to buy hir a saddle to
my son Bartly Seventy five dollars to buy him a horse beast when he arrives
at the age of twenty one and the remander my wife Mary is to have to buy
necessary for hir support Item 6th I allow my Daughter Rachel to have one
cow & calf of the increase of my stock of Cattle and at the death of my
wife Mary all the property left to hir Except the land which I have
willed to my son Bartly to be immedeately sold and the money arising thire
from to be Equally sold and divided beteen my son John & Bartly & my
Daughters Rachel & Eastly I do here by constitute & appoint my wife Mary
and my Friand John Scarbrough Executive of this my last will and Testament
here by Revoking all others are former wills or Testaments by me here to
fore made and Witness where of I have here unto sat hand & seal this 26th
of November 1831. Signed Sealed published & recorded to be the last.

                                   John Tover
                                   his X mark
                                    (seal)

Will & Testament of the above named John Tover in the presents of us who
at his request in his personed hand hereunto subsented our names as Wit-
nessed the same   Samuel Davidson
                      James J. Nickle

43   Inventory of the Estate of Cornelues Evans

        1 lot of books 1 cupboard & furnature   1.25
        1 table 1 candle stick e set knives & forks   1.00
        1 table 1 Beauro 1 Bead steal & Clothe   2.50
        1 Bead 1 trunnell do do   1.75
        10 Chairs 1 looking glass   .65½
        1 Bead Stead & furnature 1 Chest & Bead Cloth   3.75
        1 do 1 parcel of thread wool & flax & cotton   3.50
        3 pr. dogirons parcel Iron Kitchen Cupboard   3.50
        1 Kitchen table 2 Jugs 1 Churn & 1 basket   1.25
        1 Loom 3 Spining wheels   .50
        2 Axes 1 Mattack 2 foot adds & two iron wedges   1.25
        1 hand saw 3 Bull 1 Auger & 1 drawing knife   .50
        1 sat of Breck Moulds   .06½
        1 Saddle Sadle bags 2 bredles blanket Skin   2.50
        1 lot of Cooking & water vessels   1.75
        1 pot rack & 2 hooks Sythe & Cradle   1.25
        2 Grinding Stones 1 hoe 2 tubs 2 barrels   .50
        1 lot of gurs Checkins & ducks 24 Hogs   9.75
        4 Calves 4 bee hives 1 Cradle   4.75
        1 wagon & Gears 1 cow hide & 1 cow   36.00
        2 Cows 2 Heifers 1 Cow   10.87½
        3 Cows pr. Steers   25.12½
        1 yoke of Oxens 1 Brindle Steer   14.62½
        1 Spotted and one black Steer   10.75
        1 read steer & one cow   22.62½
        1 read Bull & 1 Sorrel Mare & 1 Colt   48.87½
        2 Sorrel Colts 1 Cutting Knife & reap hook   21.75
        2 Plows 4 plow Stocks 1 bay mare   49.87½
        1 Carrel horse 2 Sorrel Mares   175.87½
        4 parcels of Sheep   20.00
        Ledder & Oats   3.12½
44   Sterling Smith Note   22.50
        Judge Bowling Smith $20.50   43.00
        Abraham Lovings ok.   2.00
        Thomas Harts Note   5.00   26.00
        Joseph Moress ok.   13.00
        James Kirkpatrick Note
        William Hartlys o.k.   2.50
        David Redenour a note for 57.
           for bee salt Probably North   50.00
        13 head of Hogs lately found   7.00
        North paddle
        1 old Mattack & some Iron   1.50

                Amounting to $126.87½
        Sarah Evans & Jesse Pepper
             Administrator & Administratrix

An Inventory of the sale of the Negroes Belonging to the Estate of Wm.
Lamør Decd. Charles Lamør Negro Alexander $4.00
Elijah Adkins 4 Negros   8.20
Wallace Dewin 2 do   5.25
John Smith   1 do   237.50
Austin Moore 1 do -   275.00
Charles Luallen 1 do   127.50
David Wallace 1 do   40.00
Hugh B. Lamor 1 heifer   1.50
Charles Lamor 1 do   3.00
                    (out standing note)

1 Note on John M. Lamor   29.00
1 Elijah Adkins   50.00
James Still   8.33 2/3
Wm. Harroll   2.75
Charles Michard Luallen   7.14
Charles Luallen John Totten   5.86

                                           $2532.58 2/3

John M & Polly Lamør
      Adms. & Admx.
45   Inventory of the Estate of Isaac Sarton decd.
1 lot of book 12½   1 table & 2 water pails 25
1 looking glass 50   1 filly $20.06½
1 Cupboard & furnature 25   1 young mare   57.00
1 bunch spun thread 18 1/3   1 mare & colt   61.87½
½ doz. chairs 06¼   4 head of sheep)
3 beds & furnature 75   1 cutting box)   1.31½
1 saddle & blanket 25   1 pr. grars   .25
1 Counterpin   12½   1 Sifter 1 spur   .06¼
1 trunk of Cotton 12½   George Scruggs
1 Iron Shovel & firetongs 06½ Dr. to Sc. Estate   150
2 Axes gig & to plows 56¼   John Scruggs   35.00
1 washing tub   06¼   Money collected from Daniel Clap 39.00
1 lot of Pots   3.56½
1 Grind Stone 31½ $253.80½
1 loom   50
2 Wheels 1 Churn 2 tubs 1 cog 25   John Scruggs adms.
furnature in Smoke house 06½   Nancy Sartin Admx.
parcel of Corn 06¼   The above is the amount which
flax & fadder 06½   they returned.
Lot of Hogs 50
1 Heifer   4.56½
1 Cow & Calf 4.56½
1 yoke of Oxens 4.56½
1 Heifer 4.56½
1 do   4.56½
2 yokes of Oxens 6.56½
1 Cow & Calf   5.50

John Scruggs Will
in the name of God amen I John Scruggs of the County of Anderson in the
State of Tennessee being sick and wead of Body but a sound mind & disposing
memory for which I think God & calling into mind uncertainly of human life
do dispose of all such wortly Substance as it hath pleased God to bless
me with I give & bequath the same in the manner following vizist to my
beloved wife Elemlea Scruggs I give after (after) paying all my Just debt
all my Estate both real my personal during her natual life except a hors e
beast to each of my sons as they may grow up to want them provided she
dose not marry which if she dose it is my will that she shall have but
one one third part of my Estate during life after which my desire is that
my Estate be divided az following (to Wit) that all my Estate may be
Div ided in such a manner that all my children have a equal portion except
Thomas whom I will as much more as to any other one of my children because of his Decriped condition if they can not agree in the division it
is my will that it shall be done be disinterested valuation and if my wife
Emilia Scruggs dose not mary after hir death all my Estate to be equally
divided among my children only giving to my son Thomas Scruggs what may
be called a double postion but provided she dose mary then two thirds of
my Estate to be divided among my children according to the above plan
relative to Thomas

47   also the other third part after my wife death & lastly I do hereby constitute
& appoint my beloved wife Emilia Scruggs & my son James Scruggs Executors
of my last will & Testament hereby revoking all other wills & Testaments
by me heretofore made in Witness where of I have here unto set my hand &
Seal will that 16th day of November in the year of our Lord 1824.
                                        John Scruggs
                                           his X mark

Signed Sealed and published & Delivered to be the last will & Testament of
the above named John Scruggs in presence of us who at his request & in his
presence have herewith subscribed our names as witnesses to the same—
J. Pepper
Cornelues X Evans
       his mark
Maxwell D. Pepper

State of Tennessee   July Sessions Anderson County 1831 the with in last
will and Testament of John Scruggs deceased was produced into Open Court
by Emelia Scruggs the Executrix named the same and a appearing to the
Satisfaction of the Court that Cornelues Evans and of the Subscribing
Witnesses thereto is dead & that Joseph Pepper & Maxwell Pepper have re-
moved beyond the Limits of the State to parts unknown the hand writing of
said Joseph Peper & Maxwell Pepper two of the Subscribing Witnesses there
to was proved in open Court by the oath of Charles Y Oliver & that the
name of Cornelues Evans was Signed by Joseph Pepper it is ordered by the
Court that said will be reccorded at full length.
                                        N. W. Barton Clk
        by his deputy J. M. Mc Corum

48   Marmaduke Bookout Will in the name of God amen I Mermaduke Bookout of the
       County of Anderson State of Tennessee considering the uncertainly of this
       morlal life & being of Sound mind & memory blessed be Almighty God for
       the same do hereby make & publish this my last Will & Testament in manner
       & form following (that is to Say) first I give & bequath to my Son Jesse
       Bookout by my first wife Rachael Bookout one track of Land which I pur -
       chared from Burton & Wm. Underwood as attorney in fact for Dr. Urnsstead
       by in the County of Anderson & State of Tennessee also one horse worth
       fifty dollars which he has alread recovered & further that after my decease
       for him to have one dollar to have & to hold to him & his bodly heirs
       forever. Second I give & bequath to my Daughter Nancy Vaugher one cow
       feather bed & furnature & one Spinging wheel which she has alread Received
       & further I will that after my decease that hir body Heirs have one dollar
       for them to have & to hold forever at being since she so recived the above
       named goods & Chattles that the Almighty has called hir unto hirsalf.
       Third I give & bequath to my Daughter Rachel Wood one cow one feather
       Bead & furnature & Spinning wheel which she has allread receved & furthm r
       I will that after my decease she have one dollar to have & to hold to hir
       & her bodely heirs forever forth I give & bequath to my son Joseph Bookout
       one tract of land which I purchased form Wm. Underwood
49   Attorney for Urnstead bying in the County of Anderson & on the waters of
       Hands Creek also one horse worth fifty dollars which he has already received
       I further will that after my deceased he have one dollar to have & to hold
       to him & his bodly heirs forever fift I give & bequath to my Daughter
       Elizabeth Lumpkins one cow one feather bead & furnature & Spinning wheel
       which she has alread recived & further I will that after my decease hir
       husband James Lumpkins have one dollar. Sixth I give and bequath to my
       Daughter Eda Lumpkins one cow one feather bead & one Spinning wheel which
       She has already receved & further I will that after my bequath she be
       allowed one dollar to have & to hold & hir bodly heirs forever. Seventh I
       give & bequath to my son Marmaduke Bookout one horse worth fifty dollars
       which he has receved since that time the Governor of the universe has
       called him to himself. Eighth I give & bequath to my son Charles L. Bookout
       one track of land on the Chesnut Ridge lying in Knox & Anderson Counties
       which I purchased from Jesse Cole & Dr. Urnstead by his attorney Wm.
       Underwood & one horse worth fifty dollars which I contracted from him
       feeding a young colt of his to Winters Seasons which he has already re-
       ceived and further I will that after my decease he have one dollar to have
       & to hold to him & to his bodly heirs forever ninth I give and bequath
       to my son John M. Bookout
50   one tract of land which I purchased from John Gibbs attorney in fact for
       Charles Mc Clung in the County of Anderson & an Byrams fork of hands Cre ek
       also one horse worth fifty dollars which he has already received & further
       I will that after my deceased he have one dollar to have & to hold to him
       & his bodly heirs forever. Tenth I give and bequath to my son James Book-
       out one tract of land which I purchased from dr. Underwood by his attorn ey
       Wm. Underwood bying in the County of Anderson on the North side of the
       Chestnut ridge & in place of a horse worth fifty dollars I give his so much
       Time before he becomes of age as in eqevalent to the horse which he has
       already recived and furthmr I will that after my deceased he have one dollar
       to have & to hold to him & his bodly heirs forever. Eleventh I give and
       bequath to my Daughter Chearety Lemer one cow one feather bead & furnature

& Spinning Wheel which she has already recived and further I will after
my decease she have one dollar to have & to hold to hir & hirbodly heirs
forever. Twelft I give & bequath to my Daughter Delila Lumpkins one Cow
one feather bead and furnature and one Spinning wheel which she has already recived & further I will that after my decease she have one dollar
to have & to hold to hir & hir bodly heirs forever. Thirteeth I give & be
bequath to my Son Thomas

51   Bookout one tract of land which I purchased in a body from D. Urnstead
by his attorney William Underwood have since Divided to my others sons
as before mentioned in the County of Anderson on the north side of the
Chesnut ridge & one horse worth fifty dollars which he has already recived
& further I will that after my decease he have one dollar to have & to
hold to him & his bodly heirs forever fourteenth I give & bequath to my
youngest son William Bookout the tract of land which I now live and one
horse worth fifty dollars when he marries or becomes of age the land to
remain in his mothers possession as hir night & property during natural
life time or madonhood to assest hir further production thireof in rairig
remaining children that has not married or left hir & if she should die
before he becomes of age or has any bodely heirs the land which I give
unto him must be valued by two disinterested free holders & then my son
Thomas Bookout if he choose may pay the one half of the valulation to be
equally divided among my Daughters then living occupy the land otherwise
for it to be sold & then one half to be paid to him and the other divided
as above directed never the less not untail(?) after my wife shall decease
or marry another man. Fifteenth and lastly I give unto my wife Elizabeth
Bookout all the rest resided & remainder of my personal Estate goods &
Chattles of what kind nature so ever & the stock of all kinds & if she
should be so prosperous to have

52   any thing to spare as hir Daughters marries or all becomes of age that she
divide to them poshon as she may feel disposed & I hereby appoint hir my
sale Executrix of this my last will & Testament during hir widow hood or
naturnal life time & if she should die or marry before hir Daughters all
all marry or becomes of age I appoint Ezekial Taylor his successor as
Executor here by revoking all former wills by me made in Witness so here
of I have hereunto sat my hand & seal this 22nd day of Feb. 1830 signed
sealed & published in presence of

                                   Moses Right
                                   Bennett D. Marcus

                                                        his
                                            Marmaduke X Bookout
                                                       mark
                                                        (seal)

I Marmaduke Bookout of the County & State aforesaid do this 22 day of
february 1830 make this codicel(?) to my last will & Testament in manner
following(that is to Say) that if my wife Elizabeth Bookout should die
before hir Daughters all marry or become of age that they live on the
place in the mansion house when I now live & live on that may be left
after hir death and if any left after after they all marry or become of
age the ballance to be equally divided among all younger Lucendia
Clarkson & hir to have one cow & one dollar in Witness so here of I have

hereunto set my hand & seal the day & date above written Signed & Sealed
in the presence of
                    us Chesley H. Boatright   )
                       Moses Right   )
                       Bennett D. Marcus   )
                                         Marmaduke Bookout
                                                (seal)

53   Settlement with Richd. Oliver administrator of Powel Hughs deceased
        Richd. Oliver Administrator Dr. as pr. return of the inventory $761.63
        To this Sum Called for interest   28507.90/3
        to ballance the above Sum of 790.13 the administrator produced the
        following vouchers to Wit
        1 note on Aledr. Davidson & Alvin Hughs $303.50
        1 do an do   do   13.92
        1 do To Collins Roberts   23.38
        1 do To John Hughs   41.78
        1 do To Joseah Davidson   40.96
        Tax receipt from Olvina Hughs
           the widow for one year Support   25.00
        Tax receipt for 1828   .87½
        1 proven ok from Luke Peak   5.76
        1 do Henry Beetler   1.23
        1 do Lesay Howel   1.00
        1 proven account on John Lensly   15.00
        1 do do by Wm. A. Butler   4.12½
        1 do do do Jacob Butler   1.23
        1 do do Samuel Cowvers   7.55
        1 do do Saml. Dickey   1.87½
        1 do do Nancy Hughs   27.78
        1 do do Isaac Freelds   2.00
        1 do do James Noel   .80
        1 do do Spencer Keath   1.00
        1 do do James Galbreath   4.16 2/3
        1 do do Collins Roberts   5.50
        1 do do Eyra Russell   3.00
        1 do do Soloman Aldred   .75
        1 do do Elizabeth Hughs   32.75
   (54) 1 do do Wm. C. Griffith   4.00
        1 do do Johathan Scrbrough   .75
        1 do do Richard Oliver   19.25
        1 do do Joseph Vance   23.70
        1 do do Henry Russell   5.00
        1 do do Hugh Crozier   62.37½
        1 do do John Nollan   2.75
                                                  _____
                                                   $762.09½
        The amount which the administrator is chargeable with $790.13
        Amt. of Vouchers   726.09½
                                                               _____
                                                                 64.03½
        By Clerks receipt   10.25
        The balance   53.78½

We tender this statement and pray your worships to recieve it as such
                              Alexander Galbreath
                              Robert Galbreath
                              Commissioners

Julius Rutherfords Will in the name of God amen I Juluis Rutherford in
the County of Anderson & State of Tennessee being of sound mind and dis-
paring memmory for which I think God & Calling to mind the uncertainty
of Hummons life and being desirved to dispose of all such worldly substance as it has pleased God to be bless me with I give and bequath to
the same in manner following that is to say 1st I dseire that all my
Just debts and funeral expences be Paid and I give and bequath to my wife
Rody Rutherford the Plantation where I now live and all the household,
(55)   furnature and one third Part of my estate to hold and enjoy forever. 3rd
I give and bequath to my children the names that follows Isaac Reatherford
Joseph Reatherford Sally Wilson Michael Reatherford Jacob Reatherford
Aberham Reatherford Robert Reatherford Rachel Mitton William Reatherford
Nancy Whitton John Reatherford and Thomas Reatherford the ballance of my
Estate to be divided Equally amongst them to hold and rejoy forever 4th
I do hereby constitute and appoint James Mitton and my wife Rody Reather-
ford Executor of this my last Will & Testament revoking all other or
former Wills or Testament by me heretofore made in Witness whereof I have
unto set my hand and offered my seal this 22nd day of July 1831.
                                      his
                            Julus X Beckout
                                    mark   (seal)
Signed & Sealed in the presence of Isaac Miller, John B. Mitchell

Amount of Sale of the property of Lewis Rector Deceased

Benjamin Rector whole amt.		$ 28.75
Eliza Rector	do	80.62½
Jacob Rector	do	18.32½
Wm. Rector	do	33.18¾
Powhatan Rector		12.54¼
John Rector Jr.		1.00
Thomas Rector		10.25
D. M. C. Rector		11.00
A. Manley		4.00
Amt. Total		$ 199.69¾

(56) Inventory of the property of John Scruggs deceased (to Wit)

1 Negro man named George	$ 1.00
1 Negro woman named Claressa	.50
1 do do do Jesse	4.00
1 do girl do Lucenda	3.00
1 do woman do Esther	3.30
1 do do do Patsy	3.30
1 do do girl do Lusan	2.00
1 do Boy do Ephraim	2.50
1 do do do Lansom	2.00

1 do girl do Mohulda	2.00
1 do do do Rachel	1.50
1 do do do Dartheda	1.50
1 gray mare 30$	45.00
1 gray colt 15$	
1 Bay horse colt 10$	
5 Mask Stud 6$$	79.00
1 waggon 50$	
5 Milk Cows 40$	90.00
2 Heifers 5.506 Calves 8$	
8 head of Sheep 12$	25.50
30 Hogs 30$	
1 Set black Smith tools 35$	65.00
3 beads and Cloathing and Steads	35.00
1 Cupboard 18$ 1 table &	
Chest 6$	24.00
1 pair fish Irons 2$ 1	6.00
large Kettle 4$	
1 Large Pot 4$ 3 ovens & ten	13.00
leds 9$	
1 Weaving Loom $18.00	
1 Space Mortor 4$	12.00

Of which a Division was made by consent of the heirs in the following
manner (to Wit) George Claresea Dorthula was giving to Thomas Scruggs, the
land to John Scruggs, Jesse to James Scruggs,
(57) Lucenda to Nancy Sartin,(Inventory of John Scruggs deceased conttuned) Patsy
to William Scruggs, Ephran to George Scruggs, Lawson to Rachel Scruggs,
Mahulda & Rachel to Carter Scruggs, and the ballance returned by me

                           Milly Scruggs
                             Executor
of the last Will & Testament of John Scruggs Deceased.
    November 28th 1831
recorded November 30th 1831

Isaac Robbins Will the last will and Testament of Isaac Robbins I will ꞏꞏt
that all Just debts as shall be by me owing at my death togather with my
funeral Expences and all charges touching the proveing of or otherwise
concering this my will shall in the first place out of my personal Estate
and Efferts be fully paid and satisfied and from and after payment there
of and Subject thereunto then my will is that all the rest due of my
goods stocks Chattles and household furnature shall be sold at twlve months
Credit and the money Equally divided in four parts with my wife Faacy and
my three children Samuel & William and June and my land I want sold at a
Credit of two years and one fourth of the money paid to my wife and the
ballance divided with my children I wish my two sons to have twenty five
dollars forevermore then my Daughters the money is to be put out on Interest untill my children comes to be twenty one years of age my will and
wearing is that in can any of my said children shall depart this life be-
(58) fore such time as the part portion of him hir or them so dying becomes
payable to the others heirs of this my last will & Testament hereby re-

voking all former wills by me maid in Witness whereof I have here unto sat
my hand and seal the 30th day of September in the year of our Lord one
thousand Eight hundred and thirty three.   Isaac Robbins
Signed Sealed published and declared by the above name Isaac Robbins to be
his last will and Testament in the presence of us who at his request and
in his presence have Subscribed our names as Witnesses hereunto.
(   )
(recorded 13th feb 1834   )
(John Juragurn   Clerk   )
                       John Wallace Junr.
                       Samuel Robbins

State of Tennessee   )
Anderson County   )   Court house
January Sessions 1834
     William Jones administrator of all and Singulor the goods & Chattles
rights and Credits of Abraham Jones Decd. returns the following Envoice 3
head of Sheep 1 yoke of Steers 18 head of Stock Cattle 1 road waggon Gear-
ing 20 head of Sheep 40 head of Hogs 1 set of Black Smith Tools a quantity
of Farmer Tools one Crop of Corn Sufpor R ye 3000 Bundles of Oats a quantity
of Hay another one Crop Cut 1 hand Saw 1 Set of Junior tools 4 Sedes of
Sole leather 1 Side of upper Leather 2 Sythes & Cradles 5 Sickles one Cutting
Box & three Knives 2 Mans Saddle & one pair of Saddle bags one side Saddle
79 Lbs. Iron & some Still one pair of Steel gards one Cones. 3 Bee Hives   a
quaintly of plank one grind Stone 12 Gars

(59) 10 ducks a small quantity of Clover seed one set of Shoe maker tools one
set of Cooper Tools 3 beads and frunature & Stead one Buro & Cupboard 2 tables
8 Chairs 2 Spinning wheels one Real 12 pices of Castings one pot trowel one
pair of fire dogs one fire Shovel one pair of fire Lougs one Lantern one
Trumpet 2 bails 2 tin buckets a quantity of Knives & forks togeather with
plats & dishes of Delf & puter one large Chest one paten Clock too large
gugs 2 Smothing Irons 2 Churns 1 loom & C. 800 lb. Salted pork 3 Barrells
& one pair of measures one Keg of vinegar 4 Baskets 2 Small Keggs one Broad
axe one crow Bar, alist of the folling debts to Wit.
Abner Pars Note $75.00
John Bakers Note & Security for   130.00
William Readers Note   10.00
William Evans Note   11.00
John Sharp Note   8.00
David Sharp Note   5.07$\frac{1}{4}$
John Kincads & Jones Glurns Note $40.00 William Bridges Note $12.00 Wallace
Dew Note & Security $62.50 D. D. Williams Note $5.00 Lewis Baker & Bowling
Baker Note $72.25 William Lindsay Note 70 pounds Iron William Sharp Note
$4.00 of the above debts the following is doubtful   Abner Pars debt $75.
William Bridges $12.00 William Sharp $4.00 proven to & Subscriber in open
Court this 13th January 1836.
                        William Jones

H. Barton   Clerk
Recorded 14th Feb. 1834
J.J. Clerk

(60)   State of Tennessee   )   County Court
        Anderson County   )   January Sessions 1834

amided Envoice of William Jones Administrator of all & Singular the goods
& Chattles rights and Credits of Abraham Jones Deceased one hundred and
Seventy five dollars & Seventy Cents in Silver Six dollars in paper Money
adjudged to be Counterfeit. William Jones sworn to & Subscrebed in open
Court this 15th day of January 1834
                    J. J. Clerk
                    recd. Feb. 14th 1834

Inventory of the personal Estate of Rachel Peters deceased one Cupboard
one bed & furnature To bed steads one Spinning wheel one oven & one Pot
some Table furnature and some money redc. by the Court.   John Peters
and ordered to be recorded recd. 14th Feb. 1834 J J Clerk

State of Tennessee)   County Court   Oct. Sessions 1833
Anderson County   )

    I Richard Oliver Administrator dibouismon of the last Will & Testament
of Henry Durrett deceased to return the following Invoice of personal property to Wit twenty Negroes Sworn to & Subscribed in Open Court this 14th
Oct 1833
                    Hugh Barton Clerk
                    recd. 14th Feb 1834
                    J. J. Clerk

(61) report and Hire of the negroes Slaves of the Estate of Henry Derrett deceased
to Wit recived this Sum from Thomas Butler for Jacks Hire from 8th July to
8th August 1833 $5.00
Jack Hired to Henry R. Butler from 8th August to 24 of decr. 1833 for 500½
15 th March   22.78
          which is for the whole time
George Hired to John Nail for $4.00 pr. month for the Hire as above stated
which is Harreed Hired to F. H. Robertson for the time as above stated at
2.15 cets. pr month which is for hir Hire 9.67½

Patsy Hired to Richard Oliver at 26 cents pr month which comes to   1.17
                                                                    56.62½

          which I now Submit to the worshipful Court respectfully
                              Richard Oliver
          Administrator debouismon of the Estate of Henry Derrett deceased

State of Tennessee)
Anderson County   )   We who names are hereunto Subscribed being appoint-
                               ed Commissioners by the Court of Pleas & Quarter
Sessions for said County to make Settlement which George Winton administrator
& Martha Thompson deceased having meet & proceded to make said Settlement
the results of which is as follows to Wit the administration produced vouchers
to the amount of five Thousand five Hundred & forty Seven dollars fifty
three & one half cents given under our
(62) hand this 30th Novr. 1833
                              William Tennell
                              John O. Neal   Commissioner
                              Robert Galbreath

N. B. We the Commissioners as aforesaid have made an allowance to the
aforesaid administrators the Sum of forty dollars Telve & ½ cents each

recorded Feb. 15th 1834
  J. J. Clerk

William Tunnell
John O. Neal
Robert Galbreath

We the Commissioners being appointed by the Court & Quarter Sessions for
Anderson County To Settle which Jacob Rector Executor of the Estate of
Leives Rector deceased have proceded to make the said Settlement and which
stands as follows to Wit Jacob Rector Executor of the Estate of Lewis
Rector decd. for Settlement for the Clerk of said Court $217.47½
Cr. pr. vouchers produced on Settlement to the amount 199.69½
Debts of   17.77½
Which leaves a ballance dur from said Estate to said Executor to the amount
of Seventeen dollars Seventy Seven & ¾ cents all of which we Submit as our
report of said Settlement
       Respectfully   John O Neal
              William Tunnell
Recorded 15th Feb 1834   Robert Galbreath
  J. J. Clerk

(63) Report & Division of Negroes of H. Durrett in pursuance to an order from
the Worshipful Court of please & Quarter Sessions of Anderson County we the
undersigned Commissioners having met at the house of F. H. Robertson on the
first day of January 1834 and proceded to alot and Divide the negroes of the
Estate of Henry Durrett deceased amongst the Several Hiers ligatus of said
deceased which are ap follows to Wit
Jack & Harriet valued at $800.00 To Douglas Oliver
Thomas Peters & Old Peggy To Thos. Carwell
             valued at $750.00
Synthia Fany America & Cyntheas Child George to JohnG. Durrett valued at
             $775.00
Elizabeth Wright, Rhoda Angland, Allen and Tobitha valued at 825.00
Thomas Cllarshell Drue Mariah Peggy Wyitt and Isaac valued at 800.00
Jacob Robertson
Young George Patsy and old George valued at   750.00
               $4700.00

Negroes amounted to this Sum of forty seven hundred dollars the Negroes were
Div ided as above respective owners Except Thomas Marshall which were delivered to the administrator said Marshell not being present all of which we Lender
as report to your worships respectfully Thomas Butler
          Samuel Galbreath
recorded   William Tunnell
15th 1834   John Childs
J. J. Clerk   Jacob Peak

(64)

Inventory and amount of the Sale of the Estate of Mary Miller Deceased
Eleneazoe Gamble 1 Sprouting hoe & another hoe   .50
H enry Right 3 Hoes   .33¼
John Hwoling(?) 1 Iron wedge 2 other hoes   .25
John G. Durrett 1 Pitcher & Jug   .06¼
Elizabeth Right 1 Crock   .13
William Wright 1 large Jar   .32
Josiah Montgrmery 1 Coulter   .12½

William Deggs 1 tubpucket	.15
John G. Durrett 1 Coffepot	.06½
William Right 1 Jar lied	.40
William Johnson 1 Coffee Cellier	.18
William Butler 1 Chopping Axe	1.25
West Peak 1 Small Axe	.75
Edward Freels 1 Candlestick	.50
William Diggs 3 Bowels	.15
John D. Durrett 1 Bowel	.07½
Douglas Oliver 1 pr 6 Tea plates	.33½
John G. Durrett 1 Jar & Jug	.25
Thomas Carwell 1 Pitcher	.25
William Right 2 pepper Boxes	.27
William S. Freel 1 Set Teaspoons	.25
John Heeling 1 Set teacups	.50
H Wright 1 Small Pitcher	.06½
H Wright Saltseller	.12½
George Gallaher 6 Delph Pleats	.50
George Gallaher 6 " " " "	.37½
William Butler 4 Teaspoons	.06¼
(65)James Turpin, Cups & Saucers	.12½
John Pitman 1 Dish	.19
Douglas Oliver Senr. 1 Larg dish	.30
Henry Wright 1 Smothing Iron	.91½
Douglas Oliver 1 Puter basen	.30
Josiah Montgomery 1 Churn & dash	.06¼
Henry Wright 1 Shovel & C	.13
William Wright 2 glass Tumbler	.18¾
John G. Durrett 1 Kettle	.67
F. H. Robertson 1 Baker	1.52
J. Montgomery 1 Pot & Hooks	1.25
John Hewling 1 Pot & hooks	2.07½
John G. Durrett 1 pocket Knife	.41
William G. Buttler 1 Skillet	1.02
Douglass Oliver 1 oven & lead	1.30
Jonathan Cox 1 Check Reel	.27
John Hagler 1 Wheel	.08
Henry Wright 1 Jug	.13
Henry Wright 1 Clevis & Pin	.40
John Petman 1 Shovel Plow	.08
John Cllitton 1 Single tree & Clevis Pin	.15
Cleming Kincaid 1 Barrel Sugar	.21
George Gallaher 1 Shovel Plow	1.00
William Oliver 1 Plow	1.06¼
Tho. Gollaher Scythe & Cradle	1.06¼
Henry Wright 1 Plow	1.06¼
Douglas Oliver 1 Cotton Wheel	.26
J. W. Wallace 1 Cotton Wheel	.75
Lewis Byant 1 Stay Harness	1.06¼
Tho. Hudson 1 Stay & Harness	.76
Wist Peak 1 Slay	1.00
(66) G. W. Johnson 2 Slays	.66
Thomas Carnell 1 Book	.25
William Digs 1 pair Scissors	.06¼

Rachel Nichol 1 Vial	.12½
Rachel Nichol Gemblet	.20
Jonathan Cox 1 Bucket & Tallaer	.27
R. Cox 1 Basket & Spools	.60
Henry Right 2 Tubs	.07
Douglas Oliver 1 Jug	.30
Isaac Freel 2 Baskets	.27
Jonathan Cox 1 Basket	.07¼
Henry Right 1 Side Saddle	1 .00
William Digs 1 Goard 1 Soap	.28
James Galloher 1 Barrell	.26
George Johnson 1 Barrell	.26
Saml Pouyear 1 Pail	.12½
William Wright 1 Pail	.12½
John Henley 1 Table	.26
George Johnson 1 Table	.06¼
George Johnson 1 Tub	.06¼
John Manley 8 Chairs	1.26
James Pelshaer 2 Piggons	.25
John W. Wallace 1 pair Gears	1.25½
William Warren 1 pair do	1.00
Isaac Feel 1 Trunk	2.51
D. Oliver 1 Chest	.75
Thomas White 1 Chest	1.80½
Lewis Bryant 1 bed & Furnature	8.58
Lewis Bryant 1 bed & Furnature	5.00
James Petman 5 Cotton Hanks	.68
Henry Right 1 Bed & furnature	10.12½
William Davidson Towells	.28
(67) Henry Right 1 pair Lance	.29
Douglas Oliver 1 Sheet	.50
do do 1 do	.80
Isaac Freel 1 Cewlet	.28
E. Freel 1 Sheet	.38
Vincor Burnett 1 Bed & Blanket	2.00
Douglas Oliver 1 white Counterpain	2.00
H. B. Butler 1 do do	2.41
D. Oliver 1 Bed Quilt	1.00
William Davidson 1 do	2.06¼
do do 1 do	1.00
James Bowling 1 Coon led	3.00
Douglas Oliver 1 do do	4.64
Henry Wright 1 do do	1.37½
do do 1 Glass	.64
James Petman 8 Hanks Yarn	1.10
Eleneazor Gamble 1 Loom	.06¼
John Petman 1 Roaw Mare	30. 18 ¾
Jonathan Cox 1 Cow & Calf	6.32
Wm. G. Butler 1 Cow	7.28
Wm. Digs 1 Cupboard	.12½
C. G. Crozier 1 Cow & Bull	7. 18¾
do do 1 Bay Mare	6.12½
Benjamin Galloher 1 Heifer	3.08½

do do 1 do		3.06¼
do do 1 do		2.12½
J. H. Nichol 4 Hogs		5.50
John Hewling 4 Hogs		3.26
do do do "		2.08
John Cellitton 4 "		1.50
C. G. Crozier 6 Sheep		4.60
William Oliver 6 Sheep		3.32

(68) Thomas Garnell 1 Chest .06½
    do do 2 Gums & hogshead .06¼
Cabb Law 1 Wire Seive .25
Isaac Freel 1 Pad Lock .41
William 1 Battle .27½
$178.72½

The amount of Sale of Mary Miller deceased on the 8th August 1833 Erors
Excepted the amount of sale the 7th Dec. 1833 and property sold

Richard Oliver 1 Side leather	2.06¼
do do 1 Reap Hook	.13
Ladle & fork	.06¼
10 bushels Corn	2.31¼
Henry Wright Warpin Pars	.06¼
Jonathan Butker Spun Morter	.06¼
Do do 100Lbs. Corn	32.52
Francis Orven 1 Stack fodder	1.31¼
do do 65 Lbs. Corn	20.31¼
Wm. Digs 1 Stack fodder 1	1.06¼
Lewis Bryant 65Lbs. Corn	19.66¼
John G. Durrett 88½ Iron	3.54
do do 4 Bushels Salt	4.32
do do 1 Lot of Corn	.55
	$266.42¾

Taken Thomas Butler note for for Jack Severs
  Dec. the 8th August 1834 for   11.75
$278.17¾

all ofwyhich is Respectfully

                    Submitted
recorded 17th Feb. 1834   Richard Oliver
      J. J. Clerk   Administrator of the Estate of Mary Miller

(69) to the worshipful Court of please & Quarter Sessions of Anderson County the
following is the amt. due to the Estate of Isaac Robbins decd. Secured by
good notes of hand with good Security due from the following dates to Wit.
1 Note on Moses Overton due twelve months after date the 3rd of Feb. 1834
   for $1.50

1 Note on James Still do do do for	8.50
1 Note on Nancy Robbins do do for	18.31¼
1 Note on James Still do do for	2.12½
1 Note on John W. Crozier do do for	27.57
1 Note on Phillip Harless do do for	4.99½
1 Note on George Miller do do for	2.56¼
1 Note on Henry Snodderly do do for	2.06
1 Note on Wm. C hildress do do for	3.72½
1 Note on Hirman Brogans do do for	3.56¼

```
1 Note on Samuel Robbins  do  do for              14.00
1 Note on do due Six years the 29th Nov. 1833      50.00
1 Note on John Wallace due the Sixteen years the
    9th day of November 1833                       35.07
1 do pr. James Kerwood bal. due had note            8.84
Cash recd. by Isaac Fox                             5.62½
Cash on hand                              62½
            Apr. 14, 1835    6500        188.38¾
```

April 14th   Floyd Rutherford
                  Administrator
recorded June 4th, 1834
       J. J. Clerk

(71)   Inventory of the Estate of William Scarbrough Decd. ViZ
3 feathers Beds and furniture 1 cow & Calf one Brass Clock 11 Chairs 1 ten
bucket parcel of ham Scraps 1 Goard and ham Scraps 1 birier hook 1 Sive 1
hone 1 prinning knife 1 hawel 1 Bread Baker 1 Check Reel 1 pair Stutyards
2 plows Hatchet 1 Teakettle 1 Chisel hand Saw 1 Crack 1 Churn 1 Coffee Mill
1 Jug 1 Pot 1 Pot Hooks 1 Tub 2 Set fire Dogs 1 Shovel & Tongs 1 pan 1
Hackel 1 Oven & led 1 Kettle & Hooks 1 pan Candle stick 1 Lamp 1 Brass Candlestick 1 Cotton Wheel 1 Lanthern 1 Strainer 1 Conk Shall 12 puter Plates
Knives & forks 2 puter Dishes 7 Spoons 1 Razor 1 Hoe 2 Puter Bains 7 Bowls
2 Pales 1 Small piggin 1 Candle Mold 2 pitchers & fork 1 Set Cups & Saucers
1 Bread pan 1 Cream mug 1 Coffee Pot 1 Funnell 2 books 1 looking glass 1
Sugar Stand 1 Chest 1 Cupboard 4 Large Pots & hooks 1 Small Pot 1 Pot rack
1 Basket 1 Wheel Barrell 1 dresser 1 set Spoons 1 Grind Stone
       this 23th Sept. 1830 C. Y. Oliver Executor of the last will & Testament
of William Scarbrough Decd. recorded June 4th day 1834
                                          J. J. Clerk
Amount of sale of the Estate of William Scarbrough decd. Sold 23rd. Sept.
1830
Joseph Black 1 bucket 1 pan Scraps 3 Chairs & 1 Lamp
Michael Scarbrough 1 Goard & pan Scraps 1 adge 2 palins 1 Hatchet 1 Teakettle
1 Jug 1 Shovel & Tong 1 Brass Clock 1 Brass Candlestick 1 Razor 1 feather
bed & furniture 1 Pot rack

```
                                               .80½
                                             53.98½
            Amt. Carried over                54.79
(72)  Amt. Brot. forward                     54.79
Robert Gamble 1 Byor Hook 1 Bee Stand          .43¼
Richard Oliver 1 Sive                          .69½
David Scarbrough 1 grind Stone
1 pot & Hooks                                 3.03½
William Davidson 1 prinning Knife
1 pail 1 Sugar Stand 1 Bee Stand              2.60
Willis Leath 1 Bread Baker
1 Bee Stand 1 Wheel Barrell                   4.36¼
Sally Jackson 1 Check Reel 1 Cotton Wheel     1.08.
John Loverly 1 pair
Stutyards 1 Candlemold                        1.07
Isaac Griffith 1 Chisel 1 pan                  .69
Alexander Mc Clure 1 Saw
```

1 Crock 1 Churn & 1 tub	.80
William Scarbrough 1 Coffee Mill	.64
Samuel Taylor 1 Pot & hook 1 pail 1 pitcher & fork	.92¼
John Petman 3 Chairs	
Julis Turpin 1 Pitcher	.59½
James Cross 2 Chairs Knives & forks	1.11½
Jonathan Scarbro 1 Set fire dogs 1 howe 1 Conk Shall	
1 Cupboard 1 Meat tub Spoon Mold 1 Kettle & Hook	13.67¼
George Whitaberry 1 set fire dogs 1 Basket	1.31¼
Spencer Keeth 1 Hackle	3.25.
Gideoer Taylor 1 Oven led & Basin	2.68
Priccia Freman 1 Pan & Candlestick 1 Chest and one	
Bed & furniture	20.37½
Thomas Dale 1 Lanthern 1 Strainer 1 Bed & furniture	11.68¾
Isaac Freel 4 plates	1.07
Zachariah Prince 6 plates	1.19
Elizabeth Shannon 1 Peuter Dish & to do	2.03
Dennis Vann 7 Spoons	.38
Martha Thompson 1 piggin	.06¼
Willim Oliver 1 Bread pan Cream Mug	.20
(73) Walter Vann 1 Coffee Pot 1 funnell 1 Bed Stead & Cord	.84½
George Winton 1 looking glass	.91
Henry J. Yarnell 1 Bee Stand	.50
Henry Peters 1 Bee Stand	1.88
James H. Nickol 1 Cow & Calf	5.51
William Scarbrough Senr. 1 bed Cord	.54
Amount	146. 83

Recorded June 4th 1834
     J. J. Clerk

                         Charles Y. Oliver
                         Executor of the last
                         Will & Testament of
                         William Scarbrough
                            Decd.
                         October 12th 1830

Inventory of John Asherst decd. a Schedule of all the property of John
Asherst Decd. June 5, 1831
Which is to pay to 2 negroes and four head of horses Ten head of Caddle
15 head of hogs 6 head of Sheep 2 Side Saddle one mans Saddle 3 Bridles 4
pair of gurs & Some other coal Chains & one fifty Chain 3 Plows 5 weeding
hoes one Matlock 2 Sprouting Hoes 4 Axes 2 Sythe Blades & Cradle 1 Reap
hook one hand axe 1 drawing Knife 1 Auger one Chisel 2 Bultonges 1 Sang hoe
1 Wedge 1 Shovel 1 Tomahawk 2 Clevises 3 Single Trees one Leather line 4
head of Geese 6 walnut Plank 5 robbing Stand three Barrells 4 Kegs 3
Buckets 3½ Bushels one note of hand on Sterling Smith to the amt. of forty
dollars also one note to the amt. of thirth five dollars having credit o f
twenty too dollars dollars leaving a ballance of thirteen dollars 2 feather
Beds.
(74) & Furniture 3 Bedsteads 1 Cupboard 1 doz. Plates 6 Bowels four teacups &
Saucers Knives & forks one Dish 1 Coffee Pot 2 Jars 1 table 1 Chest 1 Chest
of drawers 1 Candle Stand 6 pot vessels 1 flat pan 1 wheet Riddle 1 pot

handle 2 pair of pot Hooks 1 mans Saddle 1 flesh fork 4 water vessels one
Churn 1 Gind Stone 1 Curry Comb 1 loom Reed 1 pair of Harnesses 1 Cotton
Wheel 5 Chairs 3 Butcher Knives 1 pan 1 note of hand on James Roberts to
the amt. of five dollars & one on Nelson Roberts to the amount of Seventy
five cents 2 Bells 1 Scythe Stake & Hammer Seventeen dollars in Cash in hand
Seventy dollars on a pade Contract on Joseph M. Asherst which property shall
be put up   Joseph M. Asherst
recorded June 10th   Administrator
1834 J. J. C.   Milly Asherst
                                 Administratrix

Inventory of the property of Martin Hill decd. January 10th 1832
One negro woman & Child 1 Mare & Horse seven head of Caddle 11 head of Hogs
1 Ox Cast 3 plows & plow Hoes 3 weeding Hoes 4 Axes 2 pair Traces & Harn es
3 Collars 4 feather beds & Clothes 1 Cupboard 1 Bureau 1 Table 1 Loom Stay
& Harness 4 Bedstead 1 Rifle Gun 12 Pot vessells 1 pair of fire dogs 3 pair
Pot Hooks 1 pot Rack 2 Cotton Wheels 1 Mans Saddle 1 flax Wheel 1 Looking
Glass ½ doz. Knives & forks

(75) 14 Delf Plates & to Dishes 1 pueter Dish 1 Bason 1 Sugar Box 1 Honey & Butter
Plates 3 Bottles 1 Hackel 9 Split Botton Chair 1 Large Bible 1 Small Bible
1 frow 1 Back Chair 1 Hammer 1 pr. Stutyards 2 Testaments 1 Dictonary 1 Check
Reel 1 fire Shovel 1 flat 10 dollars Cash 300 Bushels Sound Corn at home 150
bushels of Sound Corn at the River farm Supposed to be 500 weight of Pickeled
Pork 400 bundles fodder.
A Memorandium of Articles Sold on the property of Martin Hills Decd. this
february 2nd 1832

Hamilton Scott 1 piece of Chain	.81¼
Willis W. Talley 2 boreshmer Plows	1.06½
Arthur Crozier 2 Shovel plows	.37½
Willis W. Tally 2 do do	.30
Alfed Narres 1 Bell	.31¼
Hn. Barton 1 pitch fork	.31
Enoch Foster 1 Old Hoe	.29
William Lunsford Sundrie	.25
Willis W. Tally 1 pair bridle Bits	.13
John B. Crozier 1 fro	.31½
Samuel Moore Sundry articles	.32
William Lunsford 1 Axe	1.26
H. L. White 1 do	1.37
Samuel Moore 3 Clevises	.71
Moses Roberts 1 pr pincers & f Iron	.36
Samuel Frost 1 Hand Axe	1.75
John Prier Broken Gur	.80
Arthur Crozier antoher pair Gears	3.50
William Hansford 1 Cast	7.25
William Hansford 1 Gars eere	2.50
(76) Isaac Martin 25 Bs. Corn at 32 cts. pr Bs.	8.00
William Mc Comick 25 Bs, Corn 37 cts. Bs.	9.25
John Howard 25 Bs. Corn 40 cts. Bs.	10.00
do do do 39	9.75
William Mc Comack 25 Bs. 37½	9.37½
Polly Hill 1 flax Wheel	1.50
Polly Hill 1 family Bible	5.00

do do 1 Hackel	1.00
Polly Hill 1 Smoothing	.26
do do 1 Spinning Wheel	.34
James Overton 1 bible	.26
Polly Hill 1 looking glass	.12½
William Stephens 1 Loom	4.02
William Howard 1 wheel	.63½
Polly Hill 1 Saddle	3.00
Arthur Crozier 1 Sickle	.41
Polly Hill 1 Chest	1.01
Polly Hill 1 Bed	3.00
do do 1 do	2.00
Polly Hill 1 Set Loom Gus	.18¾
Arthur Crozier 1 Old Saddle	.52
Polly Hill 1 Side Saddle	.12½
Polly Hill Some Cotton	.50
do do "feathers	.25
Bolly Hill some wool	.12½
Polly Hill 1 Keel	.25
Polly Hill 1 trunk	.12½
do do 1 Bed	2.00
Polly do 1 do	2.00
Polly Hill 7 Chairs	.50
Moses Roberts 1 Iron Wedge	.40
	99.90¼

(77)	Amt. brot over	99.90¼
	Hugh Barton 1 fodder Stack	2.75
	Moses Roberts 35 Bushels Corn at K	3.00
	John Lackey Some Ducks	1.01
	William Hansford 13 Geese 25	3.25
	Hugh Barton 25 Bs. of Corn 30	7.50
	John Lackey 25 " of Corn 31	7.75
	Hugh Barton 25 " " " 31	7.75
	Polly Hill 2 pair fire dogs at 25	.50
	John Childress fire do	.12½
	Hampdue S. Scott 1 negro woman and Child	311.00
	Charles Mc Cormick one Black & White Cow	6.02
	John Childress 1 Cow & Calf Noted	9.25
	Banister Vowell 1 Heifer	2.50
	James Overton 1 Calf noted	1.26
	Charles Mc Cormick 1 Cupboard note	16.25
	Saml. C. Young 1 Beauro	14.38
	William Hansford 1 table	2.00
	William Stephens Stack Hay	9.06
	Polly Hill 1 Mare	50.00
	William Hansford 1 Gray Horse	10.00
	Polly Hill 1 Pot	1.50
	William Hansford 1 Skellet & lid	.33
	William do do	.51

William Hansford 1 Gid Iron	.38
William Hansford 1 Oven & lid	.63½
Polly Hill 1 Camp Kettle	.52
Polly Hill 1 Skillet	.52
Polly Hill 1 Pot Rack	1.50
(78) Polly Hill 1 Pot & Soap	.75
Polly Hill 1 Pot Lard	2.00
Polly Hill 1 pair Steelyards(?)	1.00
William Hansford 1 Plow	1.15
William Hansford 1 degon Plow	.63½
	583. 71¼

75

One note on James Wallace 3.75 due on the 25th Dec. 1830 with a credit on
the Same of $300 one on Harve Milicon Due 15th March 1831   2 75
one do Moses Milicon 75 due September 7th 1831   75
one do on Soloman Webber 5.25 due 2nd Jan. 1830   5 25
one do on George Hope & Sterling Smith for the value of 7 tubs   1 62½
    corn 29 Bundles of fodder & 25cts. worth whiskey with a credit on
    the same for $2.00
one note on Charles Price for   50
one do on Soam Sorton & Wm. Martin $1.25 Due 23rd Sept. 1831   1.25
one note on William Mellicon 3o Bs. Corn Due 15th Nov. 1831   56.00
Total amt. added   602.58¾
The above is a true perfect Inventory of all the personal Estate of
Mastin Hill Decd. which has come in to my hands as Administrator togather
with the Sales of the Same to the person above named at at the prices amexed
to the same togather with the debts due to said Estate which this day by
me returned unto Court this 10th day of April 1831.
recorded 10th June 1834
J J Clerk   William Hansford

Amount Sale of John Asherst Decd.

1. James Bunch 1 pair Geers	$1.86
2. George Haskins 1 pair Geers	1.91
3. George Haskins 1 pair Geers	2.00
4. John Tober 2 Chairs & 1 back band	.68¾
5. James Bunch fifth Chain	1.00
6. George Haskins Strechers Neck Chain	.37½
7. George Haskins 1 Blind Bridle	0.06
8. George Haskins 1 Blind Bridle	1.00
9. George Haskins 1 Blind Bridle	.59
10. George Haskins 1 Hipstrap	.57
11. Emelia Asherst 1 Flax Wheel	1.00
12. Emelia Asherst 1 Check Reel	.25
13. Richd. Anderson 1 Little Wheel	.06¼
14. Emelia Asherst 1 big wheel	.50
15. Saml. C. Young 1 frow Axe & 16 1 weeding hoe	.34
17. Joseph M. Asherst 1 Bridle & Belley Band & Bell	.76
18. Abraham Bowling 2 Sprouting Hoe & Axe	1.37½
19. John Haskins 1 weding hoe	.62½
20. John Roberts 2 weding hoes	.81

```
         21. Joseph Ashert 1 Madack                    .42
         22. Henry Bulter 1 Shovel                     .65
         23. John Roberts  1 hoe & Bulltongue          .67
         24. William H. Johnson 1 Plow & Clevias       .26
         25. James Ross 1 Plow Clevis & Tree           .56
         26. Richd. Anderson 1 Horse                 68.00
         27. Milley Nuntey 1 Horse                   32.00
         28. William Roberts 1 Mare                  46.57½
         29. Emmellia Asherst 1 Horse                21.00
         30. Abraham Bowling 1 big plow hoe           1.00
         31. Sib Baley 1 Keg                           .31½
         32. Richd. Anderson 1 Keg                     .52
  (79)   33. David Doherty 1 handsaw                   .82
         34. Emila Asherst 1 pickling tub              .25
         35. Emila Asherst 1 tub                       .25
         36. John Tober 1 Reaphook & drawing knife     .50
         37. James Hickey 1 Whitstone                  .39
         38. Abraham Bowling 1 Howe                    .29
         39. Richd. Andrews 1 Butcher Knife & Tomahawk .28
         40. Sib Baley Trumpet                         .27
         41. Abraham Bowling 1 Anville & Hammer         .62½
         42. Joseph M. Ashert 1 Axe                   1.50
         43. Sib Baley 1 Bucket & aperatices           .60
         44. Daniel Doherty 1 Saddle                  2.66½
         45. Elizabeth Roberts 1 Side Saddle          8.62½
         46. Emilia Asherst 1 Side Saddle              .50
         47. Richd. Andrews 1 Scythe & Cradle          .52
         48. John Pain 1 Scythe & Cradle               .50
         49. William Keeny 4 Hogshead 1 Barrell       1.55
         50. John Haskins 1 waggon whip                .22
         51. Charles C. Bowling 1 half Bushel          .31
         52. William Keeny 1 half Bushel               .33
         53. Richd. Oliver 1 Kiddle                    .12½
         54. John Pain 1 Half Bushel                   .43
         55. Nelson R. Asherst 1 Large Kettle         3.61½
         56. Charles C. Bowling 5 head Sheep          5.00
         57. John Cross 1 Negro boy                 557.00
         58. Joseph M. Asherst 1 Kettle              2.06½
         59. Charles C. Bowling 1 Cow & Calf          9.00
         60. James Rector 1 Cow & Calf               9.25
         61. Charles C. Bowling 1 Cow                 9.00
         62. Sterling Smith 1 Steer                   2.98
         63. Richd. Andrews 1 Heifer                  6.25
         64. William Breaden 1 Oven & led             1.25
  (80)   65. Joseph M. Asherst 1 Mole                  .38
         66. Emilia Asherst 1 Skillet                  .06¼
         67. Emilia Asherst 1 Coffee pot               .25
         68. Sib Baley 1 pot & fork                    .25
         69. James Cross 1 pair Pot Hooks              .06¼
         70. Nelson R. Asherst 1 Pack Saddle           .06¼
         71. Joseph M. Asherst 1 Spider                .31
         72. Emilia Asherst 1 Pot Tramel               .50
```

73 Joseph M. Asherst 1 Jar	1.20	
74 James Roberts 2 Pails	.40	
75 Emilia Asherst Plates & Bowls	.50	
76 James Breaden 2 Plates	.40	
77 Sib Baley Plates	.29	
78 George Enbs Cups & Saucers	.40	
79 James Cross 1 Bowl	.20	
80 James Cross	.20½	
81 Abraham Bowling 1 Auger	.25	
82 David Daugherty 1 Dish & Box & Cup	.70	
83 James Hoskins 5 Spoons	.26	
84 Micajah Philips	.50	
85 Craven Johnson 1 Candlestick	.43	
86 Saml. Dunn 1 Chest of Drawers	2.00	
87 Milley Nunly 1 Table	1.50	
88 Henry Butler 1 Keg	.36	
89 Melley Nunly 1 Loom	1.50	
90 Charles Shenliver 1 Cupboard	11.00	
91 Emilia Asherst 1 Bed & furniture	4.00	
92 James Langhery 1 Sted & furniture	8.61	
93 Saml. Dunn 1 Grind Stone	.68¼	
94 James Broden 1 Chest	.50	
95 Emilia Asherst 3 Chairs	.25	
96 James Roberts 2 pair Cards	.06¼	
(81) 97 Emilia Asherst 1 Churn	.12½	
98 Richd. Andrews 3 pair Hanes	.06¼	
99 Charles C. Bowling 3 Bushels Rye	1.50	
100. James Bunch 3 Bushels Rye	1.50	
101 Nelson R. Asherst 3 Bushels Rye	1.50	
102 Emila Asherst 1 Pot	.31	
103 John Ross 1 Raw Hide	.30	
104 Emilia Asherst 1 Pot	.50	
105 Joseph M. Asherst 1 Slay	.16 2/3	
106 Charles C. Bowling 2 Bushel Rye	1.06¼	
107 John Pain 2 Slays & 1 Gears	.55	
108 Emilia Asherst 1 Pitcher	.06¼	
109 Emilia Asherst 1 Negro Woman	5.00	
110 Micijah Philips 1 Lot of Corn	3.65	
111 Jane Bray 1 Lot of Corn	3.70¾	
112 Jane Bray 1 Lot of Corn	4.41	
113 Amilia Asherst 1 Oat Stack	1.00	
114 Benj. W. Hackney 1 Cow & Calf	6.50	
115 Joseph M. Asherst 1 Home(?)	50.00	
116 Philip Smith 1 Lot of Corn	3.50	
117 Amilia Asherst 1 Lot of Corn	2.06¼	
118 Joseph M. Asherst 1 Lot of Corn	4.12½	
119 Richd. Andrews 1 Lot of Corn	6.25	
120 Joseph M. Asherst 4 Walnut Planks	.25	
121 Amilia Asherst 1 Barrell	.31¼	

```
The above is a true Copy          $  987.61
Was accepted this the 14th Jan. 1833      )  Joseph M. Asherst
     recorded 17th June 1834               )  Administrator
          J. J. Clerk                      )
```

(82)   State of Tennessee   )
       Anderson County   )   Settlement with S. Dunn, Administrator

of Spessard Decd. pursuance of an appointment made by the Court of pleas
& Quarter Sessions of said County at the last April Court we William
Mc Kamey & Arthur Crozier Two of the Commissheraners then appointed to
settle with the Saml. Dunn Administrator of the Estate of John Specard
Decd. have this day met at the Court house in Clinton George Haskins not
atending and report as follows to Wit To Amts. of Sales appears to have
been returned by said Admr. as Certificate of Clerk of said Court 354.82¾
Amount due the Estate by note as pr. Certificate interest   17.00
Collected   13.99¾
                                      Supera   385.82¾

1. By one Note on Moses Stout which was returned in the
     above amt. of notes as pr. Debit   2.02½
2. Dickerson & Jarnajins O K
     as pr rect   6.76½
3. Paid George Haskins for
     Spesards note   6.06¼
4. Paid James Ross as OK &
     Note & rect   14.83
5. Paid Wm. Mc Kamey as pr
     Voucher   .50
6. Paid Joseph Stout as per
     Voucher   4.96½
7. Pd. Wm. Mc Kamey Junr. per
     Voucher   3.50
8. Pd. Carles Y. Oliver per
     taxes pr rect   1.89½
9. Pd. Joseph C. Strong pr do   .81¼
10.Paid Sam Vandagriff pr do   4.25
11. Pd. John Luallen pr do   3.00
12. Pd. Wm. Ammbrester pr do   1.25
13. Pd. Michael Specsard pr do   12.00
14. Jno. Jarnagin pr do   1.40
15. Samuell Dunn pr do   1.62½
     A. Crozier & Mc Kanney (?) pr do   2.00
Amt. Brot over   382.82½
  do   do   66.78½
The Administrator rendered   12.00
    at Different terms   78.98½
To rect from Trustee of P.
     County Claim   306.84½
Due Spesard in his life time   4
                                                                  310.84¼

This above Correct Statment we William Mc Kanney and A.
        Crozier do Certify this 11th July 1834
        recorded 22nd August 1834   )
) A. Crozier
) Wm. Mc Kanney
)   Commissioners

A Statement with C. Y. Oliver Executer

(83) State of Tennessee   )in presuance of an order
      Anderson County   )

of the Court of plas & Quarter Sessions of said County made at this April
Sessions 1834 We Samuel Dunn and A Crozier to of the Commissioners Wit
this day at the Court house in Clinton George Haskins absent and made
Settlement with Charles Y. Oliver Executor of the last Will & Testament
of William Scarbrough Decd. and report as follows ViZ amt. of Sales as
reported Executor & Certified by Clerk 140 38 No. 1 & 2 Clerks recipts 4.70
3 pd the Clerk for Copy of Will & pd Crees   2.50
an fees as Commissioners   2.00
Executor for his Services   7.50
                                                                     16.70
                                                                 _____

                                                                    130.13

That the above Statment is correct we do certify this 11th July 1834
    Recorded August 22nd 1834
    John Jarnagin Clerk
              A Crozier   Comms.
              Saml. Dunn
(84) Sale of Rachel Peters Estate

John Tober 3 Plates   .12½
  Cups & Saucers   .12½
1 Bed   3.31¼
1 Bed Quilt   .41
1 pr. Spectacles   .06¼
1 pr. do   .14
                                                         4.17½

William T. Lightfoot 1 Bottle   .12½   .12½
John Peters 6 teaspoons
  6¼ & Salt Barrell 2)   .08¼
1 fat Tub 15¢ bed Quilt 53¢   .68
1 Book Case   .13
1 Flax Wheel   2.02
                                                         2.91¼

Lucy Farmer 1 Bottle   .18¾
Betsey Kesterson 1 Pot & Hooks   .76
1 pair Spectacles   .19
                                                          .95

Samuel Tunnell 1 Oven & Led   .75
1 Bed Stead & Cord   .62½
                                                         1.37½

William Williams 2 tubs   .25
1 pair Spectacle   .03
                                                          .28

Willis Seins 1 tub   .04
1 Bed Quilt 78¢ 1 Basket 6   .84
                                                          .88

Nathan A Farmer 1 Counterpain	1.56
1 Coverled	2.38
1 Bedstead & Card	.76
	4.68
Isaac Armstrong 1 Sheet	.58½
1 Do	.61
1 do & Counterpain	1.40
1 Coverled 3 31½ & Do 3.01	6.32½
	8.90½
Peter Johnson 1 Cupboard	13.06½
	13.06½
	37.57½

I do Certify that the written is a True return of the amount of sale of the
personal Estate of Rachel Peters deceased July 14th 1834.

Recorded August 22nd 1834　　　　　　　John Peters
　John Jarnagin Clerk　　　　　　　　Administrator

(85) Inventory of the property Sold on the 15th August 1833 Richd. Luallen Decd.

John Luallen 1 Yoke Steers	$34.00
Samuel Moore 1 Yoke Steers	26.00
Samuel C. Luallen 1 Yoke Steers	31.00
James Kirkpatrick 1 Lot Hogs 17 head	10.00
William Stephen nd 2 lots of Hogs 28 head	29.25
William Lindsay 3rd Lot Hogs 13 head	21.50
William Lindsay 4th Lot Hogs 17 head	40.12½
John H. Cane 1 Steer	11.00
Richard B. Luallen 1 Steer	8.75
Joshua Epperson 1 Cow	5.00
Richard B. Luallen 1 Steer	7.25
Melly Luallen 1 Cow & yearland	6.67½
Parzidda Luallen 1 Cow & yearland	6.00
Isaac Maysden 1 Cow & Calf	9.18¾
Samuel Luallen 1 Steer	12.00
Parazidda Luallen 1 Cow	7.00
Francis Lovett 1 Cow & Calf	6.25
John Lynart 1 Steer	2.62½
Elijah Wallace 1 Heifer	2.00
John Lynart 1 Heifer	2.01
Milly Luallen 1 Cow & Calf	5.00
John Severs 1 Bull	13.06½
William Severs 1 Bull	6.75
William Webb 1 Heifer	6.25
Rrichard B. Luallen 1 Heifer	6.00
Francis Luallen 1 Heifer	6.00
Moses Overton 1 Cow	4.13½
James Kirkpartick 1 Cow	8.25
Richard Luallen 1 Heifer	4.25
John Lynart 1 Yearland	3.12½
Jesse Noel 1 Cow & Calf	10.00
	358.32½

(86) Amount Brot forward	358.32¼
John Severs 1 Heifer	6.81¼
Parazidda Luallen 1 Cotton Wheel	.25
Parazidda Luallen 1 Bed Stead	.25
Parazidda Luallen 1 Flax Wheel	.50
Charles Luallen 1 Matack	.99
Charles Luallen 1 Hoe	.01
Parazidda Luallen 1 Churn	.12½
Parazidda Luallen 1 Table	.29
James Kirkpatrick 1 Table	.50
Samuel Moore 1 Log Chain	2.77
Samuel Moore 1 Clevis	.38
Parazidda Luallen 1 tub	.33
Charles Luallen 1½ Bushel	.01
Enoch Foster one Barrell	.12½
Samuel Moore 1 Barrell	.13
Parazidda Luallen Two Barrels	.38½
Enoch Foster 1 Barrell	.12½
Charles Luallen one Kag	.06¼
Samuel Moore 1 Plow Scrue	2.
Parazidda Luallen 2 pots & oven Kittle hooks	7.63¼
& Loom	.30¼
James Moore 1 Matack	5.00
John Jarnagin four Beef hides	1.52
John Luallen 1 pair Stellyards (?)	1.58
Samuel Brooks one Sifter	.20
Parazidda Luallen 1 Sifter & Barsher Plow	1.46¼
James Kirkpatrick 1 Handsaw	1.37½
Calvin Slaver one Fro	.37½
Samuel Moore one Matack & Plow	1.06¼
Samuel Moore 1 Single tree	.25
Aron Slaver 1 Single tree	.37½
Samuel Moore 1 Double tree 1 Chain 1 Clives 1 Rod	1.44¼
Samuel Moore 1 Barsher Plow	.50
James Kirkpatrick one Horse Collar	.06¼
	394 .97
(87) Amount Brot Forward	394.97
James Dikes one Singletree	.25
James Kirkpatrick one Shovel	.68¾
Samuel C. Young 1 pair Harness & Chain	1.75
James Moore one pair do	2.02
Jesse Noel one Collar	.43¼
Charles Luallen 1 Bridle & Plow	1.06¼
James Dikes one Bell	1.00
James Kirkpatrick 1 Cotton Wheel & Reel	1.31¼
James Kirkpatrick 1 Heifer	5.62½
Richard B. Luallen 1 Steer	3.75
John Lynard one yearland	1.50
William Roysden 1 Heifer	5.62½
Richard Taylor 1 Steer	5.00
Elijah Wallace 1 Steer	3.52
John York 1 Heifer	4.06¼
Moses Millicon 1 Cow	6.00

Richard B. Luallen 1 Steer	4.00
David Keesling one waggon	10.37
Samuel S. Luallen one do	42.06½
Parazidda Luallen 1 Sorrell filly	21,00
Richard B. Luallen 1 do	40.00
Richard Wheeler 1 Horse	56.75
Moses Millicon 1 Mare	15.75
Charles Luallen to hire of Negroes Ruben Lucy &	
Nancy	60.50
James Kirkpatrick hire one Hanseah	8.00
John Luallen to hire of Aron	1.00
Samuel S. Luallen to hire of Jorden	22.25
Ann Luallen one Saddle & table	.12½
Parazidda Luallen two Saddles one Briddle	3.44 2/4
Samuel S. Luallen to one Coulter	.50
Samuel Luallen one Smoothing Iren	.70
Hugh Barton three Stocks of Oats	3.75
	676.77¼
(88) Amount Brot forward	676.77¼
Samuel Moore one Sow and Shoats	8.00
Joseph Keeny one Rifle Gun	5.00
Parazidda Luallen to Chairs 1 Chest 1 dresser	
2 beds	7.32½
Milly Luallen 1 Bureo	2.56½
Hugh Barton 15 head Sheep	12.56½
Samuel Moore one Hacksl	1.56
Charles Luallen 1 Steer	8.50
Moses Millican one let Hogs	10.00
Calvin Childress 11 head Sheep	8.36
Charles Luallen 100 B. Corn at 33 1/3 cts. pr. B.	26.00
Samuel S. Luallen to 90 B. Corn at 33 2/3 cts.	
pr. B.	30.00
Charles Luallen to 19 B. Corn at 33 2/3 cts. pr. B.	6.33 1/3
James Kirkpatrick to Calvin	500.00
Samuel Moore to Robert	550.00
Arthur Barton to Anthony	560.00
Richard B. Luallen to Campbell	605.00
Ann Luallen to Reubin	350.00
John Luallen to Aron & Child	200.00
John Luallen to Lucyan	351.00
James Kirkpatrick to Hansiah	50.00
Samuel S. Luallen Jorden	502.00
Samuel S. Luallen Harrietta	181.00
James Kirkpartick Nancy	235.00
Anna Luallen Anderson	403.00
Charles Luallen Mary & three Children	1000.00
	$6290.05¼

recorded August 22nd 1834
  John Jarnagin
    Clerk

(89) Settlement with William Handsard Administrator

State of Tennessee)
Anderson County   )   We Samuel Dunn John O Neal & A Crozier
                        Commissioners appointed at April Turm last to Settle
with William Handsard Administrator of the Estate of Mastin Hill Decd. have
this met at the Court house in Clinton & report as follows to Wit to Amt.
of Sales and Debts pr. Sertificate of Clerk $602.58¾
        Sufera

No 1 & 2 R. Rogers Rect for fees $10.60
3 D. Baker OK as pr. voucher   10.75
4. William Armtrester as pr voucher   5.37½
5. A Crozier as pr voucher   6.50
6. Note to academy a pr voucher   53.00
7. Hardy F. Marshell as pr do   3.98¾
8. James Mc Canns Note   10.00
9. Jarnagin OK as pr voucher   131.02½
10. James Millican OK as pr do
    Interest on last 3 Sums   10.70
11. Hardy F. Marshall as pr do   3.75
12. D James King as pr De   4.25
13. John & Polly Lamar as pr do   5.45
14. Mastin Hill as pr voucher on Note   1.22
15. Charles Mc Cormack as pr voucher on Note   2.50
16. C. Y. Oliver for taxes pr do   3.97½
17. Lewis Miller for note pr do   15.58
18. William Stephens for O K as pr voucher   3.66½
19. A Crozier for rect   3.00
20. Tho. Dikes as pr do   2.12½
21. Saml. C. Young as pr do   2.00
22. John B. Crozier as pr do   24.58
23. Charles Mc Cormack as do   2.00
24. Lewis Miller (Guardian)   42.16
25. Do   do   do   1.25
                                          $370. 56¾

(90) Amount of Debts bfot over   620.58¾
      Amount of Cr. Brot over   370.56¾
      No 27 William C. Mc Cormack as pr voucher 3.12½
      28 Dickerson & Jarnagin do   69.50
      29. George M. White do   1.00
      30 Crozier & Armbuster do   3.50
      31 William Stephens do   12.75
      32 A Crozier & Son do   1.87½
                                                    462.34¾

33 By 300 Bushels of Corn $100.00 $140.27
640 Pork   19.20
& $30. for Sugar & Coffee   30.00
                                    $149.20
the last three Items are the Widows Daier and he Handsard took the widow
home with family & Supported hir & Sold the property for the benefit of the
Estate.

```
By Insolvent Notes & Judgment              $16.37½
By Services to Admrs. for Two years          40.00
By Services pr to Commissioners               3.00
By Court paid on Suits                 300   64.37½
Amt. of Cr. Brot up                        $ 213.57½
To Ballance Debt brot up                     140.27
                                              73.10¼
34 By Clerk Fees                               2.40
                                           $  75.50¼
```

that the above is a Correct Statement Due Saml. Dunn John O Neal & A.
 Crozier do Certify this 11th July 1834

       A. Crozier)
       Saml. Dunn) Commer.
       John O Neal)

recorded Sept. 1st 1834
 John Jarnagin Clerk

(91) Settlement with Joseph M. Asherst Admor.
 State of Tennessee)
 Anderson County) We Samuel Dunn, William Mc Kamey, George Haskins
         appointed by the Court of said County at April
Term 1834 to make Settlement with Joseph M. Asherst Administrator &
Amilia Asherst Administratrix of the Estate of John Asherst Decd. Wit
Samuel Dun & William Mc Kamney, George Haskins not present and being
furnished the amount of Sales of the Estate nine Hundred & Eighty Seven
dollars & Sixty one Cents Cash in hand Sixty dollars all amounting to
1047.61 recd. the following vouchers of Joseph M. Asherst Administrator

```
No. 1 Vouchers                             $115.00
    2 pr do                                  13.60¼
    3 pr do                                   3.52½
    4 pr vouchers                             3.00
    5 pr vouchers                             1.50
    6 pr vouchers                             1.25
    7 pr vouchers                             1.25
    8 pr vouchers                             2.08½
    9 pr voucher                              .37½
   10 pr voucher                             15.00
   11 pr voucher                              1.32½
   12 pr voucher                              2.50
   13 pr voucher                              5.00
   14 pr voucher                             88.87½
```
the Amt. allowed Admr. By Commissioners for his Services & Expences   50.00
 15 pr voucher   2.00
Insolvency by note Charles C. Bowling & Sterling Smith 2000)$326.28¾
Ballance in the hand of Administrator   721.32¼
We have Examined the above vouchers & belived the Settlement Correct this
  12th of July 1834   Saml. Dunn
           William Mc Kamney
           Commissioners

recorded Sept
1st 1834
 John Jarnagin Clerk

(92)   William Griffith Will in the name of God Amen know all men by thire
presents that I William Griffith of the County of Anderson and State of
Tennessee being old & infirm but in perfect mind & memory callin to mind
the certinaly of death and the uncertainly of life do make this my last
will and Testament I first recommend my Soul to God who gave it and and
my Body to its Mother dust to be burried in a Christain manner and my
property which God gave to me I dispose of in the following manner first
I wish all my Just debts to be paid out of my Estate I will & bequath
unto my beloved wife Susanna two Negro women by the name of Caroling and
Lucinda and thire increase to dispose of as She my think before I give my
wife Susanna one bay Horse and bay mare and hir increase I give to my wife
Two Cows and five head of dry cattle and twelve head of Sheep twenty Six
head of hogs all to my wife Susanna and thire increase to dispose of as
She my think proper I also give to my wife Susanna all my house hold &
Kitchen furniture to dispose of as she my think proper I give and bequath
to my son Amos Griffith my nigro man Lewis I give to my son Thomas Griffith
one dollar I give to my son Benjamin Griffith my negro man Jacob I give to
my Daughter Bonnie Sullins one hundred dollars out of my Estate I give to
my son Jacob Griffith Lawful Heirs thirty dollars I give to my Daughter
Anna Hickey one dollar to my son Isaac Griffith Lawful

(93) Heirs one dollar I give to my son William Griffith one dollar I give to my
son David Griffith one dollar I give unto my Daughter Susanna Hendrix one
dollar the ballance of my Estate which is two tedious to name every par-
ticular I give and bequath to my wife Susanna and all the deeds and dues of
givts that I have made I wish to stand good in Law and equity and tortly(?)
I do hereby Constitute & appoint my wife Susanna and my son Amos and
William C. Griffith executors of this my last will & Testament hereby revoking all others or former wills of Testaments by me heretofore made in
Witness where of I have here unto set my hand and Seal this third day for
May in the year of our Lord 1834.

Stephen Marshall   )
William Right   )
John Hoskins   )   William Griffith
Mary X hir mark Hoskins   )
Recorded 24th October 1834

                          John Jarnagin   Clerk

(94) Benjamin Lockets Will
     I Benjamin Lockets of the State of Tennessee and County of Anderson do here
by make my last Will & Testament in manner & form following that is 1st I
desire that all my Just debts and funeral expences be paid 2nd I give my
wifw wifw Alsay Locket three Beds and furniture with all house hold and
Kitchen furniture also five head for Cattle also my Stock of hogs and Sheep
two head of horses also my black Smith tools with my Crop of Corn and all my
bacon also the tracrt of land on which I now live an also one note on
Richard Oliver under one Hundred dollars with all the plantation Tools with
all my debts by book and open account own use for during hir lifetime then
to be Equally divided among all my Children making the youngest equal with
the oldest balesting with what has heretofore given 3rd I give my Daughter
Francis Locket one Bed and furniture one cow & calf 1 Loom 4th I give my Son
William Locket 1 Coalt and Saddle and Lastly I do hereby constitute and
appoint my wife Alsay Locket and Harry Pryer Executors of this my last will

& Testament in Witness where of I have hereunto Set my hand and Seal this
twenty fifth day of February in the year of our Lord one Thousand Eight
Hundred & Thirty four.   his
                              Benjamin X Locket
                                      mark
                                              (Seal)

(95)   B. Locket Will Continued

Signed Sealed published and declared to be the last Will & Testament of the
forgoing named Benjamin Locket in presence of us who at his request and in
his presence have hereunto Subscribed our names as Witness to the same.
                              William C. Griffith   (Seal)
        recorded October   William Right   (Seal)
        24th 1834   Reubin William   (Seal)
        John Jarnagin Clerk

        Settlement with Willis Leath Administrator
        State of Tennessee   )
        Anderson County   )   W. John Chiles
                                    Martin Asherst &
                                    A. Crozier
Commissioners appointed by the Court have this day settled with Willis Leath
Administrator of the Estate of Elizabeth Johnson decd. and find from the
voucher produced to us by said Administrator that the Estate is indebted to
said Administrator Twenty two dollars and one cent this 13th Oct. 1834
Commissioners   )   A. Crozier
for Selling $1. Each is $3.00)   Martin Asherst
recorded Nov. 5th 1834   )   John Chiles
        John Jarnagin Clerk   )   Commissioners

(100)   Inventory & Amt. of sale of Abraham Jones Decd. Procedes of the Sale of
        Abraham Jones Decd. 17th of February 1834

        1 Scyth & Cradle $2.37½
        1 do   do   .75
        2 Cythes   .62½
        1 pair Harness & Chains   2.37½
        1 pair of Gars   2.00
        1 do   do   2.06¼
        1 pair Harness & Collar   .25
        1 Collar   .75
        1 Blind Bridle   1.01¼
        1 Log Chain   2.43
        4 Collars   .06¼
        1 Bell & Collar   .52
        1 do   do   .31
        1 do   do   .25
        1 do   do   .27
        1 Halter Chain   .50
        Chains   1.06¼
        Strechers   1.15
        1 pair Gears   2.12½

	Strechers	1.25
	2 Breast Chains	.50
	1 fifth Chain	1.67
	1 Frow	.25
	1 Cutting Knife	1.50
	1 Bridle	1.00
	1 pair of Bridle Reins	.28
	2 Shovel Plows	.12½
	1 Basket of Tools	25.
	Carried over $	
(101)	1 Sled trap	.18¾
	1 Clevis & Gopher	.56¼
	1 foot Adze	57.
	1 Barshear plow	27
	1 Axe & Iron Wedge	.26
	1 Axe	.12½
	1 Cutting Knife	.20
	3 Augers	.37½
	2 Augers	.80
	2 Chisels	.30
	3 Chisels & 1 Gauge	.28
	1 Barshear Blow Irons	2.25
	1 Copper Adze & other Articles	.75
	1 Waggon	85.00
	1 feed Trough	1.12½
	1 pair Breach Bands	2.50
	1 pair of hip straps	1.25
	1 Waggon Corn	1.18¾
	1 plain Auger Compass	.76
	1 Waggon Bows	.12½
	1 Matack	1.37½
	8 hogs	10.00
	9 hogs	13.12½
	1 Sow & Pigs	1.37½
	1 Sow & Pigs	4.00
	1 Hog	1.50
	1 Yoke of Oxens	57.56¼
	2 Steers	21.00
	2 Steers	20.00
	2 Steers	14.00
	1 Steer	5.06¼
(102)	1 Cow	14.00
	1 Cow & Bell	13.00
	1 Heifer	3.50
	1 Cow & bell	9.56¼
	1 Cow	8.00
	1 Calf	2.00
	1 Calf	2.14½
	1 Cow	9.25
	1 Calf	2.00
	1 Horse	77.00
	1 Horse	86.00
	1 Sorrel Horse	73.00
	1 Black Boy Ed.	560.00
	1 Muttatto Woman & Child	441.00

1 Black Child	257.00
1 Bee Stand	1.75
1 do	1.40
1 do	1.80
6 Sheep	5.00
5 Sheep	6.00
5 Sheep & 1 Lamb	6.26
1 Bag of Clover Seed	1.06¼
4 Bushels Rye at 52 cts. pr. B.	2.60
1 Spade	1.37½
1 Set Black Smith Tools	35.00
1 piece of Steel	.25
4 Bushels wheat at 63 cts. pr. B.	2.52
4 Bushels of wheat at 62 cts. pr. B.	2.50
1 Lot of Bacon	22.50
1 Side Sole Leather	1.56¼

(103) A. Jones Continued

1 Side of Sole Leather	3.12½
1 Quantity (?)	2.06¼
1 Side Sole Leather	2.18¼
1 Side Sole Leather	3.75
1 Side upper Leather	2.50
1 Sadle & Blanket	12.50
1 pot & Skillet	.06¼
76 Lbs. Iron	4.50
1 Clock	10.01
1 Bed Bible & Trunk	3.00
1 Cupboard	10.50
1 Flax Wheel 1 Side Saddle	1.00
1 Beauro	8.00
1 Bed	10.00
1 Bed	11.56¼
1 Pot & Hooks	.75
1 Pot	.71
1 Pot	.75
1 Oven & Led	2.00
1 do do	1.62½
1 Pot	1.80
1 Skillet & Led	.94
1 Tar Bucket	.22
fire Tongs & Pot Hooks	1.50
1 Barrell	.67
1 do	.50
1 Keg Vinegar	1.40
50 bushels of Corn	26.00
do	26.00

(104) A. Jones Sale Cont.

25 Bushels Corn	15.00
25 Doz. of Oats	6.37½
1 Cutting Knife & Box	2.00
25 doz. of Oats	5.25
do	5.00
do	5.00
do	5.00
do	4.93¾

do	4.68¾
do	4.75
do	4.68¾
do	4.12½
8 doz. of Oats	1.22
1 Rye Stack	3.40
1 Stack of Straw	.27
1 Hay Stack	.50
1 Lot of Hay	2.31
1 Hay Stack	.76
1 do	.81¾
1 fodder Stack	2.40
1 do	5.75
1 do	2.41
1 do	3.62½
1 do	2.12½
1 Hay Stack	3.43¾
1 Bridle	1.25
1 pair of Saddle Bags	4.00
1 Tire Bucket 1 Basin	.54
1 Coffee Pot & pan	.52
(105) 6 Puter Plates	2.50
5 Puter Plates 2 pieces	1.57
5 Plates	.52
Cups Saucers & Teaspoons	.81¼
Screw	.62½
1 Lot of Puter	1.00
1 Set of Knives & forks	1.93¾
1 Lantirn	.63
1 Plate	.06¼
1 Set of Spoons	.25
1 Candle Stick	.57¼
Powles & 2 Glasses	.76
1 Dish	.81
1 Plate & Dish	1.00
1 Coffee Mill	.95
1 Crock	.10
1 Churn	.12½
1 Kettle 1 Hooks	.81¼
3 Lins & Other Articles	.27
1 Churn	.37½
1 piggin	.06¼
1 Hatchet	1.25
1 Cross Cut Saw	6.75
12 Geese	3.41
11 Ducks	1.00
1 Sheep Skin	.18¾
3 pair of Sheep Shears	1.01
2 " " do	.54
1 Lot of Lumber	.50
1 Set Coopers Tools	.50
1 Crow Bar	1.06¼
(106) A. Jones Continued	
2 Plains	2.50

4 do	1.55
1 Bell & Collar	.30
1 Smothing Iron	.50¼
1 Candle Mole	.37½
1 loom	9.00
1 State	.20
1 Saddle	2.36
14 Shuttles	.50
1 Slay	.25
1 do	.40
1 Meal Sive	.75
1 Slay	.25
1 Oven & led	2.50
1 Set of Harness	.75
1 Wheel	1.50
4 Sheep & 1 Lamb	4.30
Harness	.30
do	.25
1 pair of Shears	.75
1 Check Reel	.55
2 Hoes	.68¾
1 Set of warping Spools	.90
1 Meal Seive	.50
1 Matack	.52
5 Single trees & 1 Hoe	.50
1 Axe	1.00
1 Cockel Seive	.25
1 Sickel	.50
1 Table	1.31
1 Cow	8.80
(107) A. Jones Sale Continued	
1 Sheep Skin	.50
3 Sickels	.78
1 Barshear	1.00
3 Crocks	.50
1 Shovel Plow	.25
2 Grind Stones	.31
1 Shovel Plow	.30
1 plough Swingle tree & Clevis	.45
1 Bushel of Flax Seed & Barrell	.50
Shoe Maker Tools	2.40
1 Bed	.50
2 Chairs	.56¼
1 Chair	.25
1 Almanac	.12½
1 trumpet	.13
1 Handsaw	1.25
1 pair Bridle Reins	.25
1 Chair	.30
Fire Dogs	.25
1 Bottle of Whiskey	.50
1 Hogshead	.30
1 Flax Break	.55
1 pair Sheep Shears	1.01
½ deer Skin	.62½

	50 bushels Corn	12.75
	25 Bushels of Corn	12.75
	4¼ Bushels	2.16 1/3
	1 Pen of Shucks	.50
(108)	A. Jones Sale Continued	
	1 Honey Jar	.25
	1 do	.25
	1 pad lock	.25
	1 Bottle	.18¾
	1 do	.18¾
	1 do	.31½
	1 do	.21
	1 Broad Axe	2.12½
	1 Tray & Basin	.68¾
	1 Dish	.71
	Powder & Lead	.45
	1 Bible	.25
	Leather	.77
	1 Arithmetic	.12½
	1 Pail & tumbler	1.56¼
	1 Axe & Pot rack	.25
	1 pair of Steelyards	1.87½
	1 Blind Bridle	.72
	1 Meal Bag	.42
	1 do	.77
	1 Drawing Knife	.43
	1 Bucket & Shovel	.20
	1 tub & pick	.12½
	1 Chair & frame	.20
	1 Canoe	1.00
	1 Half Bushel & 1 half Peck	.42
	1 plow & Pot Hook	.06¼
	1 Bridle	.25
	3 do	.18¾
	1 Tinbucket	.83¾
	1 pair Pincers	
(109)	A. Jones Sale Continued	
	three Acres in Rye	11.25
	3 Acres in wheat	4.06¼
	3 do do	6.00
	1 lot of wheet	2.25
	1 do do	1.50
	1 do do	6.00
	1 Chair	.26
	1 do	.25
	1do	.25
	1 Axe	1.00
	1 Axe & Hoe	.20
	1 Note on Majah Lindsay for To Lbs. Iron	2.15
	3½ Acres in Rye	10.18¾
	1 Hogshead	.26
	1 do	.12½
	1 do	.37½
	1 do	.26

1 Lot of Staves	.06¼
1 Hogshead	.25
2 Pails	.25
1 Gun	.06¼
1 Trough of Soap	1.56¼
2 Kegs	1.06¼
A Sundry of Small Articles	7.31¼

State of Tennessee   )
Anderson County   ) County Court

       I William Jones administrator of all & the goods & Chattles & Credits of Abraham Jones do make oath that the forgoing is a True & perfect Inventory of Sale of said Estate up to this time Jan. 14, 1835 Sworn to in open Court.

                                William Jones

John Jarnagin
       Clerk
recorded Feb. 12th 1835
              J. J. Clerk

(110)   Inventory and Amt. of Sale of Thomas Butler Decd. (to Wit)

Spencer Keith Bot

1 waggon Box & Hams	.26
1 funt Band & G.	.08
1 Axe	.25
1 White Spotted Cow	10.33
1 Black Seded Cow	8.29
1 Cutting Knife Blade	1.00
1 Cutting Plain	.65¼
1 Spade	1.06¼
2 book of Astronomy	1.41¼
1 Bottle	.13
1 Jug of Spirits of Terpentine	.75
1 Gum of Timothy Seed	.12½
1 Yoke of work Steers Spotted	32.00
	55.25¼

Jacob Peak Bot

1 Bull Tongue Plow	.25
1 Stone Hammer	.37½
1 Scyth & Gradle	1.25
1 Jacks Crue	1.00
1 Large Still	50.50
3 lunty(?) Barrles	.06¼
1 Broad Axe	1.86
1 pair of Winding Blades	.50
1 Cross Gut Saw	5.25
1 Brass Clock	.27
1 Whiskey Barrell	.12½
1 Paruciall Blue & White	1.37½
1 Hogshead	.63
220 Bushels Corn	55.00
1 Book Rize & progess of religion	.21
2 Augers	.50
	174.41

(111) Thomas Butler Sale Cont.
Jesse Noel bot

1 Bool Tongue Plow	.37½
1 Lot of Iron	1.75
1 Axel Tree	.25
2 Barrles of Tare & Trough	.30
3½ Bushels of Rye	1.99½
1 Bed & 2 Pillows	9.00
1 Bee Stand	.57
1 Bed & 2 Pillows do	9.12½
1 Counterpin	.62½
Bed Curtins	.62½
Window Curtins	1.06½
1 Lot of Cabbage	.25
1 Bottle	.12½
	24.99¼

William Taylor Bot

1 Bell & Collar	1.50
1 Large Oven	1.63½
1 Under Bed & Cover	2.75
1 Barrell of Salt	.06¼
1 Quilt	3.01
1 Quilt do	1.91
1 Mans Saddle	1.50
1 Keg of Turnip Seed	.50
1 Sheep Skin	.15
1 Dirk	7.02
50 Bushels of Corn 1st Lot	18.75
50 do do 2nd Lot	18.75

William R. Butler Bot

1 pair of Strechers	.55
1 Bell	.37½
1 Axe	.25
	84. 59¼

(112) Thomas Butler Sale Cont.

1 Hoe	.25
1 Barshear Plow	.76
1 Axe	.50
1 Sythe & Cradle	2.06¼
4 Sheep	3.12
4 do	2.45
4 do	3.31¼
1 Red Cow	11.06¼
1 Plow	.56¼
1 Gray Plow	1.10
1 Waggon Tongue & hound	
1 Axel tree	.26
1 Set of Smith Tools	10.00
1 Set of Cups & Saucers	.31¼
1 Washing tub	.53
Candle Moles	.25

1 Table	.75
1 Small Kettle	.75
1 Black Horse	61.00
1 Bay Horse	54.25
1 Large Black Horse	65.00
1 Razor	.27
1 Shovel	.12½
1 Slay	.26
1 pair of Steelyards	1.06¼
1 Looking Glass	1.52
1 Bed Stead	.75
The wood works of a Waggon	36.00
2 pair of fore Gurs & Harness	5.12½
2 pair Hendger & C	6.54
1 pair of Geers & C	3.06¼
	231. 06¼

(113)   Thomas Butler Sale Cont.

1 Counterpin	1.50
1 Blanket	2.93
1 do	2.85
50 Bushels of Corn 3 rd Lot	13.50
50 do 7th Lot	13.50
1 Lot of Cabbage	.25
1 Large Kettle	3.56¼
John H. Kington bot	
1 Cow	8.00
1 Lot of Iron	3.42½
1 Bed Stead & Cord	1.00
7 Chairs	1.12½
1 Arm Chair	.75
1 pair of Steelyards	1.06¼
69 Lbs. Iron	2.75
1 Coverlid	1.55
1 Quilt	1.91
1 do	1.96
1 do	1.25
1 do	1.81
1 Coverlid	1.75
2 table Cloths	1.00
50 Bushels Corn 12th Lot	12.75
Henry R. Butler bot	
1 Garden Hoe	.25
3 pair of Chains	.65
All the oats in the Barn	7.56¼
All the Flax in the Barn on	3.00
on a additional Quenity do	.37½
1 foot Adze	.75
Black Smith Tools & ballows	35.00
	140. 76¼

(114)   Thomas Butler Sale Cont.

1 Lot of Iron	.27
1 Cool body	.88¼

1 Iron Band	.06¼
the running of Gear of Waggon	30.75
1 Washpan	.19
1 Oven	2.00
Chains	.25
1 Dicktionary & other books	.13½
1 Jug of Oil	.51
1 fat Tub	.12½
1 Large Pot	1.26
1 Water pail	.28
1 Coverlid	1.00
1 Quilt	2.01
1 Counterpin	2.01
1 do	2.06¼
1 Sheet	.63
1 Toylet	.41
4 Pillows Cases	.37½
50 Bushels of Corn 9th Lot	12.75
50 Bushels of Corn 10th Lot	12.75
2 Shovels	.75
1 pail of Iron	.25
1 Flax & Hackel & C	1.75
1 pail	.13
1 Saw	5.00
Alexander S. Galbreath bot	
1 Cart	17.00
1 Bushel of Sault	1.12½
Ezra Russell Bot	
1 Barrell of Sault	.88
3.49 Lbs. Seed Cotton	8.89¾
	109.88
(115) Thomas Butler Sale Cont.	
1 water pail	.18¾
1 pair of dog Irons	1.12½
1 Sheet	.63
6 Grees	.84
Alexander Noel bot	
1 Log Chain	3.26
1 Side upper Leather	3.41¼
Thomas Darnell bot	
2 Iron wedges	.62½
1 Calf	1.50
1 do	2.00
1 do	1.78
2nd Lot of Hogs	9.00
1 Plow	.36
1 Coffee Pot	.62½
1 Black band & Harness	1.37½
Ansel Manly bot	
1 Side Saddle	6.56¼
1 Plow	1.06¼

	1 tingallon Pot	2.00
	1 Large Grindstone	1.31¼
	John Butler bot	
	1 Shaving Cup	.12½
	1 Gray Mare	53.37½
	1 Jug	.30
	1 Bed & furniture	8.00
	1 Counterpin	2.25
	1 Sheet	.50
	1 do	.63
	1 Toylet	.34
	50 bushel of Corn 4th Lot	13.50
	1 Clock	7.00
(116)	Thomas Butler Sale Cont.	
	Ansel W. Nanly bot	
	1 Sow	3.31¼
	1 Hog	6.20
	Simon Jackson bot	
	1 Anger	.27
	1 Lot of Spools	.56¼
	Benjamin Rector bot	
	1 Harrow	5.00
	2 Sptted Sows	2.31¼
	3 Hogs 1st Lot	4.50
	1 Sandy Saw	3.06½
	1 Anville	4.25
	Drawing Knife	.26
	Joseph Galbreath bot	
	1 Stack of fotter	2.00
	1 Cutting Knife blade	1.00
	2 mowing Blades	1.15
	1 pair of Sheep Shears	.50
	Doct. George F. Black	
	5 Hogs 4th Lot	15.25
	50 bushels of Corn 8th Lot	13.00
	1 table Cloth Cover	.25
	William Mc Kanney bot	
	1 Grubbing Hoe	.31¼
	Craven Duncon bot	
	1 Bell & Collar	.43¾
	John Cox bot	
	1 - 700 Slay	.50
	1 Barrell of Clover	.12½
	1 Barrell do	.12½
	1 Loom	3.00
		67 . 50½
(117)	Thomas Butler Sale Cont.	
	1 Quilt	1.00
	15 Gars	2.06¼
	James Scarbrough bot	
	12½ lbs Wool at 37½	4.93¾
	4 Lbs. do at 38	1.50
	1 Stack of fotter	2.00

James Hudson

1 Box of Knives & forks	1.25
1 foalding table	7.01

Thomas Hail bot

1 Cow	9.42
1 Set of unbound books	.25

William Williams bot

1 Mare Mule	65.25
1 fly Bush	.50
1 pair of Horse Phliquers	

Andrew Mc Kanney bot

2 Crocks	.57½
1 Crock	.13
1 Butter Crock	.07½

George Hoskins Esqr. Bot

Seal Chains	1.41

Andrew Mc Kamey bot

1 Cotton Wheel	.26
1 pair of working Bars	
1 Spooling frams	.09
2 head Bells & Bridle	.16½
1 Bed Stead & furniture	1.53

Nancy Hail Bot

1 Dish & Plates & C	1.75
3 plates Salt Sellers & C	.37½
1 Set of Knives & forks	1.19
1 Tin	.12½
	192.66¾

(118)   Thomas Butler Continued

1 Set of Spoons	.25
1 Glass Pitcher	.50
1 Teakettle	.75
1 Bed Cord	.50
1 Bed Stead & Cord	.25
1 Blanket	2.50

Elizabeth Butler Bot

1 Coffee Mill & Bench	.57

Elisha Prewhit Bot

1 Cotton Wheel	1.12½

John Kesterson Bot

1 Cag & pothooks	.13½

Richard Cox bot

1 Cutting Box	.75

John Tober Bot

4 Sheep 1st Lot	4.07
1 Collar Harness & Chains	.76
1 tin water Bucket	.06¼
1 Chain & 2 Singletrees	1.06¼
	45. 67½

(119)   Thomas Butler Sale Cont.

John Thompson Bot

1 Stack of fotter	2.00

1 Sugar Box	.44
Horse Shoes & C.	.27
1 Jointer & Croze	.25
1 Cag of Tallor	1.31¼
14 bushels Shattered & unsound Corn	14.70
Jacob Ryan Bot	
1 Wheat fan	24.00
1 Cary Plow	.62½
1 Grind Stone	.88
Ievy Hrwit	
1 Ox Chain	3.12½
1 Shovel & Tonge	1.00
1 Sack of feathers	1.31¼
1 Coverlid	1.18¾
1 Counterpin	1.00
1 Coverlid	2.06¼
Thomas Jack Esqr. Bot	
1 Backband & Chains	1.93¾
John White Bot	
1 Beef hide	1.75
	.37½
Brass Candlestick	.62½
Robert Galbreath Esqr.	
1 Lot of Chains	.83¾
William A. Butler Bot	
1 red Sow unmarked	2.57
Douglass Oliver Junr. Bot	
1 White Sow	3.31¼
6 Hogs 5th Lot	9.00
	$74. 52½

(120)   Thomas Butler Sale Cont.

Henry Childs Bot	
1 Large Kettle & Hooks	3.31¼
Alexander Galbreath Bot	
1 Stock of Oats	4.01
1 House of Hay	12.63
1 Barrell of Grass Seed	.26
Archiball Cobb Bot	
Scales & Weights	13.00
2 Shovels	27.00
1 Bed Quilt	.75
1 do do	.55
Joseph A. Mabey Bot	
1 Mare Mule	55.00
Hugh Riley Bot	
1 Stack of Oats	1.00
1 Stack of Straw	.25
1 flax Wheel	2.00
1 Bool Tongue	.50
the	
1 Cropping Hackel	.75
1 Barrell	.06¼

1 Gag & Basket	.07½
1 Counterpin	.62½
6 Gees	.78
Joseph Harding Bot	
1 pair of Cart Wheels	12.00
William Right Bot	
2 Snuff Bottles	.10
Benjamin Hrivit Bot	
1 pair of Compasses	.12½
	158.90½

(121) Thompson Sale Cont.
George Prince Bot

1 Bread Tray	.15
Apothery Scales & Weights	.30
1 lot of Window Glass	.12½
1 Water Bucket	.50
1 Counterpin	.77
1 Sheet	.30
1 Quilt	.75
1 Blanket	2.90
1 Sheet	.60
1 do	.50
1 piece of Siving(?)	.35
1 Toylett	.12½
1 Table Cover	.62½
1 Pellow Case & 4 Towels	.75
1 Small Trunk	.20
3 Toyletts & C.	.50

William T. Lightfoot Bot

1 Bed Stead	.14
1 Candlestand	1.00
1 Bed Stead & C.	.60
1 Bed	.18¾
1 Blanket	3.01
1 do	3.00
1 Sheet	.07

Benjamin Williams

1 pitcher	1.26
1 Garden Hoe	.25

Wm. Bray Bot

1 Bottle of Oil	.25
1 Waiter	.10
	19 .31½

(122) Thomas Butler Sale Cont.
Richard Oliver

1 Single Tree	.31½
1 Sickel	.06½
1 two Inch Anger	.43¾
1 Lot of Iron & C	.43¾
1 Inch Anger	.25
1 Grubbing Hoe	.13½
1 Bell & Buckel	1.40

Band Tools & Crobar	15.00
1 Heifer	2.56½
1 Still & C.	5.50
1 Oat Stack	4.31¼
1 Wheat fain	.25
foot Adze & C.	.81¼
1 Iron Squair	.50
1 Cary Plow	1.68
Clevis & C.	.25
1 Grind Stone	2.00
1 Cord Bid	4.00
1 Hog Old Saw	13.06½
1 Yoke of Oxens	32.00
1 Chain	2.06¼
1 Oar Bed	3.00
1 Coal Waggon	40. 00
8 delph Plates	.56½
1 Bottle	.31¼
1 Crevit	.06½
2 Glass Trumblers	.30
1 Teakettle	3.00
Chains	.50
Singletree & C.	.65
Gun domestic	2.00

(123) Thomas Butler Sale Cont.

1 family Bible	3.50
1 pad lock	".25
1 Slay	.26
Thread & Rags	.31½
1 Chest	1.56½
Loom Temples	.27
2 Barrells & Sifter	.12½
1 Bee Stand	1.10
Counterpin	.79
Counterpin	3.00
1 do	1.62½
1 do	2.26
1 Sheet	.68¾
Bed lace & Basket	.82
1 Lot of Husk	1.01
1 pots	.50
Shingles	2.00
1 Lot of Sale Wheat at 87½ pr. B.	
1 Lot of Sale Corn at 27 pr. B.	
William Galbreath Bot	
1 Beef Hide	3.18¾
Collins Roberts Bot	
1 Shovel Plow	1.25
1 Bread tray peuster	2.00
1 Bed & to pellows	11.12½
1 Bed 2 pillows	14.25
1 Lot of Cabbage	.62½
1 Lot of do	.50
all the beets	.50

Samuel Sieber bot
Giblet & Saw   .07
1 Trunk B & Cupboard   10.13
                                                   63.54½

(124)   Thomas Butler Sale Cont.
        Samuel Tunnell bot
        1 Gum of Millet Seed   .25
        Sam Rector bct
        1 Counterpin   1.75
                                                   2.00

Inventory and amount of property Sold at the Sale of Thomas Butler deceased
on the 1st day of January 1835.
Thomas Hail Bot
1 Sow & three pigs   4.00
Richard Oliver Bot
1 Small Chest
1 Side of upper Leather   2.75
pooleys & Slay   .50
1 Nigro woman Mariah & child Isaac   601.00
100 Cord Coal Wood 2nd Lot   5.00
100 de   do   do   3rd Lot   5.00
James Scarbrough Bot all the Tole Corn in the Mill
1 Black Listed Low   2.71
Samuel Galbreath bot —
13 year old Steer   5.00
1 Small piece of Beefskin   .62½
1 pot hannel   1.18½
1 Choping Ax   1.50
Henry R. Butler Bot
all the tole wheat at 75¢
1 feed trough
1 Negro Boy Elic   20.00
100 Cord Cole Wood 1st Lot   5.00
the ballance of the Cord wood if any at 5¢   402.00
                                               1237. 02½

(125) Thomas Butler Sale Cont.
      Benjamin Rector Bot
      4 Side of upper Leather   2.31½
      William R. Butler Bot
      1 pair of Strechers 1 Singletree   1.25
      1 tin bucket   .25
      1 Negro Man Adam   400.00
      1 Old Negro Woman Fanny   100
      1 Meal Bag   .12½
      James Willimett Bot
      1 Kifskin   2.56½
      1 Red Sandy Hog   3.56
      John Cooper Bot
      1 piece of Sole Leather   .31½
      John Butler Bot
      1 Negro Girl   275.00

Henry R. Butler Bot
1 Negro Woman Jenny   100.00
William M. Butler Bot
1 White Hog   3.56
James Noel Bot
1 5/4 Chizel $.26\frac{1}{2}$
Elizabeth Butler Bot
1 Jug   .25
William T. Lightfoot Bot
1 Hog $.87\frac{1}{2}$
                               791 .32$\frac{1}{2}$

Richd. Oliver
       Administrator
recorded Feb. 13th, 1835
       John Jarnagin   Clerk

(126)   Return of C. Luallen Admrs. of R. Luallen Deceased
Inventory of the Notes on hand of the good of Richard Luallen Deceased.
Considered not good Sib. Baley 193 bushels of Corn dated 19th January
1832.   Charles Mc Cormick one note dated September 1830 $500. Charles
Mc Cormick do dated 8th June 1831 $12.
                           17.00
William Webb one note dated 3rd of December 1812
                           15.00
William Rains one note dated 26th August 1823
                           5.12$\frac{1}{2}$
Thomas Adair Note dated 1809   5.50
James Baxter note dated 4th
    October 1825   1.00
William Mc Cormick Note
    dated 5th March 1828   8.00
James Underwood Note dated
    5th March 1828   2.37$\frac{1}{2}$
William Harrell Note with Credit   10.00
Robert Smith note dated
    August 22nd 1809   4.00
William Sartin note twenty five
    Bushels Corn
Burk Johnson note March 3rd 1828   7.25
Andrew Barden note dated
    August 27th 1828   5.00
Sib Baley note for forty three
    bushels Corn
Alfred Harris Note dated 25th
    March 1828   2.00
Juleus Millicon Note dated Feb.
    9th 1824   3.00
William Martin Note June 8th
    1830   8.00
Julius Millicon Jr. Note dated
    25th May 1832   3.00
                       96.25

Notes Considered good

```
Jacob Linard & David Vandegriff Note          150.00
Due October 11th1836 to be paid in trade,
Amount of money Collected                       80.00
one waggon Charles Luallen                      48.25
Charles Luallen 80 Lbs.
Bar Poll                                         2.00
Charles Luallen Admr.                      $   280.25
recorded June 10th 1835
John Jarnagin  Clerk
```

(127)

Lewis Miller Guardian of Alithia Hill Dr. to Alithia Hill April 14th
1835 Money Recd. of the Executer of James Hill Decd. as follows.

```
To Cash recd. 30 August 1827      )  One Negro Girl Named
Su receipt        74    77  Credit)     Seleny
to   do  do 16th Nov.
            1827    2    68¼ By Paying taxes $1412
to   do 3rd. Jan. 1828
            342    42  Credit By raising of
to   do 25 July 1828
            7      00  Negro Seleny Credit
to   do 25 July 1828
            4      00  By Services 50.00
to   do 25 July 1828
            10     00
to   do 25 July 1828
to   do 25 July 1828
            10     37½
to   do 25 July 1828
            250    00
to Rent paid up to this
            75     00
present date April
14th 1835   51     00
for hir Plantation
Interest from the
30th day of August
on the above amt. up to the
present date
April 14th 1835
            248    43
to 23½ yd. Homespun
one feather Bed
Bed Stead and furniture
one Saddle one Bridle
one Flax Wheel ½ doz.
of Spoons one Cupboard
one Negro boy named
Wesley set apart in will


recorded June 10th, 1835
John Jarnagin   Clerk
```

Bequathed By James Hill to the above
name Alithea Hill

Lewis Miller Guardian for
Alithea Hill
comes into open Court
April 15th 1835

John Jarnagin

```
            1075   68½
                64.02
```

(128)   An Sale Amount of Sale of John Goodman & Joseph M. Asherst
               Administrator of the Estate of Henry Goodman decd. 1 John Goodman
               to four head of Hogs   4.08¼
               2 John Roberts to 1 Cow & Calf   2.56¼
               3 John Seiber to 1 Mare   41.00¼
               4 John Goodman to 1 Plew Mole   1.00
               5 John Asherst to 1 Axe   1.46½
               6 John Goodman 1 weding Hoe   .50
               7 John Goodman one Seng Hoe   .25
               8 Dewey Harroll to 1 drawing Knife   .43
               9 John Goodman to one frow   .93¾
               10 William Bird to 1 pot   2.00
               11 Nathin Massengile 1 par of hains & drawing
                  Chains   1.70
               12 Milly Goodman to 1 Skillet   .12½
               13 John Goodman to 1 pot   1.75
               14 John Seiber to 1 Cotton Wheel   1.31
               15 Elijah Goodman 1 flax Wheel   1.25
               16 John Goodman to 1 Reel   1.00
               17 Nathan Massengile to one Saddle   2.50
               18 Hilly Goodman to one Churn   .25
               19 Nelly Goodman to 1 piggin   .12½
               20 John Goodman to 1 pail   .12½
               21 John Goodman to 3 peuter Basins puter dish &
                  one tin vase   4.56½
               22 John Goodman to 4 Chairs   1.41
               23 Catharine Goodman to 1 feather Bed   2.00
               24 Isaac Philips 1 handsaw   1.37½
               25 John Goodman pair of Harnesses & Slay   .25
               26 John Goodman to 1 Cow   6.25
               27 John Goodman to 1 Cow   3.62½
               28 John Goodman to 12 head Hogs   6.43¾
                                                                 ‾‾‾‾‾‾
                                                                 95.80¼

               recorded June 10th 1835
                    John Jarnagin
                              Clerk

(129)   John Cox Will
                    at being once appointed for man to Dec. I John Cox of the County
               of Anderson and State of Tennessee being weak in body, but Sound of
               mind and disposing memory constitute and appoint this my last will
               & Testament and do give & bequath all my Estate real and personal To
               my Step children Elizabeth & Joanah Earley after the payment of my
               Just debts and constitute make and appoint Trusty friend James Noel
               of this State and County aforesaid my Sale Executor given under my
               hand and Seal this 14th April 1835. Signed Sealed and acknowledged,
               in the presents of   John Cox
               James Scarbrough)   his X mark
               Jess Noel   ) recorded August 31st   (Seal)
                                    1835
                                        John Jarnagin Clerk
               Copy F 31st August 1835
                    J. J. Clerk

State of Tennessee)
Anderson County   )   We who names are hereungo Subscribe being
                         appointed by the Court of please and Quarter
                         Sessions for said County to make Settlement
with Joseph M. Asherst and John Goodman deceased proceded to make
Settlement and the amount is as follows

	00 00
1 to voucher	29.50
2 to voucher	2.00
3 to voucher	9.70
4 to Commissioners one	
dollar each	2.00
	93.20

giving under our hand this 13th of July 1835
                                    Richard Anderson
recorded 31st   Wm. Mc Kamey
August 1835
          John Jarnagin Clerk

(131)   State of Tennessee)
          Anderson County   )   Settlement with Joseph Black Guardian

in pursuance of an order we the under Signed have made the following
Settlement with Joseph Black Guardian for the menor Heirs of Mases
farmer Decd. and find Remaining in the hands of Joseph Black the
following Estate.

Michael Clardy	Jen. 1 Note	$1.31½
John Thompson	do	12.11
Martin Hardin	do	7.89
Nelson Roberts	do	14.32½
Samuel Moore	do	373.75
Robert Mc Kanney	do	78.32
Moses Roberts	do	10.45
Michael Clardy	do	26.99½
Joseph Black	do	13.30⅓
Joseph Black	do	105.02¼
William Henderson	do	37.09
George Winton	do	1 06.87½
John Clardy	Do	33.60
Joseph Black	Do	11.20
Wm. Reagan	Do	1.69½
Michael Clardy	Do	13.43
Elijah Hendon	1 Note	15.30
Nelson Roberts	Do	4.87
P. Smith	Do	4.11
		915 .74¾

Leaving in the hands of Joseph Black
Guardian for the Minor Heirs of Moses
Decd. this giving under our hand &   Jo Neal   (Seal)
Seals this 11th July 1835   John Chiles (Seal)
                                            Henry Butler (Seal)
recorded 31st August 1835   R.
John J

(131) State of Tennessee   )
        Anderson County   ) in pursuance of and order of the Court of
                      please & Quarter Sessions for Anderson County
under at act Sessions 1834 an A. Crozier Saml. Dunn & Aron Slover
have this day met in Clinton for the purpose of Settling with Isaac
Miller & John B. Mitchel Exor. of the Estate of Julius Rutherford
Decd. and find & report as follows to Wit
To Amt of Sales of said Estate as reported by the Clerk
of the Court as returned by said Executor

To Amt of Debts Due Estate	$232.11½
To Amt of Debts Due	46.32
To Amt of pension drawers	40.00
	$318,43¾

1 by paid Wm. Carden as pr. rect for carying Sale		$ 1.12½
2 By pd. A. L. Carden as Cler for Sale		1.00
3 By pd. Jno. Allbright as do		1.00
4 By pd. James Jett Constable as pr rect for (?) of Moses William Legatee		12.00
5 By pd. Jacob Rutherford Legatee		14.44½
(132) 6 By pd. Corneluis & Nancy Whitten Legatee		14.44½
7 By pd. William Rutherford do		14.44½
8 By pd. John Rutherford do		14.44½
9 By pd. Michael Rutherford do		14.44½
10 By pd. Rhody Rutherford (widow) do		85.15
11 By pd. James Milton & Wife do		14.44½
12 By pd. John Rutherford do		14.44½
13 By pd. Thomas Rutherford on proven as atto.		14.44½
14 By pd. Joseph Rutherford do		14.00
15 By pd. do for his Cow Sold as part of the Estate		8.32
16 By pd. Jno. Rutherford for gathering		1.00
Carried over		240.15½
(133) 17 By Amt. of Brot over of debts		318.43¾
By amt of Credit brot over		240.15½
by paid widow for Coffin for hir husband as pr rect		100 ?
18 By Clerks fee as pr rect		140 ?
19 By proven O. K. by Executors		30.00
20 Commissioners Rect for Settling	300?	$275.55½
the following are Insolvant		$ 42.88½

to Wit
4 Amts

1 A. L. Levely		$ 1.56¾
2 Ro. C. Brogan		9.62½
3 William Rutherford		1.43¾
4 Ro. Rutherford		5.37½
5 Amt of Judgt. against Jno. Rutherford before Lewis Miller Esqr.	9.55½	$27.55½
		$15.32½

Ballance due from Executors 15th April 1835

```
A. Crozier      )
Aron Slover     )  Commissioners
Saml. Dunn      )
recorded 31st August 1835
          John Jarnagin  Clerk
```
(134)   A Settlement with Richard Oliver Admr. of Mary Miller Decd.

```
State of Tennessee  )
Anderson County     )     We commissioners appointed to Settle with
                          Richard Oliver administrator of the Estate of
                          Mary Miller & Henry Harrell Ded. and on Settlement
```
the administrator produced voucher to the amount of one hundred & thirty
five dollars and Sixteen and it appearing from the Clirk Certificate
that he is margeable with too hundred & twenty Eight dollars seventeen
and three fourth cents which leaves one hundred and forty three dollars
and one & a fourth cents in the hands of the administrator this 28th
of Sept. 1835   John Seiber
                   Samuel Davidson
                   Robert Galbreath

```
Samuel Davidson Esqr. 1 day              $1.00
Robert Galbreath 1 day                    1.00
John Seiber 1 day                         1.00
  ordered by the Court that Each Receive
  the above Amt. recorded November 19th 1835
          John Jarnagin
```

(135)   Oct. 10th 1835

Inventory of the property Sold belonging to the Estate of Richard
Luallen decd.

```
Charles Luallenl Hoe                      .68¾
James Ross 1 Axe                         1.12½
```

Notes Considered not good
one on John Ross $1.50 Due 25th of Dec. 1832
one on John Chritchfield $40.00 due March 1832 to be
    paid in three Axes & four Hoes and the ballance in
    castings to be Delivered at Sitsusters furnace
    Speedwell on Judgement against Thomas Brummett for
                                          63.40
March 1st 1834
    before J. M. Larence Exqr.   55.67½

recorded November 19th 1835
    John Jarnagin Clerk

October 12th 1835 an Inventory of the property belonging to the Estate
of Henry R. Butler Decd. one negro man named peter about forty four
years of age, one do named Ellick about Seven years of age and the
undivided morrity of Land and Legacy as legater of the Estate of Thomas
Butler.

(136)   Smoothing Irons 1 pair of Steelyards 1 Cutting Box & Knife 2 Scyths
        1 Cradle 1 mowing blade 2 Sickles one mans Saddle 2 Oatstacks 1 hay
        stack footadz handsaw augers & C. perhaps Divers other Minior Articles
        to tidious to mention one beauro 3 tables a parsel of books one Candle
        Stand this is true Inventory So far as has come to Say Knowlidged

                                        James Scarbrough
                                        A D M of the Estate of
                                        H. R. Butler Deceased
        Recorded Nov. 19th 1835
             John Jarnagin
                    Clerk

A Settlement with Charles Luallen Administrator & C.

State of Tennessee   )
Anderson County   ) Sept. 22nd 1835
                        We Enoch Foster & John M. Lamor to of the Commission-
                        ers appointed by the Court of pleas and Quarter
Sessions for said County to make Settlement with Charles Luallen Administra-
tor of the Estate of Richard Luallen Decd. find agreable to a Certificate
Statement of the Clerk of said Court that said Charles Luallen made re-
turns of said Estate to the amount of $6570.30½   where in said administra-
tor produced the following vouchers which he clames credit to Wit
School Commissioners Rect No. 1   167.41¾
Clerk Rect No 2   2.14½

(137) C. Luallen Admr. Continued   Settlement

        J. Jarnagin & Co. No 3   4.52¾
        Wm. Cross No. 4   6.92
        J. Jarnagin & C. No. 5   1.26½
        Saml. C. Young No 6   1.75
        Charles Y. Oliver No. 7   15.45½
        A. Crozier & Son No. 9   27.24
        William Severs   No. 10   15.16½
        Charles Y. Oliver No. 11   6.25
        Richard Oliver   No. 12   191. 00
        William Hogshead No. 13   1. 39¾
        Pleasant Slover   No. 14   21. 06¼
        Sterling Smith   No. 15   2.58½
        Cartton Keeling   No. 16   .25
        Jess Worthington No. 17   300.00
        David Hall   No. 18   2.00
        William Stephens No. 19   9.07½
        J. Jarnagin & C. No. 20   2.00
                                                   _____
                                                   799.47¾

        Amt brot on
        J. R. Edmonson Rect. No. 21   14.62½
         "   "   "   No. 22   4.50
         "   "   "   No. 23   34. 34
         "   "   "   No. 24   48.40

****

Jacob B. Snider	No 25	26.62½
George F. Black	No 26	24.50
Jesse Noel	No 27	5.00
J. Jarnagin	No 28	225.89
Wm. Dickerson	No 29	15.26¾
C. Y. Oliver	No 30	18.25
James Weaver	No 32	3.25
J. Jarnagin	No 31	33.58¾

(138) Continued

Richard Oliver	No 33	4.58½
Char. Y. Oliver	No 34	14.93¼
James Childress	No 35	6.00
James Jett	No 36	1.25
Samuel Brooks	No 37	1.50
John Millicon	No 38	6.43¾
John M. Lamar	No 39	7.43¾
Mrs. Evans	No 40	10.50
Richard Oliver	No 41	10.50
E. Hart	No 42	10.77½
Michael Keeny	No 43	64.10
Willie Talley	No 44	.50
Jacob Linart	No 45	58.53
J. R. Edmonson	No 46	13.20
Peter Clair	No 47	4.50
James Ross	No 48	.25
J. M. & C. Lamar	No 49	1.80
Richard Oliver	No 50	184.82½
" "	No 51	166.20
" "	No 52	115.62½
" "	No 53	113.29¾
Amt. Carried over		$2 050.40

(139)

Amt. brot over		$2050.40
J. R. Edmonson rect No. 54		5.78¾
A. T. Crozier	No 55	25.93¾
Carter Scruggs	No 56	35.33½
Richard Oliver	No 57	10.85
M. Late "	No 58	21.62½
J. Jarnagin	No 59	3.65
J. Jarnagin	No 60	80.31½
Voucher	No 61	93.00
do	No 62	49.30
do	No 63	9.00
William Mc Kanney Rect No 64		1.50
Andrew Breaden Rect No 65		5.00
A. Crozier "	No 66	25.13
Robert M. Anderson " No 67		15.00
John R. Edmonson " No 68		3.50
Richard Oliver " No 69		119.81
John Chiles " No 70		1.00
Isaac Mabery " No 71		11.00
Saml. Rodgers " No 72		25.00
Robert Mc Kanney " No 73		5.00
		$2579.13¾

Amt of Sale said Estate being from
   which deduct above

leaving ballance $6570.30½
          against   2597.13¾
                                                         3973.16½

Said Administrator of Enoch Foster
   Comms. 2 days   2.00
John M. Lemar 2 days   2.00
John Gibbs 1 day   1.00
recd. by the Court

                                        Enoch Foster
                                        J. M. Lamar
                                              Commissioners

recorded Nov. 19th 1835
John Jarnagin   Clerk
(140)   Inventory of Luke Farmer Estate Decd.

State of Tennessee)
Anderson County   ) A Skadool of the property of Luke Farmer Deceased in
                     April 1835

1	to 1 waggon & Gears	27	to two Leather Collars
2	" 17 head of Cattle	28	to 1 Halter Chain
3	" 5 head Horses	29	to 5 Hogshead
4	" to a Stock of Hogs	30	to 1 pickling tub
	Supposed to be 50 or 60 head	31	to 1 Set Shoemaker tools
5	to 12 head of Sheep	32	to 1 Saddle
6	to 1 Log Chain	33	to two mans Saddle
7	to 1 pair of Strechers	34	to two riding Bridles
8	to 1 Scyth & Cradle	35	to Six Bee Stands
9	to 1 Mooving Scythe	36	to two Barrels
10	to 2 Reap hooks	37	to Six Bells
11	to three bridles & Blew	38	to 1 bar of Iron
12	to too Shovels Plow	39	to one Cupboard
13	to two Collars	40	to one Chest
14	to two Bulltonge Plows	41	to five Beds Bedsteds &
15	to two Shovel Plows		furniture
16	to one Matack	42	to 1 big Kettle
17	to five weding Hoes	43	to two pots & 2 ovens & too
18	to 1 Cuting Box		Kettles & Hooks
19	to 1 hand Saw	44	to one Bridle
20	to three Augers	45	to three Clivises
21	to one Chisel	46	to two Single trees
22	to too drawing Knives	47	to one Loom
23	to 1 Rifle Gun & Shot pouch	48	to one Iron pitchfork
24	to 1 Iron wedge	49	to to Some Sole & upper Leather
25	to Six Axes	50	to one hammer & stake
26	to three Blind Bridles	51	to one old cuting Knife

Sworn to in open Court
   Nathain Farmer
recorded Nov. 29th 1835
John Jarnagin
          Clerk

52 to 1 pair of Steelyards
53 to 1 Sprouting hoe
54 to one froe

(141)   William Botler Will
       In the name of God Amen know all men by these presents that I William
Botler of the County of Anderson and State of Tennessee being old and
inffirmbut in perfect mind and memory calling to mind the certainly of
Death and the uncertainly of life I do make this my last Will and
Testament I first recommend my Soul to God who gave it and my Body to
the Mother Dust again and my property God has given to me I Dispose of
the following manner I will & bequath to my son Thomas Botler my negro
Girl Elizabeth & Nelly and my Daughter Elizabeth Manley my nigro woman
Jane and Samuel and to my son Jacob Botler my negro woman Barbary and
negro woman Clee and my negro woman Fan and Negro Boy Moses to my son
Henry Botler and to my son William Botler my negro man Joseph and negro
Girl Margaret and to my Daughter Mary Rector my negro woman Jude and hir
child Sittany, and my grand daughter Elizabeth Pryor my negro girl Maria
& too my two grand son Jacob & Benjamin Rector forty dollars in money
each and to my grand daughter Nancy Rector my negro boy James .
       Signed and acknowleged in presence of
                    Witness
A. T. & L. B. R. & Jth   )
         his   )   William Botler
    James X Crow   )   (seal)
         mark   )
    James X Rector   )   recorded January 16th 1836
         his mark   )   John Jarnagin
                                                  Clerk

(142)   John Cooper Will
       In the name of God Amen I John Cooper of the County of Anderson and
State of Tennessee being Sick and week of body possesing a sound mind
and disposing memory and call ing to mind the Shortness of life and
Certainty of Death do nominate apoint my last Will & Testament in
manner and form following last I give & bequath and to the dust from
where it was taken and recommend my Soal to God who gave it I wish my
body to be dcently Burried and my funeral Expences paid out of my perish-
ableproperty and all my Just debts be paid I request my Land to be Sold
and the provides to be Equally Divided between my four Children first
frances Cooper Charles Cooper Martha Webb & John Cooper Lastly I nominate
Constitute apoint William Mc Kanney Senior & Robert Mc Kanney Executors
of this my last Will and Testament requesting the fully the contents of
this will fully executed according in Witness where of I here of have
Set my hand and fixed my seal the 2nd of November in the year of our
Lord 1834
                              John Cooper
                                (Seal)
request
   Subscribing Witnesses to the
   Same
        William Wilson
        I Cross

An Inventory of the personal Estate of John Cooper deceased To Wit one
Gray Horse one Sadle and bridle grest Coat one Caster(?) Hat one Bed &
furniture two Chests one Hackle one Cutting Knife and Steel one Shovel

plow 4 Chains Some peuter
(143) one pair of pot Hooks one pair of Grab Hooks one Chopping Axe one pair of
Shears one Bottle two razors toogimblers one Collar one Hammer and Stake
one Coutler plow one dollar & fifty cents in cash and some books.

Daniel Jenings Will
   In the name of God Amen I Daniel Jenings of the County of Anderson and
State of Tennessee do make this my last Will and Testament revoking all
other prvious to this date that is I give to my wife Sarah Jenings all
my Estate both real and personal land goods and Chattles that I may die
Seized and prossessed with and at hir Death the Land to fall to my youngest
Son Heram Jenings provided that he takes good Care of us both during our
natural life if not my wife Sarah to have the disposal of it at hir wish
and will and appoint Hardy F. Marshall Executer of this my Last Will &
Testament given under my hand this Sixteeth day of January one thousand
eight hundred and thirty Six.
                         John Wilson
                              his
                         Spencer X Aultom
                              mark   his
                                             Daniel X Jenings
                                                   mark

Richard Whelans Will
   In the name of God Amen I Richard whelan of Anderson County State of
Tennessee do make and ordain this to be my Last Will & Testament in the
first place I order that all my Just debts and funeral Expenses be paid
out of my cash which I have on hand Secondly I will and bequath to my Son
one Dollar thirdly I will and bequath
(144) to my Son in Law William Brown one Dollar fouretly I will and bequath to
my Son in Law Isaac Scarbrough one dollar fifthly I will & bequath my
Daughter Polly one Dollar Sixthly I will & bequath to my wife Peggy all my
Cash and property of ever description and the use of my Land during hir
life and after hir death what may remain of my property I order to be
Equally Divided amongst the names legatus I nominate and appoint Edward
Hawkins Esqr. to be Executor of this my Last Will and Testament in Witness
here of I have unto Set my hand & Seal this 22nd day July 1835
Saml. Taylor   Richard X Whelan
Richard Cox   his mark   (seal)

              recorded May 4th 1836
                    William Cross
                    OK by his Depty
                    C. Y. Oliver

A Return and amount of Sale of the Estate of Henry R. Butler deceased on the
4th Nov. 1835 as returned by James Scarbrough Administrator Nancy Ann Butler.

1 Lot of Cupboard ware $4.   1 Cupboard $5.   1 Clock $10. $19.50
1 Bureau $5.   1 Table $6.   11.00
1 Bed 1 Sted & furniture 1 do do
1 do & Tunnel $1   9.00
8 fall back Chairs $1.   4 Chairs Common .18¼   1.81¼

1 Baker & Led $100 752 pots 2 Skillets 3 pair of Hooks	$1.75
1 Shovel 25cts. 1 Coffee Pot & C. 75 1 table 2 pails 1 Bucket 2	1.25
1 Loom and Harness $41 Cotton wheel 50cts. 1 flax wheel 75cts.	5.25
1 Smoothing Iron $00.50 1 Reel 75cts. one Cotton wheel 1.	2.25
1 pair of Sad Irons $1.50	
1 handsaw 81¼	2.31¼
	$56 .37½

(145)

1 Grind Stone 25cts. 1 Bed Stead 25cts. 1 trunk Box 37½	.87½
1 plough 21cts. 1 Coffe Mill 6¼cts. 1 Auger 25cts.	.52¾
1 Hoe Single tree 1 Mowing Scythe 1 pair of Gears 33¼	2.43¾
1 pair of Streatchers and Shovel 50cts. 1 pair of Saddle bags	1.51
1 pair of Steelyards 50cts. 1 young horse to L. Thompson $40.25 1 Horse Sadle & Bridle $54.	94.75
1 Bed & Stead & furniture trensferd to W. C. Arery	6.87
1 Cutting Box & Knife 1.00	
1 Bull Tongue plow 37½	
Syth & Cradle 75	2.12½
1 plough 87½ 1 Cow red & white 6.12½	7.00
1 piging 1 Barrel fat Tub Half Bushel & Barrell	.87½
1 Jug 12½ 1 Table 1.12½	
2 Axes 1 bottle 87½ 2 washing tubs 50	2.62½

James Scarbrough

5 Chain 37½ 1 Large Pot 1.00	
1 Spece Morter 31¼ 1 Saddle $8.	
1 handy Saw $300 1 Hay Stack 326 cents	14.57½

Andrew Mc Kanney

1 Larg Oven $2.00	2.00

Isaac Freels Senr.

1 Auger returned not being of Estate	
William S. Freels 1 Bell	.70
Edward Freels 1 Hoe	.40
John C. Mc Kanney 1 pair of Chains	
1 pair of Log Chains	2.29½
Robert Brazeal 1 Plough	.80
Richard Oliver 1 Set of Black Smith tools	65.00
Jesse Noel 1 Bull tonge plow	.28
William Taylor 1 Syths & Cradle	2.42
Alexander L. Galbreath 1 foot Adze	.68¾
Jacob Butler wood works of a waggon	20.50
Ancil Mandley Senr. Promes Curvin Irons	3.44

Elizabeth Russell 1 Cow Black & White	9.40
Francis H. Robertson 1 Cow white face	4.00
1 Sow the 6th white 1.87½	
the 7th do do $1.31¼	3.18¾
Joseph K. Robertson 1 Sow Red & White	
back Shot $3.1 do black and White $3.20¢	
1black Spotted Shot 2.12½	8.14½
	254.66½

(146)
Hugh Reley 1 Hog White Stump tial	3.39
John Taylor 1 Hog	1.88¾
William R. Butler 1 Keg	.55
Spencer Keith 1 waggon & Side of waggon bed	28.81¼
Alexander Galbreath	
1 Large Hay Stack	4.14
1 New Hay Stack	8.51
	19.29¼
	47.29

An Account of Sale 28th Nov. 1835 returned by James Scarbrough Administrator of the Estate of Henry R. Buttlor decd. reccived by the amt. (to Wit)

James Scarbrough 4 Sheep	3.3¼
Andrew Mc Kanney Senr. 1 Bull $7.1 Heifer $4.00	11.00
George Prince 2 Hogs 1st Choice	3.12½
Hugh Biley 2 do 2 do	2.88½
Douglas Oliver 2 do 3rd do	2.6¼
do do 24th Lot	2.00
James Scarbrough 1 reap hook	.37½
Nancy Ann Buttlor 4 Sheep	2.00
Isaac Russell 5 Sheep 81¼ each	4.7½
Andrew Mc Kanney Senr. Black Ram	.75
do do 1 Reap hook	.37½
	31.68¼

Recorded the above returne 9th of May 1836   31.68

Wm. Cross O.K.
by his Depety
C. Y. Oliver

return of the amount of Sales of the Estate of Luke Farmer decd. Sold the 29th of October 1835 viz five Bed Bed Stead and furniture Jane

Farmer	5.00
1 Cupboard 1 furniture	3.00
fourteen Chairs	1.00
1 Looking glass 5 beds 1 Chest	.50
5 Stays and Harness	.25
1 pair of Cords James Farmer	5.00

(147)
1 Slate 1 flax wheel	
1 reddle and Shoemaker Tools	.68¾
1 flax Iron Stake & Hammer 12½ to Cotton	
Wheel real and Loom 50cts.	
washing bord and Spools 6¼	.56¼

1 flax Hackle Knife Box & Knives 12½
1 Cag 1 Jar 2 Coffeepots   .43¾
1 Churn 2 tables 18¾¢ 1 Kettle 2 pots
2 ovens & Skillet and Hooks 1 Bucket 1 pale
1 meal Gum tray & Coffee mill   1.31¼
2 pair of Sheep Shears and four Crocks 18¾ 1 plow &
Single tree 1 Clevis 50¢ 2 plows Bull tongue
  Coulter & Clevis 50   1.18¾
4 weading Hoes Mattack
1 Sprouting Hoe 25¢   .25
1 Swingletree & Clevis   .25
W. B. Farmer
1 Coulter John Haskins   .12½
1 plough John Ray   .95½
1 Barshear plow 31¢ 3 Axes 1 Log Chain Wm. Smith   .25
1 Ax to Robert Lively 37½
too Axes to William Cross 18¾   .56¼
2 Hars Iron 2 Collars
2 Pair of Gears 1 half Bushel   1.1
to James Farmer
3 plows W. Smith 28¢ 1 Hammer
B. T. Hackey 43¾   .71¾
1 plow Nathan 64¢ 1 Haulter Chain W. B. Farmer
25¢ 1 Reap Hook & Cutting Knife W. Smith   1.15
2 Bells Ezra Russell 50½
1 Bell & Collar do   .79
1 Bell Wm. Griffith 25¢
1 do E. Russell 25   .50
1 Bell reap Hook & Saddle 43¾¢ 1 Handsaw and
drawing Knife 50¢ 1 pitch fork 12½¢ J. Farmer   1.6¼
6 Hogsheads two Saddles
3 Blankets 2 bridles   1.56
1 Bridle 31¼ John Taylor   1.81¼
2 Barrels and 3 Bee Gums 52¢
4 do 1.44¾ to
Robert Seiber   1.96¾
1 Cradle Cutting Box and Mowing Sythe 50¢
and one waggon John A. Hindson $76.   76.50
1 pair of Hind Gears $6.
18¾ D. M. Rector   6.18¾
1 pair of Hip Straps and 1 bridle 62½ 1 Sorrel
Mare $22. John Haskins   22.62½
1 Roan Cloat $28. to Mose Duncan   28.09
(148)   3 horse beats $60. Jane Farmer   60.00
1 Sandie Sow & 8 pigs to Jo. Seiber   5.75
6 Hogs $5. Jane Seiber
1 Hog Robt. C. Glively 1.37½   6.37½
2 Sows and 2 Shoats Samuel G. Galbreath   9.00
1 Sow & 3 Shoats to Jhon Carnall   7.12½
10 Hogs first Choice to Robt. C. Lively   39. 75

2 Sows to Janw Farmer 6.6¼
1 Sow & 3 Shoats to I. Freels
$5.32½ 2 Sanded Shoats first Choice
Elizabeth $2.37½
1 Sow & five Pigs to Janw Farmer $2.00 15.76¼
1 Sanded barrow to Robt. C. Y. Levely 4.00
1 deen Cow & 1 pidded Heifer Jane Farmer 6.50
1 Branded Steer to A. Thompson $1.31 Deen Stear
to George Winton $10.00 1 Red & White Stear
John Taylor $5.31¼ 28.31¼
1 Deen Heifer to Benjamin Lively 5.31¼
1 Red Cow & Calf to William G. Buttlor 11.25
2 Small Stears to Isaac Duncan 7.67 1 Ox Yoke
G. Winton 31¼ 19.23¼
1 Black Stear John B. Crozier $90. 1 Pidded to
Benjamin Thacker $8.25 1 Rifle Gun to James
Farmer $5.00 22.25
1 Armed Chair to Henry Chiles 61¢ 6 heep(?) first
Claim .61
to Jane Farmer 13.00 3 Sheep 1 Choice to Solomon
Lively $2131 ½
3 Sheep 3rd Choice Wm. Smith $2.50 7.81¼
1 pair of Steelyards Jane Farmer $2.00 2 Hay
Stacks to Solomon Lively $8.56¼ 10.56¼
407 .70

Will Cross Clk.
by his Deputy
C. Y. Oliver

Inventory on amount of Sale of the Estate of Thomas Buttlor Decd. on the first day of January 1835 and Subsquent Sales up to the 1st January 1836 returned by Richard Oliver administrator of said Estate (to Wit)
Thomas Kail 1 Sow & Pigs $4.00
Richd. Oliver 1 Shoat 50
James Scarbrough Corn in the mill 24.50
$20.94½ at 29½ cts. pr bushels .94½
(149) Samuel Galbreath 1 Stear $5.
Henry R. Buttlor wheat in the Mill $3.75 Saml.
Galbreath 1 Small piece of Leather 62½ James
Welmatt Kipskin 256¼ 5.93¾
John Cooper Leather 31¼c
R. Oliver Pulleys & Slay 50 .81¼
Samuel Galbreath 1 pot Trammel 1.18¾
William R. Buttlor Tin Bucket 25¢ .43¾
Richard Oliver Negro woman Mariah & Child 601.00
Henry R. Buttlor Negro Boy Alexander 200.00
John Buttlor Negro girl Pertrica Ann 275.00
Henry Buttlor one Negro woman Jenny 100.00
William R. Buttlor 1 Negro man Adam 400.00
Wm. R. Buttlor 1 Negro woman Fanny 1.00
Saml. Galbreath 1 Ax 1.50 James Walmatt 1 Hog 3.15 4.65

```
           William R. Buttlor 1 Hog  3.56
           James Scarbro 1 do 2.75                          6.27
           James Noel 1 Chisel 56¼
           H. R. Buttlor loo Cord Wood $5. Richard
           Oliver 200 Cords wood $10.                       15.56¼
           Elizabeth Buttlor 1 Jug 25¢
           Wm. R. Buttlor 1 Bag 12½                           .37½
           Henry R. Buttlor
           Negro Man Peter                                  402.00
           Richard Oliver
           wheat 1.76 F. H. Robertson
           1 wheat 76                                         2.52
           Richard Oliver Rye 1.
           George Prince Flax 12½                             1.12½
           Samuel Galbreath
           Flax 31¼ Robt. Brazel Gutting Knife $1.13¢         4.50½
           Richard Oliver Stack oats 3.61¼ Francis H.
              Robertson 1 Stack Oats 3.12½ Richard Oliver
              Sythe & Cradle 25¢
              Berry Hudson Leather 2.76                       6.13½
           James Walmatt 10 Bls. Corn $3.40 Wm. R. Buttlor
              10 do 3.20 William R. Buttlor 10 do 3.40
              Saml. Galbreath 10 do 3.20                     19.70
           Wm. R. Buttlor 10 do 3.40 Richard Oliver Leather
              68¾ B. O. Farmer Do 2.20                        2.38¾
           John H. Kington Leather 4.76
              B. D. Farmer D. 3.99½                           8.75½
   (150)   John H. Kington Leather 3.88½ Oliver do 2.78½      6.57
           this Sum Collected from John Oaks                 24 .67
           from William Scott 90¢ from James Jones            4.38
           the for going the amount of Sale up to the 1st
           of January 1836 inclusive and the property then Sold
           of Thomas Buttlor decd. all of which is Respectfully
           Submitted
                            Richard Oliver
                            Administrator of Tho. Buttlor
           recorded the foregoing amount of Sale and Inventory the 9th of May 1836
                                    Will Cross
                                        Clk.
                                    by his Depety
                                    C. Y. Oliver
           return of the Settlement of John Witson and John Sharp Executors of the
           Estate of John Sharp Senr. decd. (to Wit) John Whitson and John Sharp
           Executors of the Estate of John Sharp Senr. Decd. Dec. 1830
           May 13th To Amount of Sales personal Estate         $197.76¾
           By amt. paid Mc Clung                   139.39
           paid to Mary Ridenhour                    5.00
           as pr. rect.
           D. Nicholas Sharp Do.                     5.00
           Do paid Isaac Foster do                   5.00½
           Amt. paid Paul Hammer as pr. recpt.       4.00
```

```
Amt. paid Adam Moser                                    8.00
Amt. paid David Sharp                                  13.25
                                                      170.01½

by amount paid John Sharp for Service
   as Executor of paid Estate 500
   amt. paid John Whitson for his services
   do                                                   5.00
By paid Clk. of the County Cour                         1.20          11.20

                                                       11.20        181.21½
```

(151) By Balance Due $16.55¼
      By Amount paid John Sharp his part
      as one of Ligatus $43 by amount
      paid to Jacob Weaver and Enoch Foster
      forther Services as
      Commissioners $2.00   6.03
                 6.03

```
James Loveday 1 Box
Bell Double tree                                         .25
John Webb 1 Chest & Sickle                              .50
James Cooper 1 pair Scissors bokin Buttons            1.75
James Cooper 1 Lot of book                              .37½
William Mc Kanney 1 Stake & Hammer                     .41½
Aron Slover 1 Gimblet & Collar                         .16¾
William Webb 1 Bottle                                  .18¾
Conrod Lindsay 1 Tumbler Tin Cup                       .15
James Cooper 1 razor                                   .50
James Cooper 1 razor & Shaving Box                     .06¼
```
(152) Aron Slover 1 Lot Sewing thread   .07
```
George Webb 1 Hackle                                   1.40
Joseph Webb 1 Shovel & Pot Hooks                        .37½
William Webb 1 pair of Spectacles                       .37½
Joseph Webb 1 Lot of Pewter Plates                     1.31¼
paid John Sharp do                                      .18¾
                                                      6. 21¾
                                                        .18¾

                                                      6 . 21¾
```
                                           due   10.33½

Signed   Jacob Weaver
                Enoch Foster
January 7th 1836
recorded the above Settlement 9th of May 1836
                        Will Cross Clk.
                     by his Depety
                        C. Y. Oliver
Amount of Sale of the property John Cooper decd. of Anderson County
May the 7th 1836

```
James Loveday,    1 Box Bell Doubletree                    .25
John Webb         1 Chest & sickle                         .50
James Cooper      1 Pair Scissers  Booin Buttons        1 .75
James Cooper      1 Lot of Book                            .37½
William McKamey   1 Stake & Hammer                         .41½
Aron Slover       1 Gamblett&& Collar                      .16½
William Webb      1 Bottle                              118¼
Conrad Lindsay    1 Tumbler Tin Cup                        .15
James Cooper      1 Razor                                  .50
James Cooper      1 Razor & Shaving Box                    .06¼
(PG.152)
Aron Slover       1 Lot Sewing Thread                      .07
George Webb       1Hackle                               1.40
Joseph Webb       1 Shovel & Pot Hooks                     .37½
William Webb      1 Pair of Spectacles                     .37½
Joseph Webb       1 Lot of Pewter Plates                1.31¼
Paid John Sharp   do                                       .18¼
                                                         6.21¾
                                                          18¾

                                                         6.21¾
                                       due              10.33½
```

```
        Signed    Jacob Weaver
                  Enoch Foster
```

```
        January 7th 1836
Recorded the above Settlement 9th off  May 1836
                     Wm. Cross Clk
                  By his Depety
                     C. Y Oliver
```

Amount of Sale of the property John Cooper Dec'd of Anderson County
May the 7th 1836

```
James Loveday     1 Brier Hook                             .81¼
                  1 Cleves & Singletree                    .43¾
                                                                1.25
William Webb      1 Plow                                   .37½
William John      1 Cutting Knife & Steel               1.50
William Webb      1 Bull Tongue                            .37½
James Cooper      1 Hat                                  4.50
William Webb      1 Bed & Stead & Furniture             3.56½
James Cooper      1 Pocket book & Buttons                  .50
do    do          1 Peice of Lennon                        .25
C. C. Bowling     L Choice Pale & Pocket Book              .83
do   do           1 Chest                               1.50
William Webb      1 Vial & Bemblet                         .08
John Webb         3 Chairs                                 .12½
Aron Slover       1 Craut Cutter                        1.50
James Andrew      1 Big Coat                           15.00
John White        1 Saddle Blanket Sersingle            3.06¼
H. B. Bowling     1 Horse bridle,& Collar              50.00
James Cooper      3 Tracts of Land                    310.00
Jacob Hatmaker    1 Lot of Plank                        2.12½
William Webb      1 Ax                                     .50
                                                      405.17
```

Recorded 9th of June 1836

William McKamey
Robert McKamey
Will Cross Clk
By his Deputy
C Y Oliver

An Inventory and amount of Sales of the Estate of John G. Darrett
dec.d (to wit)

Elizabeth Darrett	1 Palling		.31¼
do do	1 Mattock 40¢		
	1 Shovel plough 30¢		.70
	do pot rack 30¢ 1 pot & Hooks		
		25¢	
	2 Oven hooks 25¢		.80
do	1 Oven lid & Hooks	37½¢	
	1 sprouting hoe	26¢	.63½
do	3 Beds & furniture	$9.00	
	1 Table	1.00	$10.00
Pg (153)			
E Darrett	1 dresser &	8.00	
	Furniture	4.00	
	7 Chairs	.50	4.50
Do	1 Looking Glass	.25	
	1 Chick real	.12½	
	1 Basket	.25	.62½
	1 Lot of Bed Cloths	1.00	
	1 Side Saddle	5.00	5.06½
	1 Bee Stand	.25	
	1 Shovel Plow	.50	
	1 Plow	.50	
	1 Kag	.25	1.50
	1 Gear	.50	.01₇
	1 Hoghead	.01	
	1 Lot of Sheep 3 Eus &		
	Lambs	1.00	1.51
	1 Lot of Sheep	1.06¼	
	1 Bay Mare	40.00	
	1 Great Coat	8.25	49.31¼
	1 Bridle	.26	
	12 head of Hogs & 3 pigs	11.50	
	1 Barrel	.25¢	11.75
	1 Hogshead	06¼	
	2 Water Pales	.25¢	
	1 Falling ax	.25	56.00
	1 Weading Hoe	.18¾	
	1 Basket	.06¼	
	6 head of geese	.06	.31
	1 Churn and to crocks	.25¢	
	1 Bottle Seive & Trumpet	.25	.50
William Peak	1 Cotton Wheel	.50	
	1 Pot & Pail	.50	1.00
Ebenezer Gamble	1 Falling ax	.12½	
	2 Hogshead	.06¼	.18¾

John Jones	1 Falling ax		18¾
Isaac Freels	1 Bell	$$10001	$1.19¾
Robert Gamble	L Hoe & wedge		.31¼
James M Nickle	1 wedge	.37	?
	1 plow	.40	.77½
	1 Harness & Single tree	2.81¼	
	1 Log Chain	1.12½	2.93½
	1 Lot of Irish Potatoes		
	5 bushels 25¢ per bushel		1.25
	1 Cow	10.06¼	
	1 White face steer	4.00	
	1 red steer	6.38	20.44½
	1 Red Heifer	3.51¢	
	1 White backed Heifer	3.25¢	6.79
	2 Little Bulls		5.56
John Hail	1 Iron wedge	.25	
George Harden	1 Frow	.75	1.00
Mary Locket	1 Lot of iron	.06¼	
	1 candle stand	1.25	1.31¼
Thomas Carnalle	1 Hackle	2.50	
	1 Hiddle	.18¾	
	1 grind stone	1.00	3.68¾
Martin Watson	1 Slay	.12½¢	
	1 Coutter	.52¢	.64½
Mary Ann Durrett	1 Chist	3.00	
	1 Block	5.00	8.00
	2 Beds & furniture	8.00	
	1 wheel & Cards	.50	8.50
	1 Looking Glass	.25	
	1 Box	.06¼	
	1 Small trunk	.06¼	
	Warping Irons	.06¼	.43¼
	1 Loom	2.00	
	1 Gray Mare	25.00	
	1 Bridle	.18¾	
	1 Cow & Cald	13.00	40.18¾
Richard Oliver	1 pot & half bushel	.25	.25
	1 Washing tub	.06¼	
	5½ Bushel potatoes	1.37½	1.43¾
(Pg 154)			
Robert Gamble	1 Mans Saddle	2.00	
	1 Small wheel	.25	2.25
George Whetaberry	Slays	.25¢	.25
William Davidson	1 Bee stand		1.00
Richard White	1 plow	.56¼	
	1 Large Flow	2.18¾	2.75
	1 plow	.18¾	
	1 Sythe & Cradle	.75	.93¾
Clingon Kincade	1 plow	1.00	1.00
John Hagler	1 Gear	1.25	
	1 Beef hide	2.50	
	1 Beef hide	2.26	
	1 Collar		6.01
David Terpin	1 Collar	.13	
	1 Chest	.31¼	40.46¼

John Gammon	1 Cutting Box & Knofe	75	—
	1 Beef Hide & C	$1.31¼	
			2.10
Geary Winton	1 Cart	6.37½	
	1 Cow	8.43¾	14.81¾
John Thompson	1 Yoke of oxen		49.75
Thomas Gallaher	1 Sickle	.25¢	.25
Thomas Hagler	1 Bay filly	25.80	25.80
Barley Lovery	1 Lot of Tools		3.01
Daniel White	1 pair of Saddle bags		3.87½
John Will	1 Lot of 5 sheep	2.25	
	1 Lot of 7 sheep by the head	.37½	2.72½
			4.97½
William H. Durrett	1 Kettle & lid		.50
	1 negro man, Nelson	200.00	
	1 negro Girl, Fanny	1021.	1221.50
William Parks	1 nigro woman Syntha	6.75	
	1 negro Girl America	4.61	
	1 negro Child George	3.34	375.00
	Total		3009.50½

Elizabeth Durrett

J. H. Nickle

Administrator &
Administratrix

Recorded 11th July 1836
Will Cross Clk
His Deputy
C Y Oliver

(Pg 155)

Return of the amount of the Sale of the Estate of Elijah
Longmire dec.d   Sold 18th May 1836(towit)

Elias Dagley	1 ax & steel		.56
Elijah Longmire	1 ax	.90	
Robert Longmire	1 Bull tongue and shovel plow	$1.12½	2.02½
Anderson Longmire	1 Bull tongue & Shovel plow		1.12½
Elijah Longmire	1 Sprouting Hoe		.40
William Jones	2 Hoes and Barshear plow		.50
Henry Sharp	Shoe Maker tools		.62½
Jacob Piles	1 Rams Horn 1½ Bu.		.37½
Robert Hancock	1 pair fire dogs		1.00
Squire Williams	3 pair Horse Shoes		.62½
Elijah Longmire	1 pair Gearing & Plow stock		1.00

Kenney Stooksberry	5 sheep		3.35
Henry Sharp	1 Black Spotted cow & calf		14.37½
do do	1 Red Cow & Calf		16.50
Preston Strong	4 Steers & Bell		40.00
Elijah Longmire	3 Heifers	$15.25	
	14 Hogs	22.25	37.50
John Robbins	1 Young bay Mare & Bridle		45.50
Mahaly Longmire	1 Gray Mare		40.00
Henderson Longmire	Bee Hives		1.50
Wm. Handcock	1 Kittle & Hooks		2.62½
Hugh Davis	6 Bushels of corn		3.12½
Robert Hancock	1 Skillet		.30
William Hancock	Frying pan		.50
Preston Sharp	1 Little pot		.8½
Isaac Sharp	1 Other Pot		1.43¾
Elijah Longmire	1 Skillet & Lid		.75
Plasant Rogers	1 fire shovel		.50
Jacob Piles	1 Washing tub		.12½
Squire Williams	1 pail		.25
Preston Sharp	1 Churn		.30
			216.64¼

(Pg 156)

Squire Williams	1 Pail		.20
Preston Sharp	1 razor & Box		.37½
William Jones	1 Candle stand		.51
William Jett	1 Little Bell		.15
Henry Snodderly	1 flat Iron		.56¼
Do Do	1 Black Bottle		.12½
Pleasant Rogers	1 set of working tools		.37½
	1 white Bottle	.12½	
	4 Bowls	.40	.52½
Mahaly Longmire	5 Plates		.25
Henderson Longmire	1 Jug		.50
William Hancock	1 Set teacups & Saucers		.37½
Henderson Longmire	1 table		1.00
John Lay	1 Check real		1.00
William Jones	1 Gun & apparattus		10.00
Robert Longmire	1 Mans Saddle		8.50
Elijah Longmire	1 Fur Hat 1 Bed Stead 12.50		12.50
Mahaly Longmire	1 Bed & Bed stead		5.00
George Meller?	Geese		2.18¾
Wm. Jett	1 peace upper Leather		1.18¾
Henry Snodderly	1 peace of Sale Leather		1.50
David Branson	1 do do		3.07¼
			50.67
			316.64
			367.31

Recorded 11th July 1836
Wm Cross Clk
By his Deputy
C Y Oliver

An Inventory an amount of Sales of the Estate of William Buttlar, Dec.d returned by Jacob Buttlar administrator (to wit)

William M. Buttlar	1 Sow & 4 pigs		$4.00
	1 white Hog		2.68
	1 Spotted Sow and	$1.76	
	Invoise	.11¢	5.45
Arthur Kirkpatrick	1 Hog		4.50
(Pg) 157			
James Jones	1 Shoat	1.31¼	
	1 Brown Mare	152616	57.57¼
Elas Buttlar	2nd Shoat n	75¢	
	1 plow and Single-tree		
	1 Bed steat & Card	83¢	2.33
	1st of Corn 20 bu. at 41¢	8.20	
	2 lot	39¼	16 .05
	3rd 20 bushels	44¼	8.80
	4th Lot 20 bushels	n 41¼	8.85
	5th Lot 20 bushels	41¾	8.35
			25,00
	1 pot	50¢	
	1 Half Bushel Measure	51¢	
	2 Outs Shoats		1.50
Will C. Griffith	1 Shoat		.76
Jacob Buttlar	1 Black Yearling	3.87½	3.87½
	1 ax	31¼	
	1 poker	.20¢	1.03½
	1 Coulter	31	
	200 Bundles fodder	2.14	2.45
	1 Hogshead	.37½	
	1 pint Cup	.04	
	1 Hoe	.30¢	. 71
Benjamin Rector	1 Hammer	.50	. 50
Caleb Buttlar	1 Ax	.62½	
	Bell & Collar	.12	1.64½
	Tongs	.32	.32
Ancel Mandlysen.	1 Baker	.22¢	.22
	1 Pewter Dish	1.27	
	1 Trumpet	.18¾	
	1 Colt	11.25	12.70¾
	1 Large Bell	.25	
Andrew McKamey	6 pewter Plates	2.75	
	Candle Mold	.31½	
	Hames	.16¢	.47¼
Jane Rector	Candle Stick & Snuffers	.06¼	.06¼
	1 Wing Table	1.30	
	1 Walnut Chest	1.78	3.08
	1 Broken Oven	.06¼	
	1 Meal Tub & Salt Tub	.25	.31¼
James Crow	4 Chairs	1.04	
Will R. Buttlar	2nd Stack fodder	2.00	2.00

James Scarbrough	1 Cow & Calf		&8.00
	1 Heifer	$38.01¼	
	1 White face Calf	1.50	4.18¾
	Cups & Saucers	18.	18¾

(Pg158½)
2nd Sale

Elvica Buttlar	1 Cow & Calf		8.13
Buttlar Jacob	1 Brown Horse		67.25
	2 Bushels Salt		2.41

W Cross by his debuty
C Y Oliver

A return of the Sale of the Estate of Henry R Buttlar dec.d by James Scarbrough Administrator of Said Estate (to wit)

A Memorandum of the 3rd Sale of the property of Henry R Buttlar dec.d on the 26th February 1836

	1 Small negro Girl named Fanny broght by Obediah Ashlack		$375.00
Jacob Buttlar	1 feed trough		.38
Andrew McKamey	15Lbs Iron		.75
			376.13

James Scarbrough
Administrator of the Estate
Recorded 12th July 1836
W Cross by his Deputy
C Y Oliver

Return of the Settlement with Elizabeth Worthington now Elizabeth Wallace Guardian of John Worthington Minor Heir of William Worthington dec.d Make the following report (viz) from the Estatement of the Clerk we find that the Said guardian in chargeable with for person I Estate. Sold by the Executors of said guardian in chargeable. Sold

by the Executors of said Estate	$466.47¾
for hire of negro woman untill Febry 19th 1836)	125.11
) Carried Over	
	592.11

(Pg159)

To amount Brot Over	592.11
For rent of Plantation	45.17½
Total Amount of the Estate	637.28½

Cr by taxes paid for land and

negro	$11.91	
1 negro woman	300.00	311.91
Leaving a balance		326.37½

favor of John K Worthington of)
Recorded 12th of July 1836   )   Jacob Weaver
W Cross by his Deputy   J L Mamor
      C Y Oliver   John Gibbs

Additional return of the amount of Sale of the Estate of Thomas B uttlar dec.d being a Statement the property Sold by Thomas Buttlar dec.d Since 2nd report and the amount thire of respectively

Henry Buttlar	20 Bushels Corn	$10.00
William Buttlar	20 do	8.40
Mary Ann Buttlar	20 do	6.40
Elias Buttlar	20 Corn	8.00
Francis H. Roberson	20 Corn	8.20
William M. Buttlar	Refused Corn	5.07
Amt of Due frm, Jacpb Buttlar		11.12½
A Note of Hoover in Suit		108.10
Collected from Thomas Gallaher		2.00
Due from A McKamey		9.45

185.04½

(Pg160)
do do A McKamey   6.10
        Collected from Julian F. Scott in part payment
        of the Turn Pike road   200.00
        1 Note on Same Due January 1837 for   100.00
        One Note on Same due Jan 1838. This being the   100.00
        Amt. in full for the turn Pike which makes
        $400. the amount given for said road   406.10
        The above sumof is the balance in full of the
        assets and proved of the Estate of Thomas Buttlar
        dec.d so far as come to my knowlidge all which is
        Submitted respectifully to the Worship Court Sept.
        Term 1836
                        Richard Oliver
                                Administrator
                                        Thomas Buttlar
                                                dec.d
                        Recorded 8th Sept 1836

                        Will Cross Clk
                                By his Deputy
                                        C Y Oliver

        David Clarkson's Will in the name of God Amen I
David Clarkson of the County of Anderson & State of Tennessee being
Sick and weak of Bodybut of Sound Mind and dispasing Memery for which
I think God in Calling to Mind uncertainly of human life and being de-
sirous to dispose of all Such wordly Substance as it hath pleased God
to bless me with I give and bequeath to my Soul into the hands of
Godwho made it I give and bequeath My body to the dust from whence
it came to be burried in a Christian Like Manner I David Clarkson
of the County and State aforesaid do Make this My last will and
Testament in Manner & form following (that is)
(Pg161)

1st- I desire that 30 Much of My perishable property be immediately
Sold after My Deceased as Will pay MyJust debts and funeral Expenses

2nd- rafter payments of debts and funeral Expenses I give to my
beloved wife Ann Clarkson all my real & personal Estate during her
Natural life and at her deceased to be divided as follows

3rd- I give aa bequeath to My Daughter Sally Dunn My negro Named

Harry extraordinary My reason for giving his that much More than
any one of the rest of my children was on account of her being so
durifull a Child to her Mother and My Salf by waiting on us when we was
not able to help ourselves
4th
I give and bequeath to My Daughter Lucy Parnall the property belonging
to me that she has in hir possession at this time
5th The ballance of real & personal Estate to be Sold and the Money aris-
thire from to be equally divided among all my children except my two
negroes Peter & Rachel his wife who are to chuse thire own Mistrees among
my children but not to be considered as any part of that Child Share of
My Estate and Lastly I do here by Constitute and appoint My Friend Samuel
Dunn and My Son John Clarkson Executor to this my Last Will and Testament
hereby revoking all other former Wills and Testament by mehere tofore
made in witness where of I have here unto Set My hand and Seal this twenty
Ninth day of January in the Year of Our Lord one thousand Eight hundred &
Eight hundred & eighteen
Signed Sealed Published

                                        David Clarkson
                                        (Seal)

(Pg162)
declared to be the Last Will Testament of the above named David Clarkson
in presence of us and at his request and in his presence have here unto
Subscribe Our Names as witnesses to the Same John Cooper
                                        William McKamey
                                        Joseph Stout
                                        Robert McKamey
Recorded this 26 the day of November 1836
   e
                                        Will Cross Clk
                                        by his Deputy
                                                C Y Oliver

Return of a Settlement Made with John M. Lamar Administrator and
Polly Lamar Administrator of the Estate of William Lamar dec.d
in the following words & figurs (to wit)

State of Tennessee) October the 12th 1836 to the Worhipfull Court
Anderson County) for Said County.
We each Foster Joseph C Moore & William H Gibbs Commissioners appointed
by said Court to make Settlement with John M & Polly Lamar, administrator
for the Estate of William Lamar deceased Make the following report as
appears from voucher produced by them (to wit)

Voucher	No 1		272 00
do	No 2		272 00
do	No 3		272 00
do	No 4		7.41
do	No 5		6.00
do	No 6		3.00
			832.41

(Pg 163)

Amount of vouchers brought over			832.44
Voucher	No 7		2.04
do	8		1.65
do	No 9		272.00
		Total	1108.10

The above being a true copy of all
The Vouchers produced by said Administrator and administrtrtrix
leaving a balance in thire hand $2728.08¾ $2728.08¾

Recorded 9th December 1836) Enoch Foster
Will Cross Clk   ) Joseph L Moore
By his Deputy   )Wm M Gibb
            C Y Oliver   Commissioners

A return of the Settlement with Nathan Norman Guardian of
John Norman (to wit)

State of Tennessee   )   In pursuance of an Order of Court with
Anderson County   )   Nathan Norman Guardian of John Norman per
                         account Nathan Norman Indebted to John Norman
                                                                26.68½
                         Credit for boarding and washing   26.68¼
                         Given under our hand this 11th day of
                         November 1836
                                        John Wilson
                                        John Chiles
Recorded this 9th day of December 1836
                                        James Hall
                                        Will Cross Clk
                                        by his deputy
                                                    C Y Oliver

(Pg 164)
                    William McMunn Will
I William McMunn of the County of Anderson County and State of
Tennessee being of Sound and perfect mind and Memory do make and
publish this my Last Will and Testament in the Manner and form
following first it is My desire that whatever debts I may owe at the
time of my death Shall be paid out of my personal property or that
my personal property Shall be Sold of value Sufficint to pay the
said debts I do also give and bequeath to my beloved wife Ellen McMunn
the plantation on which I Now deside during her Natural life provided
She Should remain unmarried but Should she marry then it is my desire
and Intention that She Shall be entilled to hir devorse which will be
one third of the land during hir Natural life. It is further My Will
an Intention that at the death of My said Wife Ellen Myar above devise
Shall be sold and the money for which it May be Sold it may be Sold to
be Divided equally among My Grand Children (To wit)
Betsy Jane McMunn
Nancy Martha McMunn &
Mary Ellen McMunn, Children of my deceased Son Wm McMunn   I do further
will and bequeath to my beloved Wife Ellen McMunn all my Household
furniture for own use and benefit unconditionlly and also my farming
utentuals of ever description it also My will Intention that the ballance of my personal property which may remain after paying all my Just
debts Shall belong to my said Wife Ellen McMunn My Executrix I auth-
orise then to Settle all my debts boath that which I may owe and that
which be due to me by any person in testimony where of I have here unto
set my hand
(Pg 165)

and affirmed My Seal this 14th day of November 1836
Signed   Sealed   Published and declared

                                          his
                              William X McMunn
                                         mark
by the above Named William McMunn to be his Last Will & Testament
in the presance of us who have here unto Subscribed our Names in
the presence of Henry Clear   his
                              DavidX Redman
                                        mark
Recorded this 18th day of January 1837
                              Will Cross Clk
                              By his Deputy
An Inventory of the personal   C Y Oliver
property money and debts of
William McMunn dec.d (to wit)

              7 head Cattle 7 head Hogs 20 Geese 1 Mare 1 Sheep
              250 bushels of Corn estimated by Wm Jones
              83 doz Oats Suppoised to be 8000 Bundles fodder
              Supposed to be 1 mans Saddle An Account against
              James Taylor $20.00
                              Cash on hand $9.50   9.50
                                                            _____
                                                               29.50

The above is a correct Statement of the person property
Cash and debts due except that which is Specially bequeathed
in the Last will & Testament of said Wm McMunn dec.d
                              John Whitson
                                  Executor
                              Ellen McMunn
                                  Executrix
December the 7th 1836
(Pg 166)
In the name of God Amen I Samuel Frost be Sound Mind and in Tolerable
health Knowing the certainly of death and the uncertainly ofof life
do make this My last Will and Testament revoking all other by me Made
1st I agree and bequeath to my beloved Son John R. Frost for and in
Conderation of the Sum of two hundred Bushels of Corn and three hundred
Bundles of fodder yearly and the said J R. Frost to do the Milling for
this father and get the fire wood during his life for which I agree to
give unto him the said J. R. Frost the following discribed tract Par-
aell of land comming on a rock at the Spring   running with a conditional line made by Samuel Frost Between Said J. R. Frost & J Henderson
runing to the top of The river ridge runing with My Line to the beginning
Corner To have to hold the said tract of Land at my death & the said
J. R. Frost is to have the Possyfull Sion of the whole tract of land together with Henderson Part during My Natural life with the exception dwelling
House and Lots around it.
Secondly I give and bequeath unto My Son inlaw Jesse Henderson for con-
sideration Services done and rendered a Certain tract of or percell of
Land comming on a Rock at the Spring runing with Morrows Land Portwoods
line funing with Portwoods line a a N rth East Course to Corner on
the road that leads from My house to Clinton on a road Oak thence
running a trail line through Lovers field to the Top of the ridge then to

a divisional line between J R Frost and said Henderson then with the
conditional line to the beginning. I give and bequeath unto My grand son
John R Frost Jun.r or for the Love & affliction I have for him I have for
him one tract or Parcell of Land Beginning on Henderson road Oak Corner
running on My line a North East Course to a Conditional between said
John R Frost Jun.r & Clark Morton thence to the beginning corner
(Pg 167)
4th- I give & bequeath unto My beloved Grand Son Clark Morton one tract
or parcell of Land beginning at the Conditional Corner Between John R
Frost Jun.r and Clark Morton runing around with the upper line to the conditional J. R Frost Jun.r and Clark Morton thence with said line to the
beginning &
5th- I further appoint My beloved Son Jn R Frost & beloved Son in law
Jesse Henderson My administrators to this My Last will & Testament and
it is My desire that the Court require no Security of them for thire
performance as administrators Signed and Sealed in presence of this 20th
day of August 1836

Jn B Crozier   )   Samuel Frost
James Clardy   )   (Seal)

Recorded 3rd day of March 1837

                                             Will Cross Clk
                                             by his Deputy
                                                C Y Oliver

We bring appoint Commissioners to Settle with Joseph Black Guardian
of the heirs of Moses Farmer deceased find in the said Black hands in
Notes in $690.94
In cash   200.00

                                                              890.94

Given under our hands this 24th day of June 1837
Recorded_____   13th   July 1837

                                             William Cross
                                         By his Deputy
                                             C Y Oliver

                                             James Noel
                                             John Chiles
                                             James Hall

(Pg 168)

A report of part of the prpseed of the Estate of Thomas Buttlar
deceased to June turm of the County Court 1837
Amount of A K on John Coatney $36.20
Amt of rent Collected from James Weaver for the use of the
land in Morgan County   20.00
Due from Gray for the above Named Land   15.00
due from Thomas Gardner & James Wilson   18.00

                                                             109.20

All of which Respectfully Submitted to the Court
                                        Richard Oliver
                                        Administrator

Recorded July the 13th 1837
                                        William Cross Clk
                                        By his Deputy
                                             C Y Oliver
Additional Inventory and return Made by Elizabeth Durrett & James
H Nickle administrator and administratrix of the Estate of John G
Durrett dec.d (viz) in our hands on Settlement with Richard Oliver
Administrator of the Estate of Mary Miller decd. the Sum of $22.26¾
cents of the effect of the Estate of John G Durrett deceased
                                        Elizabeth Durrett
                                        J H Nickle
Recorded 13th July 1837)   Administrator &
Will Cross Clk   )   Administratrix
By his Deputy   )   Estate of John G Durrett
          C Y Oliver)
(Pg 169)
I Elijah Kirk of the County of Anderson and S{t}ate of Tennessee revoking the uncertainly Mortal life and the opportunity for men once
to die feeling unsound in Body but Clear in Mind do Constitute and make
this My last Will & Testament in Manner & form following (vis) first I
give and bequeath to my Wife Catherin the Land & property on the place
during his life or widowhood and My Son Solemon is to have a house out
of the property that now is My Son Matterson is to have a horse also:
and when My Son Matterson becomes twenty one the Land is to be Sold
and Equally divided betwixt the Boys and Catherine to have equal part
with them then the loose property to be Equally divided betwixt the
girls. I hereby Constitute appoint William Warwick and Catherine Kirk
Executors of this My last Will & Testament hereby I revoking all Wills
& Testament Made by Me given under My hand and Seal the first day of May
1838
Signed Sealed in the presents of us
                           John P Kirk
                           John D Marcus

                                        Elijah Kirk
                                        (Seal)
                                        William Cross Clk
                                        By his Deputy
                                             C Y Oliver

(Pg 170)
A return of the Amount of Sale of the Estate of William McMunn (viz)
The following is a Correct Statement of the personal property Sold by
Eutherity of the Worshipful County Court of Anderson County (to wit)

1 Cow			8.75
1 Do			10.00
1 Steer			8.62½
1 Yearling			3.12½
10 Bushels Corn @ 40¢		4.00	$ 30.50
10 Do 43¢		4.30	
10 Do @ 50¢		5.00	
10 Do @ 46¢		4.60	
5 Do @ 40¢		2.00	
1 Saddle		3.25	

1 Bureau	11.12½	$35.50
1 Halter Chain	1.00	
		35.27½
		$70.77½

March 6 1837   John Whitson Executor
                        Ellen McMunn Executrix
Recorded   13th July 1837

                                    William Cross Clk
                                    By his Deputy
                                    C Y Oliver

Pg
(171)
In the Name of God Amen All men have one time to die being of
Sound Mind though weak in Body do Make Ordain this My Last Will &
Testament in the following Manner & form to wit.
First I give and bequeath My body to the Earth to be Burried in a
Christian like Manner teaching My wordly Estate
Secondly I bequeath that all My Just debts Should be paid out of My Es-
tate
Thirdly I give and bequeath to My wife Mary Snotterly all the remainly
part of My Estate for the purpose of raising My said family and after hir
decease the remaining Part of My Estate is to be Equally divided among
all my Children Betsy, John Bebeary Henry, Sally Polly, Daniel and
Pence, Philip jacob Lewis & Anna Equally Excepting one horse beast to be
given to my Son Henry Snotterly at the time of his being of the age of twan
twenty one years Old to be worth fifty dollars and I do hereby appoint
My loving wife My Executrix and John Gibbs Executor to this My last Will
and Testament and Exempt them hereby from giving Bond and Security in the
Management of the said Will and Testament in witness I have here unto Set
My hand and Seal to this My last Will and Testament August 24th 1825
Signed Sealed and acknowledged in the presence of us

                his   his
            Lewis I Miller   HenryxSnotterly
                mark   Mark
                his
            John X D Minneroe
                mark
                his
            Peter K Clair
                mark

Pg
(172)
Inventory and Amount of the Estate of James Davis deceased December 23rd
1837. returned to January term County Court 1837   (viz)

Moses Overton	1 Cuting Box & Knife	.25
Isaac Going	1 Bar Plow	1.75
James Davis	1 Pole ax	43¾
Crowell Maberry	1 Single tree & tub	.25
Squire Williams	1 Hone	1.00
Austin Moore	1 Mattox	
James Overton	1 Bar Plow	.93¾
Moses Overton	1 Sprouting Hoe	.20
James Davis	1 Plow	.25
James Overton	1 Single Tree & Clevis	1.04

William Brown	1 pair of Chains	.81¼
James Kirk	1 pair of Gears	1.25
John Overton	1 Mans Saddle	3.00
John Cox	1 Iron Wedge	.54
John Cox	1 Breakfast Knife	12½
James Davis	1 Sythe Stake & Hammer	1.00
William Dail	1 bed & furniture	6.50
John York	1 Grid Iron	.50
Sally Davis	1 Trunk	6¼
James Kirk	1 Mare	$70.00
John Cox	2 Bridles & Leather	1.01
Calvin L. Childress	1 Cow with one horn	3.75
James Davis	1 Hog	5.12½
William Brown	1 Loom	1.00
James Overton	1 pair fire dogs	.75
Isaac Going	1 Sprouting Hoe	.25
Henry Baker	1 Shot Gun	1.93½
Joseph Overton	1 pair Bridle bits	. 6¼

$105.41½

                    Joseph Overton &
                    Jesse Davis
                              Administrator

(Pg 173)
Settlement with Nathan A Farmer administrator and Jane Farmer
administratrix of the Estate of Luke Farmer dec.d in account
Current with Said Estate
                    To Amount of Sale $407.70¼

This said administrator and administratrix are entitled to
Credit for the following vouchers (viz)
(1) By Clerk receipt for taking & Issuing Letters of administrator   1.00
(2) By Clerk receipt for recording amount of Sale   .90
(3) By Guardian Henry Farmer receipt   62. 6¼
(4) By Guardian Henry Farmer receipt   60.00
(5) By Guardian Henry Farmer receipt   175.00
(6) By Guardian Henry Farmer receipt   4.50
(7) By Account for Services as administrator   10.00
(8) By Guardian H Farmer receipt   108.96¾

                                                 $422.42

Balance due the administrator and administratrix from the
said Estate   12.32¼
James Nail   1.00
Wm McKamey   1.00
John Siber   1.00

                                                 $ 3.00

                    AS Commissioners
                         James Nail
                         William McKamey
                              Commissioners
(Pg 174)
A Second Settlement with Charles Luallen Administrator of the

Estate of Richard Luallen dec.d We the Commissioners appointed
by the County Court of Anderson County July term 1837: to examine
the Accounts of Charles Luallen administrator of the Estate of
Richard Oliver deceased and to make Settlement him in relation to
his administrator of said Estate have performed that duly and returned the following Settlement We find that said Charles Luallen
administrator is charged to amount $6570.30¼

We find that said Charles Luallen   has the following Vouchers
for 1.50 dollars trade on Jacob Luneirt and David Vandergriff w
which was valued at one hundred and twenty dollars Cash   2597.13¾

		No 74		30.00
Hugh Barton Voucher		No 75		6.50
John Jarnagin	Do	No 76		101.87½
John Whitson	Do	No 77		21.20
John M Lamar	Do	No 78		2.00
James Kirkpatrick	"	No 79		28.52
Richard Luallen	Do	No 80		450.00
Samuel R Rogers	Do	NO 81		62.50
Commissioners	Do	No 82		5.00
Thomas Hart	Do	No 83		.75
Alfred England	Do	No 84		1.50

We further find by Heirs receipt a Credit $1304.00
                    Commissioners on 5th August 1837   300.
                                                               _____
                                                               4013.18¼
(175)
We the Commissioners find a ballance due to said Estate of   2067.12

                              Enoch Foster
                              Wm H Gibbs
                              Hoyt Rutherford
                                   Commissioners

Inventory of Property received by me a Guardian Smtha Cross dec.d
(viz)

3 head of horses	8 head of cattle	
70 head of Hogs	6 head of sheep	
2 Beds & furniture	3 Axes four Plows	four Clevices
4 weeding Hoes	Has one Sythe & Cradle	One Mowing Sythe
one Harrow	two Bells	one pair of Steel Yards
one Chest	three pair of farming gears	

This being one fourth part on value of the above Estate on hand
This 2nd of October 1837

                              Alfred Cross   Guardian
                              Sworn to in Open Court
                                   William Cross Clk)
)

Inventory of the amount of Property Sold by Alfred Cross Guardian
of Senthy Cross which he has Exposed to Public Sale and Secured by
Note and approved Security (viz)

1 Note on Jacob McGhee	12.50	12.50
1 Do on John Wickle	20. 6¼	20. 6¼
1 Do on Isaac Duncan	9.41½	
One do on Hugh L White	5.57	5.57
One do on Isaac A Freels	6.25	6.25
One do on George W R⁴aver	11.33½	11.33½
(176) Pg		
One Note on James H Black		11.87½
One Note on Lazrius Moore		18.87½
One do on Jesse Nail		9.00
One do on Wm Davidson		7.12½
One do on B D Freeman		15.25
One do on Dickson Russell		9.53
One do on George Haskins		1.87½
		190.84

All of the foregoing property was Sold on a Credit of twelve
Months approved Security this 2nd day of November 1837

                                    Alfred Cross
                                    Guardian of
                                    Sinthy Cross

State of Tennessee   )
Anderson County   ) In obediance to the County Court by an
order to us directed to Make Settlement with Jacob Buttlar administrator of the Estare of William Buttlar deceased report to
Court as follows. We find that the Said Jacov Buttlar is charged
with   201.18¾
and the said Jacob Buttlar produced Vouchers to the amt of   18.08
              Balance due the Estate   183.10¾
              Commissioners $1 pr day each   3.00
              Given under our head this 17th
              February 1838

                                    John Key
                                    James Jones
                                    John Seiber
                                    Commissioners

Pg
(177)
Joh B Crozier Guardian of the Miners Heirs of Martin Will deceased

Dr To rent of Plantation of 1835			50.00
To do do do 1827			50.00
To Cash received of	William Cross Clk		50.00
To Amount received of	Moses Roberts		18.37½
To do	1836		50.00
To 7 Cords of wood for	Ryan		.87½
			$219.25
No 1 By cr	Oliver & Tates		8.80
No 2 By	Tates & K		10.75
No 3 By	do do		7.50
No 4	By Sheriff Galbreath recept		9.00
No 5	By Gover My recept		20.00
No 6	Crozier & Sons A k		51.00
No 7	McKamays Sheriff receipt Tax		1.85
No 8 Do	do do do		1.85

No 9 By	I Jarnagin & C ak	14.99¾
To Paid	McKamey Sheriff for Mare	
Sold at the Suit of	Noel & Brother	27.62½
1836	Paid Moore for repairing fence	4.00
	Hawling and putting up fence	26.10

Paid John Williams Attorney at Law for answering Chancery Bill
Attending Chancery Court & three days — 8.00
To 9 days attention renting receiving rent and collecting debts — 9.00
To paid Clerk for Commissioners — .25
Paid Commissioners   for setting — 3.00
J B Crozier $1.
to paid Shares for Lucy Hill   1.50   2.50
                    Ballance in Guardian
                            hands   7.85   211.40
                                    7.85

                                    219.25

(Pg 178)

We the Commissioners find in the Guardian hands after Settling
Seven dollars and Eighty Cents this 8th February 1838   7.85
                    Richard Andrew
                    William McKamey
                    John Chiles
                            Commissioners

Paid to J Jarnagin of the Minor Heirs of M Hill dec.d   8.97½
the 7th of June 1838
                    C Y Oliver

Joseph C Moore Guardian report to Court To the Worshipful
County Court of Anderson County in obediance to the Statute in
Such Cases and Provided I Make to your Worshipful the following
report of all the property which has come into my hand virtue of
my appartment vasGuardian for the Miner Heirs at Law of Richard
Luallen deceased 1st i find a Bill of Injunction in the Chancery
Court Instituted by Arthur Crozier and four Plantations undivided
in which the heirs all Claim to hold equal Share form which I have
received one hundred and forty bushels of Corn and four hundred
Sheaves of Oate and have Sold the corn in Lots (towit)
2nd 37½ at w37½   Oats
3rd 37½ bushels at   38½ Cents to Hart
4th 32½ bushels of Corn@at40½ Cents pr bushels to I Allen
5th 32½ at   40¼ Cents to S Allen and some to
                                    Seavers
not measured yet the Oats I have as handy yet

(179)
The money that is in the Administrator hands I have demanded and he
will not pay Over with out Suit is brought all of which is respectfully Submitted this the First day of January 1838
                    Joseph C Moore
                        Guardian

Lays X Cross Road Anderson County Tennessee
An Inventory of the property blonging to the Estate of John M Lay
dec.d 2nd July 1838
3 Beds & furniture   1 cupboard   1 Table   6 chairs
1 pattent Clock   1 Looking glass 5 plats   2 dishes
1 Set of Cups & Saucers   ½ " Knives & forks

1 Set of Spoons	1 Tea pot	1 Sugar Jug
1 Cream Do	2 pitchers	2 Lard dishes
P Salt Sellers	1 Lot Pheals	1 Coffee pot
5 ten pans	1 crock	2 pots
2 Ovens	1 Baker	1 frying pan
1 Skillet	1 pair of Pot hooks	1 pot rack
2 Candle sticks	2 pair Snuffers	2 Sterrips
1 flat Iron	1 Coffee Mill	1 Trunk
1 Ten Bucket	3 Pale	3 Cows and
3 Calves	1 Jug	2 pair of fire dogs
1 pair of tongs	1 Choping ax	1 Hoe
1 pair of gears	1 Lot of Hogs not known how many	
1 pair of Cards	1 Tray	1 Spinning wheel
2 Books	1 Cradle	1 Sifter
1 check real		1 Side Saddle

By Henry Smith
Sworn to in Open Court
Attest   Will Cross Clk

(Pg180)

State of Tennessee)   To the Worshipful County Court of
Anderson County   )   September Sessions 1838

I Samuel Seiber Guardian of Polly Childs, Sally & William Childs Minor Heirs of Micajah Chiles decld do here by report to Worship and account of all the Estate of said Minors which has come into my hands or Possessions   Guardian (viz)

1 Cow	Worth $10.00		$10.00
2 Sows & fourteen pigs			12.00
2 Small feather Beds & furniture			10.00
1 Side Saddle			15500
1 Sheep	1.25	1 Bee Stand 2.	3.25
2 Pea Fowls	2.00	3 pairs cartings 3.	5.00
1 Beef Hide	2.00		2.75
6 delf Plats 1 Set tea Cups & Saucers			1.00
1 Small choping ax & fir shovel			.75
In Cash			6.00
			65.75

One tract of Land Containing Ninety acres of which Seventy Acres is cleared and under cultivation this 31st day of August 1838

Sworn to this 31xt of August 1838
Samuel Shiber
William Cross Clk

State of Tennessee)   To the Worshipful County Court of
Anderson County   )   September Sessions 1835

I Samuel Seiber Guardian of Polly, Sally and William Childs Minor Heirs of Micajah Childs deceased do hereby report to
(Pg 181)
Your worship an Account of the propets and disbursements of the

Estate of said Minor Heirs for three years and nine Months inding on the 31st of August 1838

Received for rent the first year		$30.00
Received for the 2nd year		26.00
Received for 3rd Year		20.00
Received Six dozen of Oats for rent	$1.00	1.00
To Amount of said Estate as pre said Guardian Exhibit		65.75
By Cash find J		149.08 1/3

Jarnagin Clerk of Anderson County being his part of a
Judgment in form of the Commissioners for dividing and
making partition of land   6.93¾

By Tax for 1834 &	.50	
By Cash paid by for Tax 1835	.50	.50

By Cash paid Richard Oliver the difference in value
of the division of the Land between said Oliver and the
Heirs of Micajah Childs dec.d   35.00

By Cash paid Jacob Peak for Land	1.16 2/3
Cash paid Henry Chiles for making rails	3.00
Cash paid Elijah Seiber for putting up rails	3.00
Cash paid Do for repairing farm	10.00
Cash paid Clerk for Guardian	.50
Amt allowed Guardian for his Services	8.00
	72.85 2/3

The whole Amount which said Guardian is Chargable is $49.03 1/3
Total Amt of disbursement due the ward   76.22½
The above Settlenent taken and Settlement Made with Samuel
Seiber Guardian & C this of August 1838
                        William Cross Clk

(Pg 182)

State of Tennessee   )   To the Worshipful County Court
Anderson County   )   Sept Sessions 1838
I John Garnnor of Guardian of Louisa Jane Buttlar Minor Heirs
of Thomas Buttlar deceased to thereby report to your worship an
account of all the Estate of said Minor w ich has come to my hands
or possessions Guardian (to wit)
Received from the administrator of said Thomas Buttlar dec.d
in cash 3rd day of January 1827 $386.07¾
Received from Richard Oliver being so much of the Estate due
the Minor Heirs from the Estate of Thomas Buttlar Sen. deceased
hir Grandfather recived of James Scarbrough being the amount of
Toll made by the Will this 13th of August 1838   13.25
                                                      649.32 2/3

John Garnnor Guardian of L Buttlar Minor of Th Butlar dec.d
State of Tennessee)   To the Worshipful County Court
Anderson County   )
I John Garnnor Guardian of Louisa Jane Butlar Minor Heirs of
Thomas Butlar Jr deceased do hereby report to your Worship an
account Current of the profits and disvursement of the Estate
of said Minor Heirs for Nine years and some Months ending on the
18th of August 1838

(183)
John Garnnor Guardian   H Dr
To Spencer Keith Note for Money Loaned $103.25¼
Do   Do   68.47¼
To John Hagler   A Copeland & A do A Hagler   138.53
To John Nail & Wm Scott   de---   138.63
To William Scott & John Nail de---   93.85½
To George White & Wm Scott   do   11.42½
To R. Oliver & Henry Butlar   272.50
To James Scarbrough & R. Oliver   do   11.21
To Do   Do   Wm R Butlar   2.49¾
                                                                   _____
                                                                    894.27

Disbursements or Cr. by Amount Paid Clerk for Guardian Land   .50
"   "   "   Clerk for Second Guardian ben one of the
Securities deceased and new Security required by this amount
paid Clk for taking Stating Account and recording Some by as
Allowance Made Guardian for his Services for 9 Years   25.00
The whole Amount with which said Guardian Chargable is   894.27
                    Total Amt of disbursement   27.50
                                                                   _____
                    Amount due   866.77

State of Tennessee
Anderson County
I do Certify that the foregoing Guardian is above Stated was
taken by me which is Submitted to the Court for Confirmation
rejection this 18th of August 1838
                              Will Cross Clk
                              By his Deputy
                              C Y Oliver

(Pg 184)
Report of Enoch Foster Guardian) To the Worshipful County
State of Tennessee Anderson Co) Court October Term 1838

I Enoch Foster Guardian of Alexander M Luallen, Nancy Luallen
Daniel Luallen Jesse Luallen, Louisa Luallen & Freemen Luallen
Minor Heirs of Richard Luallen deceased do hereby report to
your worship on account of all the Estate of said Minor Heirs of
said which has come to my hand or possessions of Guardian (to wit)
Received of Charles Luallen administrator of the Estate of
Richard Luallen deceased impromissory Notes payable to Myself as
Guardian as aforesaid on different individuals Made Same by Se-
curity as I believe to be the amunt $1110.18
                         Sworn to in Open Court
                         William Cross Clk
                         Enoch Foster

Largest Road Anderson County 3rd August 1838
Alex of the Sale of property of John H Lay deceased
Julia Lay   1 Bed & furniture   5.00
do   do   do   5.00
do   do   1 Trunnel do do   1.00
"   "   1 Beaure   2.00
"   "   1 Table   1.00
                                                    _____
                                                     14.00

			14.00
Thomas Collins	1 Trunk		2.12½
John Baker	1 Looking Glass		.55
Julia Lay	6 Chairs		1.00
" "	1 tea pot Sugar & Cream Jug		.25
	1 pitcher & 2 Sauce dishes		.25
			4.17½
Thomas Brandlett	1 razor 1box blacking 7& 2 pairs Butts		.50
James M Turner	1 pair of waufle Irons		.50
Julia Lay	1 Crock		.05
John Baker	1 Lantern Canister & Trumpet		.12½
IsaacStuksberry	1 pale & frying pan		.52½
" "	1 Skillet & Pot		1.00
I D Aranson	1 Oven & Lid		.93¾
IsaacStooksbarry	1 Plow		1.68¾
July Lay	1 pair fire dogs & to small chairs		.25
" "	1 pair of cards & wheel		.25
Isaac Stuksberry	1 Cradle		.25
July Lay	1 ax & Tongs 1 bed tick		2.25
Lewis Miller	1 Clock		14.75
			$24.71¼

(Pg 185)

July Lay	2 dishes & 5 Plates		25
" "	1 Set of Cups &nSaucers		
	Set of knives & forks		12½
July Lay	1 Set of Spoons & Salt Seller		12½
" "	3 Ten pans & coffee Pot		25
" "	1 Jug Bowl & Plate		25
" "	1 Candle stick & snuffer		12½
" "	1 Bible		12½
" "	1 tin bucket & flat iron		37½
" "	1 Kittle & Pan	1.00	1100
" "	1 Skillet & Lid	50	.50
" "	2 pot hooks	28	.25
" "	1 pot	25	.25
" "	1 pail	6½	6½
" "	1 pan & sifter	12½	.12½
" "	1 flour barrel	6½	6½
" "	1 coffee Mill & pot rack		.25
" "	1 table & wheel	25	.25
" "	1 Side Saddle	5.00	5.00
" "	1 Strainer	.05	.05
			$ 9$ 00
Elijah Longmire	1 pair of firedogs	40	40
Anderson Sharp	1 Candle stick & snuffer & 2 bottles for	,55	.55
John Stout	2½ pairs ladys stirrups	.40	.40
James Weaver	1 Book	.18¾	.18¾

(Pg186)

| July Lay | 1 cupboard & White Cow & Calf | 6.00 | 6.00 |

July Lay	1 Calf	1.00	1.00
Jacob Lay	1 Cow	13.50	13.50
Alfred Sharp	1 Bull	4.25	4.25
John Baker	1 Cow	12.50	12.50
Allen McCoy	Jars Metal paper draft		
	3 Salt Guards		.31¼
W G Cardin	1 Pocket Book		37½
A Sharp	" " "		7½
July Lay	1 Pale		12½
Braham Cross	Chisel		.25
George Miller	1 pair of stretchers		68¾
July Lay	1 Lot of Hogs		11.00

$$50.07½$$
$$52.18¾$$

$$102.26¼$$

Recorded 6th October 1838) Henry Smith
                            Wm Cross Clk   his debuty
                                            C Y Oliver
                                                Admr.

A return of an Inventory of debts belonging to the Estate of
John Lay dec.d

1 Note on John Brummor		$127. 50	127.50
1 Do on J Reed		6. 37½	6.37½
1 Do on George Brumit		1. 75	1.75
1 Do on Jas Carnut		4. 00	4.00
1 Do on John Sharp		2. 00	2.00
1 Note on Leonard Keller		1. 00	1.00
1 Order on D Snodderly		37½	.37½
1 " A McCoy		1. 32½	1.32½
1 " John Snodderly		10. 34½	10.84½
1 " " Albert Cross		2. 10	2.10
1 " " A Moser		1. 51	1.51
1 " " Jermeah Remine		1.64½	1.64½
1 " " John Morton		.68¾	.68¾

$$185.27½$$

(Pg 187)   Amount brought forward

Josiah Oaks	3.96½
Wisly Davis	12 12½
H Robertson	2.62½
Anderson Gentry	1.87½
A Page	1.25
Wm Sharp	6.09½
Reese & Brags	3.00
H Thomas	.56¼
Sal Petibone	2.64
I Miller	25
H Robertson	68¾
J Lays	6.75

$$29.49½$$

Henry Smith
Recorded 6th of October 1838
Wm Cross Clk by his deputy
                    C Y Oliver

DAVID KISLINS WILL
In the name of God Amen
I David Kisling of the County of Anderson and state of Tennessee
being weak in body but of Sound Mind and Judgment do make this My
Last Will & Testament revoking all other viz

I give unto My wife Frances Kisling two horses that she may make choice
of two pair of Gears and all the farming utential and two choice of
Milk Cows and Calves eight Killing hogs and one big steer for this year
three breeding Sows and ten Shoats. Such as she make choice of two
head of Sheep and all the grain that is all the household and kitchen
furniture and the Plantation during his Natural life or widowed and
fifty dollars in Money
(Pg188)
two barrels of salt and two Saddles that she make choice of and I give
unto my Daughter Rebecca Kisling My Young horse Mike and the balance of
the property to be sold to pay my debts and the Remainder of the Money
to be Equally divided amonst all the children all My Notes on hand and
Book Accounts to be Put into the Executors hand for Collection and the
Money equally divided amongst the Children. I appoint John Wilson and
Thomas Ingreem to be Executors of this My Last Will and Testament Witness hand and Seal
                    This 17th day of November 1838
                            David Kisling
                                 (Seal)

Signed Sealed and delivered by the said Testator as for his last Will
and Testament in the presence of David Yarnall
                            Ransom Haskin
Recorded 5th December 1838
                    Will Cross by his deputy
                            C Y Oliver

An Inventory of all the property of Hugh Murphy deceased Estate

1 Bay horse	8 head of Hogs	two wheels
1 pair of cards	1 Bed stid & furniture	
1 Set of Carpenters Tools		1 pair Plow gears
2 weeding hoes	1 ax	2 horse wagon
one Clevis 1 iron wedge	1 Chest	1 looking glass
one ten bucket & Lid	1 Bottle	1 Slay & Parcell
		of books
1 Militia Sword & Ploom	1 Shovel	two Tribis
1 Mans Saddle	1 Set dry Measure	
(Pg 189)		
Some fodder and wheat	3 baskets 4 chairs	1 razor box & brush
Five Cakes of shaving		
soap	1 Cross Candle stick	1 Sun dial

Thomas Cole
        Administrator
Return of the amount of the sale of the Estate of Hugh Murphy
deceased sold 20th of November 1838 (to wit)

2 weeding hoes	50¢	1 ax $1.00 Clevis 40¢	$1.90
1 Iron	31¼¢	1 Trippet	.18¾
1 Do	12½		
1 fir Shovel	12¢	1 Candle stick 18¢	
1 Bucket	25¢	1 cake soap 6¼	
1 do	6¼	1 do 6¼ 1 do 6¼	
1 Razor strap & Box	27½	1 Looking glass 50¢	
1 pair Harness & chain			
chains	1.12	1 Saddle 2.75	
1 flax wheel	1.12½	1 Big wheel .50	
1 pair Cards	.25	1 Bottle 18¾	
1 Basket	12½	1 Basket 16¼	
1 do	25¢	1 pair Saddle	
		bags	
1 Set of Measures	75¢	4 Chains 62½	
1 Bed sted and furniture			
furniture	2.00	1 Chest 1.00	
1 Set of Carpenter			
Tools	20.75	1 Lot of books .12½	
1 wagon	13. 6¼	1 Book .50	
1 Slay	75¢	1 Chain 25	
1 Lot of fodder	16¼	2¼ bu wheat 2.50	
1 Lot of Hogs	3.50	1 Horse 37.00	
1 sword	.12½		

The above Inventory is a true copy as Made out by the Clerk of the
sale
This 3rd day of December 1838

                          his
                  Thomas X Cole
                 -    mark
              Recorded 5th of December 1838
              William Cross Clk
                  By his Deputy
                      C Y Oliver

(Pg 190)
A return of James Scarbrough Adms. of the Estate of Henry R Butlar
deceased of the amount of money recived on the Book of H R Butlar
which has not a ded to the amount of Sales & C

Received of James Crow		$2.12½
of Ancil Manley	$2.37½	2.37½
do John M Butlar	12.66	12.66
Robert Galbreath Esq	.52	.52
Do William Galbreath	.75	.75
Bal of Jo Seber		
O K	12½	.12½
Do John Seber	25¢	.25
of John Taylor	58½	.58½
Do Henry Pryer	31¼	.31¼
of Wesley Peters	66¢	.66¢
Do Elizabeth Russell	50	.50¢

Of Ezra Russell	1.56¼	1.56¼
Do Henry T Buttlar	.66¾	.66¾
Do of John Cox by Mary Cox	1.58½	1.58½
Do of Jacob Buttlar for		
William Buttlar	1.83	1.83
Do Do of Caleb Buttlar	.31¼	.31¼
		$0.38

By Nancy Ann Buttlar Note to James Cox Executor of the
Estate of Joseph A Mabry Admr. for which I had given my Note
to said Executor an administrator of the Estate of Henry R
Butlar dec.d which amount of the 12th Nov   11.49
which amount   18.89
brought up to the best of my recollection at this term this
15th Nov 1838

                      James Scarbrough
                            Administrator
              The Estate of H R Butlar decd.

(Pg 191)
Inventory of the Daleable property of David Kisling deceases not
disposed of in the last Will & Testament viz
State of Tennessee   )   Nov 26th 1838
Anderson County   )

1 Set of black Smith Tools and some Iron	1 Wagon
2 blind bridles	2 pairs Gears
5 pairs hip straps	8 head of sheep
3 head horses	5 head of cattle
22 head	Barrel of salt
1 Cutting Box & Knife	1 Rifle gun
8 Geese	2 beef hides
2 Mans Saddles	3 Cast Iron
washboard	six or seven hundred
feet of inch Plank	1 pair Hay ladders

1 Plow   3 axes   1 saw 1 hand vise together with some notes of hand
executed to said deceased as follows .

One Note of hand on George Moore & John Chiles for $11.00 due March
6 1837
One Note of hand on Elijah Carnall & Robert Williams for $7.37½ cents
due May 19th 1838 disperate
One Note of hand on George and Joseph C Moore for $30. due January 2nd
1838 disperate
One of hand on Elijah Carnall for $5. due March 16th 1838 disposate
One of hand on Aron Norman Sen for $3.00 and 8¼ Cents due 26th of January
1838
1 Note of hand on Samuel McCaskay and Robert E Cummings for $20.00 due
March 14th 1838
1 Note of hand on Robert Williams for $15 Current Bank Notes due November
15th 1837 disperate
1 Note of hand on John Alverson for $5. in Common Curring due Oct 5 1838
One Note of hand on Benjamin Grayhorn for $5. due December 1837 desperate
One Note of hand on Robert McKamey for $50. in Silver due 7th February
1838

A Note on Wesley Roberts for $2.50¼ due October 1832 desperate
given under our hand and you Above Written

John Wilson
Thomas Ingrum
Executors of David Keesling deceased

(Pg 192)
Amount of Sale of the Estate of David Keesling deceased

State of Tennessee)   To the County Court of the said
Anderson County   )   County January Sessions 1839

An Account of Sales made of the personal Property of the Estate of
David Keesling deceased at his late residence in Anderson County agter
advertising According to law viz)

Parnall Ingrun	three axes & one hand saw	$1.00
George Lucas	1 Plow	2.25
Wm B Smith	the fore wheel of a wagon	14.12½
Austin Jenkins	1 wagon bed	19.00
Lazruas Moore	1 wagon Wheel 3 hubs 1 axel	7.50
James Hall	39 Lbs of Iron at 3 1/3¢ per lb	3.25
Austin Jenkins	1 Iron Mereld board	1.00
Ben L Childress	1 do	1.24
Roseland Frost	1 do	1.25
George Lucas	1 wagon berelster	.12½
Anderson McClain	1 set of black Smith tools	41.00
Aron Headrix	1 peice of sheet iron	.39
Robt L Childress	8 Shoats	16.54¼
Stephen McClain	ten shoats	21.50
Lazrus Moore	4 head of hogs	15.75
Joshua Frost	1 Barrel of salt	9.00
Robt Millicon	2 Saddles & 1 Grind Stone	.75
Thomas May	3 hip straps 2 collars & 1 bridle	3.75
Thomas May	1 pair of Gears 2 pairs of Britch band	1.68¾
John McChapman	1 pair of Gears shot	2.39
Robt Millicon	one rifle gun & Pouch pot	8.00
Robt Childress	Two hides	5.00
George Lucas	one lot of Plank 83 foot pr	6.30
Robt Harper	1 Horse	42.75

(Pg 193)

F E Gentry	one Horse	35.25
Sam I M Chapman	1 Colt	41.12½
Jas Clardy	1 Cutting Box & knife	2.00
Purnall Ingrun	1 pair hay ladders	.90
Willie Young	4 head of Sheep	3.12½
James Nelson	1 Black cow	6.87½
Daniel Yarnall	4 head of Sheep	3.35
Thos May	1 Cow	5.25
Archibald Dowling	1 Bull	10.51
Jas Nelson	1 Calf	3.13
Thos May	1 Calf	1.15
Wm B Smith	8 Geese	2.25
Edward Lucas	1 hand vise	2.05

Robb Childress   41 Lbs iron at 8 1/3¢ per lb   3.41 2/3

                                                             355.86

The whole Amount of Property Sold
                    John Willson &
                    Thos Ingrun
                                   Executors
                    David Keesling Decd.

Wm Cross Clk
          by his deputy
                              C Y Oliver
Inventory of James Moore)
State of Tennessee   )   Inventory of the Estate of James Moore
                             Senr. decease to wit

Eight Negros   five head of horses   twelve head of Cattle thirty head
of hogs   farming tools   Notes $570.00 down in North Ca rolina
                              $53 land one Plantation
furniture household   5.
                       Joseph C Moore
                       Savannah Moore
(Pg 194)
An Account of the Sale of the Estate of James Moore deceased
An Account of sale made of the personal property of the Estate of
James Moore deceased at his residence in Anderson County after having
advertised according to law (to wit)

Samuel Moore	2 Bands Iron	$ .99
Samuel Moore	2 Gudgeons	1 .50
D Moore	Mill Spindle	3 .50
D Moore	Bellow & diver	1.01
James Moore	1 Spade	31¼
James S Davis	1 iron wedge	56½
Samuel Moore Sen	1 Man Saddle	4.75
Austin Moore	1 Broad ax	2.41
Elisha Childress	1 Barrel	.26
Samuel Moore	half bushel & basket	.90
Susannah Moore	1 Hoe	.50
Susannah Moore	Check reel	.25
Samuel Moore Sen	1 Hoe	.27
Isaac Goins	Sundry Articles	.21
James Ray	1 ax	.51
Sussannah Moore	1 steel yards	.50
Calvin Childress	1 double tree	.68¾
David Weaver	1 Mattock	.35
Sussannah Moore	1 Log chain	.62½
Isaac Goins	1 pair of Gears	2.00
Sussannah Moore	1 pair of Gears	1.00
Sussannah Moore	1 Bell & Collar	1.15
Sussannah Moore	1 Shovel Plow & Single tree	1.30
Sussannah Moore	1 Plow	.35
Daniel Foust	1 Shovel Plow	.37

                                                    26.45¾

****

(Pg 195)

Amount brought Over		26.46¼
James S Davis	1 Plow	.20
Sussannah Moore	1 Cray Plow	6.75
Sussannah Moore	1 Flax brake	.20
Samuel Moore	1 Scythe & Cradle	22.00
William Baker	1 Hammer	18¾
William Baker	1 Scythe & Cradle	.50
Samuel Moore	1 wagon	73.00
James Moore	1 yoke of oxen	40.00
Samuel Moore	1 ox	16.00
Moss Overton	1 Yearling	2.30
James Dyches	1 Steer	5.68¾
Calvin Childress	1 Brindle Steer	3. 6¼
Calvin Childress	1 yearling	3.68¾
Nancy M Snodderly	1 Heifer	3.76
Calvin Childress	1 Bull	8.62¼
James Dikes	1 Cow	12212½
James Dikes	1 Oat stockk	4.62½
James Overton	1 Cutting Box	2.43¾
Calvin Childress	1 Horse	67.00
Daniel Foust Jun	1 filly	41.00
Samuel Moore	1 Colt	27.31¼
Sussannah Moore	1 Barrel of vinegar	.12½
George Moore	1 Table	2.12½
James Griffin	1 Bed & stead	14.55
George Moore	1 Bed	12. 6¼
James Moore	1 hand saw	2.00
Joseph C Moore	2 Books	.62½
Cabel Moore	Sunday Books	.62½
Sussannah Moore	6 Hogs	14.00
James Moore	5 Hogs	9.31¼
James Moore	1 Cart	8.68¾
		$414.76½

(Pg 196)

Amount brought up		$414.76½
Nancy M Snodderly	5 Hogs	8.45
George Moore	5 Hogs & some pigs	10.00
George Moore	3 Hogs	10.25
Sussannah Moore	Curry Comb	00.25
Joseph C Moore	1 Broken Clevis	.37½
Joseph C Moore	Smith tools	12.00
Samuel Moore	1 Plow Shear	00.32
Samuel Moore	1 Set of Mill Stones	1.25
Samuel Moore	1 Grind stone	.25
Susannah Moore	1 iron wedge	.56¼
Caleb Moore	1 Auger	31¼
Susannah Moore	1 half bushel	.20
AustinMoore	1 peice of leather	.91
Samuel Moore	1 peice of leather	.63
James T Davis	1 Bridle	.37½
Moses Overton	1 Dulcemore	.38
Sussannah Moore	1 Coulter	.26

Sussannah Moore	1 Bottle	.27
John Dale	1 Bridle	.20
James T Davis	1 Box	.96¾
Sussannah Moore	1 Candle Stand	.39½
James S Davis	1 candle stick	6¼
Sussannah Moore	2½ bushels wheet	2.68¼
James Moore	1½ bushels wheet	1.50
Sussannah Moore	Shovel & tongs	.27
Sussannah Moore	1 Set of hand Irons	.25
Sussannah Moore	1 Little Wheel	2.04
Austin Moore	1 Spice Morter	.62½
Sussannah Moore	2 Boxes	.50
Austin Moore	1 Barrel	.25

473.44¼

(Pg 197)

	Amount brought over	$473.44½
Sussannah Moore	1 Box	12½
Sussannah Moore	1 Little Wheel	12½

473.69¼

This is all that would be Collected at present except two Beds
& furniture, cupboard & furniture and all the pot ware and bu-
reaw and Clock by order of the legatees and two Slaves left on
the farm untill Majority Says Sell and on agreement the legatees Ordered Me to leave to Mother two of the black Kindness &
Andy untill further Orders and to sell the ballance thirefore the
understatement and thirefore for the Several prices

Joseph C Moore	Bird	6.53
Samuel Moore	Betty & Child	13.55
Caleb Moore	Harriet Girl	5.66
Caleb Moore	Gilbert	5.06
James Moore	Greenberry	4.20

35.00

| | And Cash Notes | 5.68 |

| | In the Clerks Office | 50 |

North Carolina and some other dues
not settled the pen chosen have all give bonds and Security the
foregoing is a full and perfect amount of the sales of all the
property of the Estate of James Moore deceased. All the Notes
has been taken payable in twelve Months after date with the
proper credential. This 7th day of January 1839
One of the Administrators of James Moore deceased
(Pg198)
State of Tennessee)   June 6th 1838 To the Clerk of the
Anderson County   )   County Court for said County

I John Jarnagin Guardian of Lindly Hill, Lucy Hill, James Hill &
John Hill Minor Heirs of Martin Hill deceased do hire by report to
you Account of all the Estate of said Minors which has come to my
hand or possessions as Guardian (to wit)
One tract of land adjoining the town of Clinton 167 Acres

4 lots No 29, 26, 27, 55, recived from John B Crozier former
Guardian of said Minor $18.82½ This 6th of June 1838
                              John Jarnagin
                                Guardian

                              Sworn to before me
                              William Cross Clk 7th January 1839
                              by his deputy
                                   C Y Oliver
1838 John Jarnagin Guardian of the Minor Heirs of Martin Hill deceased Dr   June 6th
                         To amount received of John B Crozier
                         former Guardian   16.82½
                         Rent of farm for   50.00

                         Disbursements Cr $ 66.32½

by Amount paid Clerk for Guardian Bond and for his fees on
deed of conveyance   00.50
                                                             00.41¼

By Amount paid Register for registerying deed of Conveyance)
from Lieb to Hill   )
)
                                                             1.00
                         By Amount paid tax on land for
                         1838   1.85
                         By Amount paid for repairing
                         fences on farm 1839   22.47½

                                                            26.23¾
(Pg 199)
Amount of disbursements bret over   1838   26.23¾
By Account paid John Jarnagin & Co Bill for Merchandise
                              for James Hill   4.93 1/3
By Account paid J Jarnagin Co Bill of Merchandise for
                              Lucy Hill   8.78
By Amount Paid J Jarnagin & Co "   "   "   John Hill   5.00
By Amount Paid Gavin Miller per receipt in full for his part 8.11¼

                                                            53 . 06¼
Amount with I am charged $66.82½
                      Whole Amount of
                      disbursement   53.06¼

                                        13.75¾
By Sheriff Oliver tax recept for Tax 1835   1.56¼
By James Ross recipt to Executors proven Amount   11.77
By William Webb receipt to Do proven Do   50.00
By Cash paid to James Ross of Note of hand debt & Interest 12.77¾
(Pg200)
By Cash paid John Shinliver proven O K for coffin   5.00
By Cash paid Clerk William Cross for probating Will and for
letters Testamentary   1.00
By Cash paid Attorney J H Crozier for Council in relation to
saidm Estate   1.00

By Cash paid Clerk Cross for receiving and recording Amount
of Sale   .50
By Amount paid Clerk Willaams Cross for Settlement and recording this the same   2.50
By allowance Made Executors to said Estate for their Services   20.00

To Balance due in the hands of the Executors due to the   106.10½
Heirs of said Cooper   299.06¼

State of Tennessee   )   I do Certify that the above state-
Anderson County   )   ment was taken by and before me
and now presented to the Court for confirmation or rejection
this 7th January 1839
Confirmed by the Court & ordered to be recorded

                              William Cross
                              Clk by his Deputy
                                       C Y Oliver
Settlement with James Scarbrough administrator of the Estate of
Henry Buttlar deceased (to wit)
Dr James Scarbrough administrator of the Estate of Henry R Buttlar
deceased Dr
To Amount of the sales as returned to Court as appears of or from
the records in the Estate Book $766.27¾
                          To Balllance Cash received on
                          the Book   18.89¾
                          Amount Cr
                                                          ─────────
                                                           785.16¾
By Cash paid R Oliver as per recipt due on Shool   4.00
Articles to J hn Nickle
(Pg 201)
Amount of Credit brought over from page 200   4.00
Cash paid Jacob Buttlar as per proven account Cash paid
Richard Oliver administrator for the Estate of Thomas Buttlar
dec.d as pr H R Buttlar Note inding Interest_____   116.03

                  Cash paid John Smith as pernote   5.60
                  Cash paid William R Buttlar as
per recipt on Settlemen   .67
                  Cash paid Armistead Hoskins
                  proven account   1.16 2/3
Cash paid John Cox as per Note peunity for John Murray   11.80
Cash paid William & Buttlar as per proven account   7.87½
Cash paid Ancil Manly as per proven account   3.06½
Cash paid Robert McKamey Shff as per receipt   6.59¼
Cash paid Hugh Riley as per proven Account   1.79½
Cash paid James C Riley as proven account   1.37½
Cash paid Alexander Galbreath as per proven Statement   7.12½
Cash paid James Hones as per proven acccount   7.21½
Cash paid Joseph H Roberson proven account   4.20
Cash paid Moses Winters proven account   10.78½
Cash paid William L Freels Constable Collins Roberts admr. 64.01½
Cash paid Sylvester Kesterson proven account   3.00
Cash paid Nancy Ann Buttlar Guardian of the Minor heirs of
Henry R Buttlar deceased   154.34

Cash paid Do Do	26.00
Cash paid William Right as per receipt	2.00
Cash paid James Noel aas Clerk of sale	1.00
Cash paid Alexander Galbreath Cryer at Sale	2.00
Cash paid J Jarnagin Clerk as per receipt	1.75
Cash paid Luke Peak O K as per receipt	1.50
Cash paid Richard Oliver administrator of the Estate of	
Thomas Buttlar deceased	224.60
Cash paid H T Marshall proven account	5.00

(Pg 202)

By Cash paid Richard Oliver as per receipt on Settlement	27.47
" Cash paid J Rice Note as Security to R Oliver	3.84
Cash paid Alexander Galbreath Shff as per receipt	24.00
Cash paid Hiram Hoskins per account 1835	2.00
Cash paid John Seiber per proven account	1.68¼
Cash paid Sheriff for Tax	2.50½
Cash paid Newton McKamey as per proven account	3.00
Cash paid John Tayler proven account	3.00
Cash paid Joseph Seiber proven account	1.81¼
Cash paid Collins Roberts proven account	7.35¼
Cash paid Joseph Seiber proven account	.65 1/3
Cash paid Wm B Gallaher proven account	4.75
Cash paid Clerk Cross as fees at office	4.10
Cash paid Dr M Tate for Attenction & Medicine to H B R	5.00
Cash paid Allowed to administrator for his Services	779.69
attending to said Estate	40.00
	819.69

State of Tennessee)   This Settlement made by the Clerk of
Anderson County   )   the County Court with the administrator
James Scarbrough of the Estate of Henry R. Buttlar deceased from
which Settlement There appears to be Over paid by said administrator the some of thirty four dollars and fifty two Cents and one
fourth of a Cent above the aAmount of said Estate Confirmed by
the Court & Ordered to be recorded

William Cross
byy his Deputy
C Y Oliver

(Pg 203)

DAVID MORTON WILL
in the Name of God Amen

I David Morton of the County of Anderson and State of Tennessee being
weak in body but of Sound Mind and disposing Memory do on this
twenty first day of May in the year of Our Lord one thousand eight
hundred and thirty eight Make Ordian and establish this My Last Will
& Testament in word and for going as follows
First I will that all my Just debts be paid Out of my Estate
Secondly My Will is Short the remainder of my Estate both real and
personal be the remainder the possessions of my wife Nancy Morton
for hir comfort and Support and for the remaining Mantaining and
education of my Children during hir Natural life or widowhood
Thirdly My Will is that it the decease of my wife or in Case she
should marry then that all the Estate which may remain to be sold

-and equally divided amongst my Children
Fourthly I hereby Nominate Constitute and appoint My Wife Nancy
any My son James Morton my sole Executors of this my Last Will and
Testament in testimony where of I have herewith set my hand and seal the
day and date above written   Signed Sealed Published and declared
in the presence of us

                              James Lewis
                              Obediah Brock
                              William Turner   David Morton
                                                       (Seal)

(Pg 204)
State of Tennessee)   To the worshipful County Court January
Anderson County   )   Sessions 1839.

I Stephen Marshall Guardian of Martha J Thompson Minor Heirs of
James Thompson deceased do hereby report to your worship an account
of all the Estate of the said Minor Heirs which has come to my hand
or possessions as Guardian (to wit) One house and Tract of land
No 1 East fork of Poplar Creek Containing one hundred and fourteen
Acres R ceived from the administrator of the Estate of James Thompson
dec.d from the administrator and administratrix of the Estate of
John Thompson deceased in Cash $730.61¼

                              This first of January 1839
                              Stephen Marshall
                              Guardian of Mary J Thompson

State of Tennessee)   To the Worshipful County Court
Anderson County   )   January Sessions 1839

I Stephen Marshall Guardian of Martha J Thompson Minor Heirs of
James Thompson deceased do hereby report to your worship as account
Current of the profits and disbursements of the Estate of the said
Minor forEight ears ending the 1st day of January   1839

Stephen Marshall & C said Minor to Cash received for land rent
for the year 1832 $15.70

To Cash recived for land rent for the Do   1833   15.70
To Cash recived do   do   1834   15.32½
To Cash recived do   do   1835   14.25
To Cash recived   1836   26.62½

(Pg 205)
To Amount of disbursements brought over   87.60
To CAsh recived for rent for Land for the
year   1837   42.63¼
To Cash recived   do   do   1838   68.00
                                                          _____
                                                            $198.23½

To George Winters Note for Money loaned
and due the 20th October   1838   123.29¼
to John Chiles Note for Money loaned due on
Interest from the 20th Oct   1838   51.97½

To Spencer Keith & Richard Oliver Note Money loaned
due 31st Oct   1838 $200.00¾
To Richard Oliver and Spencer Keith Note for Money
loaned due 31st Oct   1838   161.19½
To John Wilies & Wm Scott Note for Money loaned due
2nd of Nov   1838   144.55
                                              4741.95
                                                     ─────────
                                                       940.18¼

Disbursements By this amount paid to Clerk for
Guardian   .30
by this Amount paid to Clerk receiving Exhibit
of the Estate and recording the same   .37½
By the Amount paid Clerk for stating and taking
Account on Settlement with Clerk   1.00
By this Amount paid Clk for recording Settlement   .50
By Amount paid for Schooling Miner   2.37
per Statement   8.00

By Cash paid for repairing dwelling house   85.00
By Cash paid for Making and puting up
5000 rails   50.00
By Cash paid for building spring house &
cleaning up 6 acres of land   25.00
To Cash paid Dr Hill for attending said Minor   10.00
To Cash paid for Clothing and for attention
to said Miner Estate   9/20¾
Stephen Marshall $190.18¾   750.00
Guardian for M J Marshall

(Pg 206)

State of Tennessee   )   To the Worshipful County Court
Anderson County   )   April Session   1839

I Henry Farmer Guardian of Mary Farmer, John Farmer, Henry Farmer
Elizabeth Farmer & Luke M Farmer, Minor Heirs of Luke Farmer
Dec.d do hereby report to your worship and account of all the
Estate of said Minor which has come to My hand or possessions
as Guardian (to wit) received of the administraror and adminis-
tratrix of the Estate of Luke Farmer dec.d the 2nd day of December
1837 the sum of   e $297.06¼
And received the 30th December 1837   113.46¾   410.53
Sworn to and Subscribed this 29th of March 1839   410.53

                    William Cross Clk
                    By his Deputy
                             C Y Oliver
                    Henry Farmer Guardian

State of Tennessee)   To the Worshipful County Court
Anderson County   )   April Sessions 1839

I Henry Farmer Guardian f Mary A Farmer , Nenry Farmer,
Elizabeth Farmer and Luke M Farmer Minor heirs of Luke Farmer dec.d
do hereby report to your worship and account Current of the profits
and disbursements of the Estate of said Minor from the 30th of December

1837 up to the 30th of March 1839 (to wit)
To John Coatney, James S Coatney Richard Oliver and James Noel
and A Galbreath Note for Money loaned and due 23rd of Oct 1838
bearing interest from the 23rd Oct 1837   189.87½

(Pg 207)
To Amount brought Over   175.80
To Robert Patterson and Robert McKamey Note due the 9th Jany
1838 & Interest   68.40
To William Smith & Moses Duncan Note due the 26th of Feby 1837   27.70
To Philip Davis John Duncan   Thomas Davis and Moses Duncan
Note due 9th Feby 1839   50.37½
To Note on Squire Justice and Abraham Justice ,   10.00
                                                               ──────────
                                                                $333.72½

To Cash on hand Not loaned as appears from the Settlement
of Guardian   109.
                                                               ──────────
Disbursements   442.72½
By this Sum paid J Jarnagin Clk for Guardian Bond $ .50
By this Sum Clerk Wm Cross for this Statement and recording
the same   1.50
By the sum paid Commissioners for Settlement with administrator   2.00
By this Amount paid Clerk Cross for Exhibital   0.37½
By Amount of Service of Guardian Making Settlement 2 days & C   2.00
                                                               ──────────
                                                                $6.37½

Whole Amount with which I am Chargable is $442.70½
Total of Disbursements   6.37½
                                                  ──────────
                                                    436.33
                                                    410.53
                                                  ──────────
                          Increase   26.80

                          Henry Farmer
                             Guardian & C

(Pg 208)
State of Tennessee)   To the Worshipful County Court of
Anderson County   )   the said County March term 1839

I Hardy F Martin Guardian of Martin legatee of the Estate of Samuel
Frost deceased do hereby report to your worship and account of
all the Estate of said legatee and Minor Heirs which has come to
my Possessions as Guardian of the said Clerk Martin (to wit)
One tract of land lying and veing in the said County containing
one hundred Acres unimproved adjoining the land of John Frost &
John Childs Received of Jess Henderson Executor of the Estate of
Samuel Frost dec.d in Cash twenty five dollars in the Month of
January 1838 this 16th $25.00
                          February 1839 Sworn to and
                          Subscribed before me
                                      Will Cross Clk
                                      By his deputy
                                        C Y Oliver

```
                              his
                      Hardy X Martin
                             mark
                    Guardian of Clerk Martin
State of Tennessee  )        To the Worshipful County Court for
Anderson County )   )        the said March term 1839
```

I Hardy F Martin Guardian of Clark Martin legatee of the Estate of
Samuel Frost deceased and a Minor do hereby report to your worship
and account Current of the Profits and disbursement of the Estate of
said Clark Martin Miner as aforesaid one year and up to the first day
of January 1839 to (wit) Hardy F Martin Guardian & administrator to
George Summers Note for Money loaned due
(Pg209)

February 1838 er interest one day oafter date Debt and Interest	$26.37½
No profits arising from the land Disbursemen ts	00.50
By this Sam & Clark for Guardian Bond	
" this Sum paid Clark for recording exhipet	.37½
By this Sum paid Clerk for Recording Account Current and Settlement & recording the same	1.50
By this Amount paid register for registration of deed	1.00
By this Sum paid Clerk for registering deed and State Tax	.35
	3,72½
	22.65

due said Ward this Som $22.65 from said Guardian Sworn to and
Subscribed before me this 16th of Fabry. 1839
```
                         Will Cross Clk
                         By his deputy
                             C Y Oliver
                                        his
                                 Hardy X Martin
                                        mark
                                             Guardian


State of Tennessee  )        To the Worshipful County Court
Anderson County     )        May term 1839
```

An additional Inventory of the Estate of David Keesling dec.d
(to wit) Cash received Benjamin P Hackney   4,50

```
                         Sworn to in Open Court
                         William Cross Clk
                         by his debuty
                             C Y Oliver
                         John Wilson
                         one of the Executors of David
                         Keesling dec.d
```

(Pg 210)
Inventory of the Property of James C Thacher deceased viz May
3 1839

3 Coffee Pots	1 Tea Kettle	1 Cow & Calf
1 Oven & lid	1 Handsaw	(1) pot rack
1 Draw Knife	3 Augers	1 fallen ax
1 pair pot hooks	1 Book Johnson on disease	2 broken glasses

3 Chairs	1 small basket	2 wash pans
½ doz Plates	2 Bowls	1 large Bottle
1 Black do	2 set of Knives & forks	Carving knife
2 spoons	1 large bucket	1 do do
1 Shovel & tongs	1 large pot	1 small pot & lid
do do some pamphlets 1 Set chains	1 Set chains	1 Ware glass pitcher
1 Salt Cellar	3 pairs of candle molds	1 Strainer
1 Smoothing Iron	Candle Stick	3 Milk Cups
7 Plates	2 Earthen Pitchers	2 stand Jars
1 Crock	1 small table	1 frying pan
1 small pot & lid	1 Looking glass	2 pair of dog irons
1 small pot & lid	1 do do kettle	1 Oven & lid
1 do do	1 Skillet & lid	1 Set Tea Cups and
Saucers	1 Coffee Mill	2 dishes
2 fur Hats	1 man Saddle	1 Military Book
Webster Pistelence	American dispon	Satory Sweed an
Sypillous	½ Cups & Plates	2 Beds & furniture
1 Secretary	1 Carriage & Harness	1 Shovel
1 Plow	1 Back Band	1 Blind Bridle
1 Butcher knife	Ten Cups & Spoons	1 China press
1 Small Steer	1½ Bushal Measure	

The above Property sold at six Months Credit on the 3rd & 6th of
May 1839 The foregoing is a true inventory of all the personal Property of said Estate that has come to my knowlidg

        John Jarnagin
            Administrator of the Estate of
            James C Thatcher dec.d

(Pg 211)
Return of the Amount of the property of James Thatcher dec.d May
3rd 1839

Jourden Smith	3 Coffee Pots			$00.75
do do	1 Tea Kettle			00.87½
Moses H Swan	1 Cow & Calf			12256½
do do	1 Oven & Lid			1.19¾
Do Do	1 handsaw			.75
William Cary	1 pot rack			81¼
Do Do	1 Drawing Knife 85¢ 1 fallen ax 1.25		2.08	
Do do	1 pot hooks 20½			
	1 Book Johnson on descas		25	.45½
Do Do	2 Broken glasses			.14
Do Do	8 Chairs			3.25
Do Do	1 Small Bucket 6¼			
1 Large D	44¢			.50¼
L Large "	2 Wash pans 8 tea Cups			.49
" "	½ doz plates			.76
" "	2 Bowls 37½			
" "	1 Large Bottle 50¼			83
" "	1 Black Do 2 Set of knives			
	& forks & Carver & 2 Spoons			4.51½
Joseph Peterson	1 Large Basket			.31.¼
Do , Do	1 Do Do			.31½
" "	1 Shovel & tongs			.26
" "	1 Shovel & Large Pot		$2.50	
	1 small pot & led		1.12½	3.62½
Levi Lacy	Phamphlets			12½
" "	1 Set of China Ware		5.00	5.12½

"	"		1 Set of China Glass & Pitcher	68½	
"	"		1 Salt Seller	12½	.81½
Thomas Wheeler Sen			2 pr Candle Mould & Strainer		.12½
"	"	"	1 Smoothing Iron & 1 Peggin		.37½
"	"	"	2 Brass Candle Sticks & one Iron do		.75
"	"	"	3 Milk Cups 7 Plates		0 .75
"	"	"	2 Earthen Pitchers	81¼	
"	"	"	2 Stone Jars & Crocks	1.	1.81¼
"	"	"	1 Small Table	1.00	
"	"	"	1 Looking glass	.26	

(Pg 212)

John E Wheeler	2 pair fire dogs			.37½
John H Wheeler	1 frying pan			.32
"	"	1 Small pot & led	62½	
		1 Do Do	62½	1.25
"	"	1 Kittle	62½	
		1 Oven & led	75¢	1.37½
"	"	1 Do do	1.25	
		1 Scillet & led	.87½	2.12½
"	"	1 Set Tea Cups & Saucers	.40	
"	"	1 Coffee Mill	.37½	.73½
"	"	2 dishes	.83	
"	"	2 fur Hats	3 .02	3.85

			12.07
Thomas Wheeler	1 mans Saddle		10.00
"	"	1 Book Military		.12½
"	"	1 Book Webster & Testalence	1.56¼	1.56¼
"	"	Sweed or Syphilous	.60	.60
"	"	Amer. Dispensatory		1.70
		½ Cups & Plates		00.31¼

			14.30
Warrick Thatcher	1 Bed furniture & Stead		5.00
"	"	1 Do Do		5500
"	"	1 Seretary		10.00
John E Wheeler	1 Carriage & Harness		221.00
1 Side to J Jarnagin & he is to pay		9	

313. 56

Clinton May the 6th 1839
Property Sold viz

Hiram Sparks	1 Shovel Plow		. 50
Joseph Black	1 back band		. 43¾
Hugh B Lamar	1 Blind Bridle		. 68¾
Jesse Bailey	1 ten Pan Butcher Knife		
	10 Cups & Spoons		. 40
Banister Smith	1 China press		8.62½
John Jarnagin	1½ Bushel Measure	00.25	
	1 small Steer	3.00	3.25

$327.46

The above property Sold at 6 Months bond & Security taken
The Amount except $ 7.63½ Cents

                              Cash paid
                                    John Jarnagin
                                         Admr
                              William Cross Clk
                              By his deputy
                                         C J Oliver

(Pg 213)
State of Tennessee)   To the Worshipful County Court
Anderson County   )   May Session   1839

Joseph C Moore Guardian of the Minor Heirs of Richard Luallen
deceased do hereby report to your Worship an Account Current of
the Profits andDisbursements of the Estate of the said Minor Heirs
for the time J was Guardian ending
                              Joseph C Moore & C
                              To said Minors   Dr

To Cash received for rent Corn and Oats $69.49½
By this amount paid E S Harrell for tuition   12.69¼
As per Amount and Order filed)
)
by this Amount paid Anderson & Crozier in 2 Chancery Cases
pinding at Knoxville in which the Minor Heirs of Richard
Luallen dec.d
Charles Luallen and others per recept filed   43.99¼
By the Amount Anderson and Crozier Council further
to the amount of the bill filed on Richard Luallen &
others being the bill filed last in behalf of the Minors
Heirs   2.50
By this amount paid Addison Anderson as free receipt as
part of the fee in the case in Chancery in which the Minor
Heirs of Richard Luallen dec.d are suing for their proportio
tion of the sales of the Negroes & C   7.00
By my Services to Knoxville attending to the suit A Crozier
vs C Luallen and Others   3 days $1.50   4.50
Commissioners to take Desposition 2 days   1.50   3.00
(Pg 214)
                         Amt of disbursements brot up $73.68½
                         For Services in taking desposition 1.00
July 1839 for Services attending the rules of Court 2 days 3.00
By two days Services renting & receiving rent   2.00
By this Amount paid Clerk for bonds   1.00
By this Amount paid Clerk receiving and recording
Inventory the same   1.50
                                                      ─────────
                                                      17.20¼

Ballance of $17.20¾ Cents in favor of Joseph C Moore
former

```
                          Cash paid
                          John Jarnagin
                               Admr
                          William Cross Clk
                          By his deputy
                               C Y Oliver
```

(Pg 213)
State of Tennessee)   To the Worshipful County Court
Anderson County   )   May Session 1839

Joseph C Moore Guardian of the Minor Heirs of Richard Luallen
deceased do hereby report to your Worship an Account Current of the
Profits and Disbursements of the Estate of the said Minor Heirs for
the time J was Guardian ending
                          Joseph C Moore & C
                          To said Minors Dr

```
To Cash received for rent Corn and Oats        )        $69.49½
By this Amount paid  E S Harrell for tuition  )          12.69½
As per Amount and order filed                  )
```

By this Amount paid Anderson & Crozier in 2 Chancery Cases
pinding at Knoxville in which the Minor Heirs of Richard Luallen
dec.d
Charles Luallen and others per receipt filed   43.99¼
By the Amount Anderson and Crozier Council further to the
amount of the bill filed on Richard Luallen & others being the
bill filed last in behalf of the Minors Heirs   2.50
By this amount paid Addition Anderson as free receipt as part
of the fee in the case in Chancery in which the Minor Heirs of
Richard Luallen dec.d are suing for thier proportion of the the
sales of the Negroes & C   7.00
By my Services to Knoxville attending to the suit A Crozier
vs   C Luallen and Others   3 days $1.50   4.50
In April 1837 February 1838
By Services to Knoxville to get Commissioners
to take Desposition 2 days   1.50   3.00

(Pg 214)
Amt of Disbursements brot up $73.68¾
for Services in taking Deposition   1. 00   1.00
July 1839 for Services attending the rules of Court 2 days   3.00
By two days Services benting & receiving rent   2.00
By this Amount paid Clerk for bonds   1.00
By this Amount paid Clerk receiving and recording
Inventory the same   1.50

                                                        $17 .20¾
```

Balance of $17.20¾ Cents in favor of Joseph C Moore former
Guardian of the Minor Heirs of Richard Luallen dec.d appears
from the above Statement and Settlement which was taken before
Me Sworn to and Subscribed this 6th of May 1839
```

State of Tennessee)   I William Cross Clerk of the said
Anderson County   )   County Court of Anderson

de hereby Certify that the foregoing Settlement and Statement of
the profits and Disbursements of the Estate of the Minor Heirs
of Rachard Luallen deceased was taken before me and form said
Settlement and Statement it appears that thire is Due and Owing
to Joseph C Moore late Guardian of the said Minor Heirs the Sum of
Seventeen dollars twenty and three fourths Cents which is now presented to the Court for their Confirmation by the Court or rejections

                      William Cross Clk
                      By his Deputy
                             C Y Oliver

(Pg 215)

Inventory of all the Sales debts due to J C Thatcher Estate that has
come to my Knowledge up to 26th of June 1839, viz
1 Note on Samuel Allen Due the 3rd day of February 1838
for One Hundred Dollars $100.00
1 Note on Joseph Vannoy & William Vannoy due 22nd February
1837 for $125.   125.00
1 Note   on Joseph Vannoy Due 22nd
Jun8 1831 for   25.00
the above named persons are not Citizend of the County and
Supposed to be Doubtful
1 receipt   William Cross white Cnst. for the Collection
of a note on Leonard Genner date of the receipt 12th Nov
1832 for $20. $20.00
one Ak on Lewis David for $10.   10.00
One Ak on George S Burnsides for $15   15.00
1 Ak on George Blang for $ 5.   5.00
One Ak on William Ambrister for $14.87½   14.87½
One Ak on Solomon Dirney for   1.50   1.50
One Ak on Robert Ross for   1.50   1.50
One Ak on James M Boulton   4.97½   4.97½
One on Samuel McConkey   1.50   1.50
One Ak on David Vandgriff   2.00   2.00
One Ak on James Hicks   3.00   3.00
One Ak on William Sparks   1.00   1.00
One Ak on Hardy P Martin for   .20¢   .20¢
One Ak on George Martin for   5.50   5.50
One Ak on Joseph Peterson with day
or date for   47.49½   47.49½
                                                             _____
With a Credit for   3 .00   383.54½
                      Recorded 4th July 1839   3.00
                                                             _____
Claim on all State $106.75
John Jarnagin Claims
                                                             _____
                                                                $487.29½
The Estate of James C Thatcher dec.d
                      Will Cross Clk By his Deputy
                             C Y Oliver

(Pg 216)
Inventory of the Estate of George Wintan Deceased as returned
into Court By his Administrater to wit

9 head of horse beast	1 Copper still	1 Durham Bull
2 yoke of Oxen	2 grind stones	2 pair double trees
24 head of cattle	2 Sythes & cradles	16 head of sheep
3 Mowing Sythes	40 head of Hogs	1 iron Wedge
Farming Tools	2 double Shovels	1 wagon
1 Iron tooth Rake	1 Corn Crusher	1 fork
4 Bar Plows	3 hoes	5 Shovel Plows
2 pair Stretchers	3 Bull Tongs	3 Single trees
1 Harness	3 Blind Bridles	2 Mattocks
3 Pair of Gears	2 log chains	2 pr drawing chains
1 Set of Smith Tools	4 Chopping Axes	1 Sythe Stake & Hammer
10 Books	1 wheat fan	1 Barrel containing
1 Apple Grinder & Timber	2 hand Saws	some vinegar
5 Grain Tubs	Sundry Old Barrel	1 Cockle Sive
4 Augers	6 Chisels	1 Straw Cutting Knife
1 Hand Ax	3 Cow Bells	Small Lot Bur Iron &
Sundry Old Iron	1 Reap hook	A Quantity of wheat
Corn & Oats	Sheaf	Some flax seed
2 Saddles	1 pr Saddle bags	A Small lot of leather
Small lot Coffee & Sugar	Some paints	Casks not full

(Pg 217)
Amount Continued
Some tow Cloth

1 pint Measure	1 Half Gallon Measure	Small lot of wool
Small lot picked cotton	Small lot wool	1 tin pan
4 pair hand Irons	1 ten dipper	Small lot seed
	Cotton	Small lot of cup- board ware
Small lot hames	3 bed stids	Harness Leather for
3 beds & furniture	3 Meal bags	back bands not made
1 Set Shovel & tongs	1 apple pealer	1 Clock
Small lot of Cloth	1 looking glass	Small to Flax
1 Shaving Glass	Household furniture	A small lot of walnut
4 Tables	Kitchen furniture	and Charry Plank
1 trunk	1 washing tub	2 Spinning wheels
3 Crocks	1 Reel	1 Picher
8 Chairs	6 Pails	6 Bottles
1 Bucket	1 Funnel	2 flat Irons
17 pieces Cooking Casting	A lot of soap	Some lard
1 Coffee Mill	4 pair Pot hooks	A Meat Trough
1 Meal Seive	1 Kneeding Trough	1 Wooden Bowl
1 ten strainer	2 Coffee Pots	9 Middlings Bacon
6 Joints Bacon		

(218)
Continued (viz)
We find five negros Nancy & hir Children Mary Jacob, James & John
Situation of the real Estate of the deceased. We find the Title of
the land on which the deceased Resided and of which he was possessed
of is in his father who is Now living & C

Recorded this 10th Sept 1839) John Grant
                                Robert Winton
                                Executors of George Winton Dec.d
                                William Cross Clk

Inventory and Amount of the Sale of the personal property of the
Estate of George Winton   deceased Sept 26th 1839

William Cross	1 lot of Old Iron	00.12½
Jackson Cox	1 Shovel	1.00
William B Smith	Cutting Knife and steel	.25
A Cross boal & Shovel		.88
A Cross	1 Hoe	12½
John Oneal	1 ax	67
David Hall	1 ax & wedge	31¼
William B Smith	1 Coulter	51
Mathua Road	1l Saddle & Plow	30
David Hall	1 Bull tong Plow	25
William B Smith	1 Do	18¾
David Hall	1 Mattock	75
Willie Leath	1 fork	30
J M Winton	Single tree	12½
Aron Hendrix	Horse shoes	50
		6.28½

(219)
Amount Brought Over

William B Smith	fork & Chain	.90
Samuel Johnson	1 lock Chain	.27
Jess Ayers	2 Churns	.40
Richard Oliver		
Joseph Black	1 Plow Mould	.50
John Garner	1 piece wagon tire	1.50
Jesse Ayers	Drawing knife & Hammer	.35
William B Smith	1 Anger	.30
Do Do	1 Do	.50
Marthua Roads	4 Angers	.25
Samuel Johnson	1 pair stretchers	1.12½
Willis Leath	1 Lot Iron	.90
William Oliver	1 Lot Iron	1.01
Elijah Cornall	1 Lot Iron	.57
William	1 Bar Roald Iron	1.08
William Smith	4 Moaing blades	.06½
David Hall	1 Double tree & Single tree	.75
John W Winton	1 double tree & do	1.00
William Freel	1 pair of Gears	1.50
Joseph Black	1 do do	3.06½
Joseph Black	1 do do	2.00
Jackson Cox	1 pair of hames	12½
Elijah Seiber	1 Cart	.63
Thomas May	1 Set of Black Smith tools	30.00
James Winton	1 Log Chain	4.00
John Garner	1 Log Chain	3.12½
Joseph Aldridge	1 Half bushel	.18¾
William B Smith	1 Large Harrow	3.93¼

Richard Oliver	1 Bar Plow		1.88
James McClair	1 Cary Plow		3.30
(Pg 220)			
Amount Brought Up			
Joseph Aldridge	1 small Plow		.56½
Eli Norman	Shovel Plow		1.00
Jackson Cox	1 Moving Slay		1.00
Joseph Black	1 Shovel Plow		1.27
David Hall	1 Sythe & Cradle	9	2.12½
Jackson Cox	1 Sythe & Cradle		3.06½
Aron Gentry	2 Moing Syths		.62½
Elijah Carnall	1 pair Irons		.61
John Chiles	Waggon Bed		5.30
William B Smith	1 Lot of Iron Know		5.39
John Oneal	1 Grind Stone		1.25
William Norman	1 Copper Still Caps & Worn		22.00
John Oneal	1 Cast Plow		2.58½
William B Smith	1 Cray Plow		2.30
Thomas Norman	1 Bull Teng Plow		1.02
Aron Gentry	1 Corn Crusher		3.75
Willis Leath & Parker	1 Wagon tire		3.00
Thomas Wilson	1 Set of and Irons		2.00
David Hall	1 Set of and Irons		2.01
Do do	1 hand-Saw		1.50
Roland Frost	three chisels		1.00
Jackson Cox	1 stake & Hammer		.76
Daniel Yarnall	two chisels		.74
Joseph Black	1 Seive		.52
Joshua Frost	Shovel & Tongs		1.00
Jackson Cox	Razor Strop		.06½
Jefferson Jett	1 Gimblet		.15
Michael May	1 pair of Steel Yards		1.40
John Oneal	1 Set of Plates		.75
Robert Millson	4 Cups		.50
Nancy McKamey			.91
(221 Pg)			
Amount Brought Over			
Daniel Yarnall	Tire dipper and stranner		.15
Robert Millson	2 pans		.30
Richard Oliver	Half gallon and Pint Cup		.39
Daniel Yarnell	1 Pitcher		.45
Roland Frost	1 Dish		.50
Roland Frost	1 Funnell		.06½
Roland Frost	2 Glass Tumblers		.18½
Willis W Talley	1 Pitcher		.50
Sarah Jackson	Bowls & Vials		.15
Nancy McKamey	1 Pitcher		.33
Joseph Black	3 Bowls		.20
Daniel Hall	1 Bottle & Turpentine		.25
Willis W Talley	Pepper Box		.12½
John Webber	6 Plates and Bottle		.62½
Lasrous Moore	2 Soup Plates		.46
John Garner	1 Bottle		.31¼

Lazrous Moore	2 Plates	31¼
William B Smith	1 Umbrella	1.06¼
Richard Portwood	1 paper of tax	11
J W Winton	1 Set of plates	37½
Walter Vann	1 pair Boots	2.06¼
Roland Frost	1 Looking Glass	.50
J M Winton	1 Mans Saddle	14.25
Joseph Aldridge	1 Check Reel	.50
Milton Cox	2 Books	.62½
Samuel Thompson	4 Books	1.50
Jackson Cox	1 Bell	56½
Samuel Johnosn	1 Wool hat	40
Nancy McKamey	1 pair Waffle Irons	32
John Oneal	1 hand Saw	1.00

(222 Pg)
Amount Brought Over

John May	1 Reel of webbin	28
Joshua Moore	1 keg of nails	8.87½
Samuel C Young	1 Keg	25
Spencer Keith	half keg brace nails	6.25
Jackson Cox	Barrel of vinegar	1.12
Winton J M	1 piece of domestic 7⅓ yds-7 cents	.50
Jackson Cox	1 Lot of leather	62½
Samuel Tunnell	1 Large Spotted Sow	5.25
Samuel Moore	do do	3.00
Joseph Black	5-1st Choice Hogs	12.50
William B Smith	5-2nd Choice do	10.05
Eppy Lea	5-3rd Choice do	8.00
Stephen McClain	5-4th Choice do	5.20
Joseph Black	1 Russian Sow	5.00
Stephen McClain	7-5th Choice do	6.30
Joseph Black	1 Durham Bull	81.00
William Wright	1 wagon	36.50
Lazrous Moore	1 Wheat fan	16.25
James Winton	1 Bay Mare	85.00
J W Winton	1 Bay Horse	100.00
William Oliver	1 Brown Mare	55.50
Walker Reeds	1 Brown Mare	41.00
Emit Knott	1 dark Brown Mare	30.30
Joseph Harden	1 Bay Horse Colt	18.00
John Montgomery	1 Bay Filly	48.00
Joseph Black	1 Brown Colt	38.00
Roland Frost	1 Sorrel Colt	15.00
James H Nickle	1 Yoke Oxen	28.25
Joseph Black	1 other Yoke oxen	45.50
Anthony Norman	1 spotted Sow	5.62½
Eppy Lea	1 Sow & 4 Pigs	40.00

(Pg 223)
Amount Brought Over

Eppy Lea	1 Black Shoat	1.50
Do Do	1 White Shoat	1.50
Eppy Lea	Reep of wheat per Bushel 31cts	.31
Do Do	Do per Bushel 31cts	
John Oneal	1 Stack of Hay	4.00
William B Smith	1 Pen of Hay	2.75

Amount Brought Over

Eppy Lea	1 Black Shoat	
Do Do	1 White Shoat	1.50
Eppy Lea	Reep of wheat per bushel 31cts	1.50
Do Do	Do per bushel 31 cts	
John Oneal	1 Stack of Hay	
William B Smith	1 Pen of Hay	4.00
Joseph Norris	1 Lot of flax	2.75
George Moore	20 bu of clean wheat @ 40 cts	2.03
William Runnels	20 Do do	8.00
Thomas Coward	20 Do do	8.00
Stephen McClain	20 bushels 38 ¢ per bu	8.00
Roland Frost	20½ bu wheat 40 ¢ per bu	76
Stephen McClain	2 Bushel at 38 ¢ per B	8.10
Roland Frost	20½ bu wheat a 41 ¢	7.60
Stephen McClain	Balance Old wheat a 37 ¢ p B	8.10
Moore Lazrous	1 piece of domestic per yd 11¢	
Joseph Black	1 hand thread and Flax	.21
Jackson Cox	2 Shalls	.41
Richard Oliver	1 peice of calico per yd 13¢	.42¼
William Oliver	1 peice do per yd 24 c	.78
Roland Frost	1 Set Tea Cups and Saucers	.30
Jackson Cox	5 spoons	.21
Nancy Ann Butlar	1 Pitcher	.33
Saml C Young	1 Pitcher	.40
Jackson Cox	1 Pitcher	12½
Frost Roland	1 Set Knives & forks	76
Nancy Ann Butlar	1 Set of Plates	665
Joseph Norris	Salt Cellar and Box	20
Joseph Black	Crough & Snuffers	17
Moore Lazrious	1 peice flannel per yd 48¢	96
Nancy Ann Butlar	6 Combs 17¢ a peice	1.02
(224)		
Amount Brought up		$
Roland Frost	2 bolts Ribbond	000 .30
James Black	Buttons and Paper	000 .37½
Samuel C Young	lot pish back & Buttons	000 .41
James Black	lot of Buttons	000 .37½
Simon Jackson	lot of Buttons	000 .48
Jackson Cox	Incigo & Madder0	38
Joseph Black	Set of Buttons	000 50
Willis Leath	Buttons & Lining	001 .03
Banister Smith	1 Ax	000 .83
Richard Oliver	1 peice of Steel per Lb 31 ¢	001 .55
Lazrious Moore	14 Lb Coffee 25½ ¢ per Lb	003 .57
Joseph Eldridge	1 Coffee Mill	000 .30
John Oneal	1 hand Ax	001 .63
		000 .55
William Coward	1 half Peck	000 .26½
John Nickle	1 Smoothing Iron	000 .76
Joseph Black	1 Blind bridle & Leather	000 .57
John Winton	Candle Mould & Strainer	000 .32
Samuel C Young	1 Sickle	000 .32
B B Bradley	1 pair drawing Chains	.75
Iron Hendrix	1 Shovel Plow	000 .25

Robert Millicon	1 Coffee Mill	000.10
Banister Smith	Cotton & Cards	000.50
Joseph Morris	1 Lot of wheat in Sheaf a 30¢	
Alfred Cross	1 Saddle & Blanket	002.18½
John Oneal	1 Small Chair	000.37½
Joseph Black	3 Barrels & Flax Seed	1.76
Joseph Sunday	Old Barrls	1.00
Joseph Moore	1 Oven Lid	000.15
Willis Leath	1 Mattock	000 12½
Aron Hendrix	1 Sledge Hammer	001.12½
(225)		
Amount Brought Over		$
William Norman	Barrel Kegs	000.50
Aron Hendrix	3 Barrels	000.25
John Oneal	1 Churn	000.25
James Winton	apple Pealer	000.25
Joseph Morris	2 Barrels & Shoe tools	000.77
Banister Smith	2 Pails	000.18
Joseph Black	1 Pail	000.50
Joseph Black	2 Piggins	000.40
John Oneal	1 Peggin	000.18
Banister Smith	1 large Pot & C 2 62¢	002.62½
Roland Frost	1 Pot & Hooks	000.62½
Samuel C Young	1 Seive	000.39
Banister Smith	1 large Pot	000.70
Joseph Morris	1 Tub Crock & C	000.50
Willis Young	Lot Casting	000.82
John W Winton	1 Bowl	000.20
Banister Smith	1 Bread tray & C	000.39
Thomas Coward	1 table & wagon tub	000.51
Roland Frost	1 Fielding Ax	000.62½
William Cross	Iron Saddle Tree	000.20
Banister Smith	7 Yards Tow Cloth	000.98
Willis Leath	1 Bucket of paint	2.75
Roland Frost	1 Barrel Clover Seed	.27
Samuel Tunnell	1 Do	.27
Roland Frost	1 Lot of Hamp	000.40
Stephen Julian	1 Bracken Kag of Nails	005.66½
William B Smith	Broken Keg Nails	003.53
Joseph Black	1 Barrel Dried fruit	1.01
Joseph Black	Do Do	1.26
Joseph Morris	1 Lot Timothy Seed	.37½
Richard-Oliver	Turnip Seed	.06¼
(226)		
Amount Brot Up		$
William Herrington	1 Trunk	000.21
Roland Frost	1 Bearew	10.87½
Josephn Black	1 Bed & furniture	7.25
Do Do	Do	9
Do Do	Do	9.00
John Oneal	2 Brushes & C	000 .31
CalibButtlar	1 Cupboard	008 .60
Eppy Lea	1 Bed stead & Card	2 .00
Samuel C Young	Do Do	001 .21½
Banister Smith	Do Do	1 .51
William Norman	2 hogshead	000 .50

Lazrous Moore	2 Other Hogsheads	000.75
Alfred Cross	1 Tub of Brand	000.06¼
William Cross	1 pair and Irons	000.56¼
Aron Hendrix	1 Do Do	1.00
Morris Vann	1 Side of bacon @ 11½¢ per Lb	
Do Do	Do @ 12¢ per Lb	
William S Smith	1 Do @ 10¼ Per Lb	
Morris Vann	1 Other side bacon @ 12¢	
Do Do	Do @ 9¼¢ per Lb	
Banister Smith	1 Lot bacon damage	0 0 1.37½
George Moore	4 Joals bacon @ 3¢ " Lb	
JamesWadkins	1 Barrel Soap	005.
Isaac Martin	1 Large trough of soap	1.19
Lazrous Moore	1 do do	000.50
Jackson Cox	1 Lot soap fat	000.37½
William Cross	1 large meat trough	000.38
Do Do	9 salt barrels	000.18¾
(227)		
Amount brot Over		$
Morris Vann	1 Lump of sault	000.22
John Road	1 Strap of Iron	000.12½
John Oned	11Grind stone	
Do Do	1 small lot Cherry & w Plank	76
Alfred Cross	Garden Post & Lumber	4.25
Willis Leath	All the Cabbage	3.12½
Joseph Morris	1 Lb wool rools at 51 per Lb	3.57
Do Do	37 Lbs Wool rools 36¢ per Lb	13.32
Joseph Black	1 Jug Molasses	.83
Appy Lea	100 lb seed cotton	2.50
Thomas Coward	Do Do	2.51
Appy Lea	the balance of cotton at 2 cts Lb	
Nancy E McKamey	Whole of the Picket cotton	1.75
William	1 Large Gun	.20
James Wadkins	Onions	.06¼
William B Smith	Apple Grinder	1.12½
Isaac Martin	1 Cow & Calf	9.25
John Road	1 Red cow & Calf	11.05
Do Do	1st Bell cow & calf	10.50
Aron Hendrix	1 Cow & Bull	13.12½
Do Do	1 Spotted Cow	10.31¼
John Road	1 Large Brown steer	14.00
William S Smith	1 Bee cow	10.12½
Hugh L White	1 red steer	11.25
Sarah Jackson	1 Spotted Heifer	8.06¼
William B Smith	two steers	15.00
Do Do	2 Small Bulls	7.05
George Moore	1st Choice of sheep	6.12½
James H Black	5 2nd Choice	
Do Do	7 3rd Lot of sheep	6.07
Thomas Coward	1 flax brake	.06¾
Amount Brot Forward (Pg 228)		$
William B Smith	1 Lot of old Corn 35½ per bu	003.52½
J M Prince	1 Lot do 35¢ per bushel	003.50
Eppy Lea	The ballance corn per B 35¢	
Richard Oliver	2 Rakes	000.83½
Sarah Jackson	1 Slay	000.75
Sammel C Young	1 Meal Bag	000.75

Thomas Coward	1 dry hide	2.50
J W Winton	1 Bell & Collar	00 0.51
J W Winton	1 Do Do	000.12½
Aron Hendrix	2 red Heifers	12.00
Do D o	1 branded do	5.00
Eppy Lea	14 Lbs Sugar	2.331/3
William Hendrix	1 Lot Cod	.25
William B Smith	Corn Crop in the field	200.00
Lewis Frost	18 Lbs Bacon	1.87½
Mr. Thompson	2 Crocks	000.25
Do Do (228) Pg	1 Haccle	1.25
Joseph Black	6 Pane windown Glass	000.37½
John Black	12 Lbs Roold Iron	.91
Charles Parker	8 Yds domestic	1.60
Jackson Cox	3 Do do	.60
Do do	2 Lbs wool rolls	1.25
Do do	2 Black woll	.75
William B Smith	apples	5.00
James Black	2 Chairs	000.75
	Some corn & fodder 8¢	2.35
Eppy Lea	1 pen of Oats in Sheaf	27.00
Do Do	Oats over burn flow per doz 12½	
Audrey Thompson	10 Lbs bacon	1.00
J W Winton	1 Meal bag	000.75
Do D o	Indian Basket	1.00
(Pg 229)		
Amount Brot Over		$
James Winton	1 pair of saddle bags	09 .00

We present the foregoing as a just true and Perfect inventory of all the goods Chattles of the personal property of the
Estate of George Winton deceased that has yet come into our
possession. We also herewith render a true account of the sales
of the goods and Chattles named in the aforesaid Inventory faith-
fully copied from the sales books of our Clerk together with the
sale of the standong crop of corn and other articles sold by us at
Private sale by the consent of the legatee to individuals given
under our hands this 3th day of October 1839 all os which we respectfully Robert Winton Submit to the Court John Grant Sworn to in
Open Court Administrator attest William Cross Clerk
                              By his deputy
                              C Y Oliver

(Pg230)
A list of the Property of John Luallen deceased

One rifle gun	two Mans saddle	1 log chain
one pair of trace chains		
and hames		1 pair chains
Hames and back band	1 pr of Old chains	3 blind bridles
two riding bridles	one mattock	1 Shovel
two hoes	1 Sythe & cradle	1 Shovel Plow
and stock	1 bor hhear Plow	One singletree
Two Bull Tongus	1 Stock & Grind stone	two iron wedges
one half bushel	one hatchet	one auger
One drawing knife	One hand saw	1One curry comb
One butcher knife	two dcoffee mills	1 pr sheep shears

One wagon	breast band	1 tar bucket
One set china 32 pc	two chist	one cupboard
one butter compshire	cream pitcher	one salt cellar
one set plates	1 pepper box	one clock
one pair steel yards	1 pair of saddle bags	one bible
A lot of books	razor box brush & glass	two bed stids&7cards
One spinning wheel	One side saddle	One large jug
2 large jars	One piggin	One bucket
One churn	One coffee pot	One grid iron
One shovel	One frying pan	& skillet
One pot rack	two cotton wheels	One quill wheel
One sifter & tray	One Loom & apparatus	7 chains
two smoothing irons	One basket	One Hackle
One Chissil	One Cutting Box Knife	&sow side
Three Oats stacks	three horses	One barrel flax
two hogsheads	slop bucket	One shoe hammer
One keg	four cows	two yearlings
Nine Geese	About fifty or sixty head of hogs	

(231) Pg

One bed	One big pot	1 small pot
One large oven	One set of plates	1 butter plate
1 Shot bag	1 Collar 1 candle stick	1 umbrella
1 pair of cotton cards	One note on Charles	

Luallen twenty eight dollars and one half cents due the 9th November 1838 Recorded the 11th October 1839

William Cross Clk
By his deputy C Y Oliver
James Ross Administrator of the Estate of
John Luallen Dec d

A list of the property of John Luallen Decd Sold and Prices

John Luallen	1 rifle gun	$5.25
John Luallen	1 new mans saddle	8.25
Michael Keeney	1 log chain	3.43¾
Nancy Luallen	Hame Chains	1.75
John Luallen	Hames Chains back band	.62½
Nancy Luallen	Chains	.31¼
John Luallen	1 Hoe	06¼
Charles Slover	1 Sythe & cradle	1.12½
Nancy Luallen	1 Shovel Plow & Stock	12½
Joseph C Moore	1 Bar shear Plow rolls cotton	1. 6¼
Nancy Luallen	Single tree	.56¼
John Lenirt	1 Bull tongue & Stock	1.06¼
John Luallen	1 Bull Tongue	.25
Joseph C Moore	1 Grind stone	43¾
John Luallen	1 iron wedge	06¼
		27.43¾

(Pg 232)

Amount Brot up		$
Nancy Luallen	1 iron wedge	00 0.32½
John Luallen	1 Half Bushel	000.37½
John Luallen	1 Hatchet	...87½
Do D o	3/4 Auger	...43¾
John Vandergriff	1 drawing knife	50
John Linert	1 hand saw	99½

****

~~J~~ohn Luallen	1 Curry Comb	$6\frac{1}{4}$
John Vandergriff	1 Butcher Knife	25
Betsy Luallen	1 Coffee Mill or spice	4
Nancy Luallen	Sheep Shears	$13\frac{1}{2}$
Nancy Luallen	1 waggon	38575
Do Do	1 Tar Bucket	25
Betsy Luallen	1 Set of Chenny	$3.37\frac{1}{2}$
Nancy Luallen	Chest	1.25
Jane Luallen	1 small chest	$.43\frac{3}{4}$
Nancy Luallen	1 Cupboard	$1.56\frac{1}{4}$
John Spesard	1 Bottle	23
Nancy Luallen	Campher & bottle	$6\frac{1}{4}$
John Luallen	2 pair of Steelyards	1.00
Jane Luallen	2 Glasses	.75
Nancy Luallen	2 Large pitchers	$.31\frac{1}{4}$
Betsy Luallen	Cream pitcher	.25
Jane Luallen	Set plates & pepper box	$56\frac{1}{4}$
Betsy Luallen	1 Clock	12.00
Calvin Johnson	1lpair saddle bags	$3.56\frac{1}{4}$
Nancy Luallen	1 Bible	$1.13\frac{1}{2}$
John Shinliver	1 lot of books	.75
John Luallen	1 razor	$31\frac{1}{4}$
Do Do	1 Do Strap	$37\frac{1}{2}$
Nancy Luallen	1 Bed & Card	25
Betsy Luallen	1 Bed sted & Card	25
(Pg 233)		68.92
Amount Brot over		$
Betsy Luallen	1 Spinning wheel	$1.\ 6\frac{1}{4}$
Nancy Luallen	1 Side saddle	$8.\ 6\frac{1}{4}$
William Webb	1 large jug	$1.18\frac{3}{4}$
Eli Rhea	1 Jar	1.00
Nancy Luallen	1 Jar	$56\frac{1}{4}$
Do Do	1 piggin & basket	.25
John Luallen	1 Churn	.25
William Spisard	Coffee Pot	.50
Nancy Luallen	1 Table	$1.38\frac{1}{2}$
Betsy Clinner	Horn	$.82\frac{1}{4}$
Nancy Luallen	3 Crocks	.25
Do Do	1 Grid iron & Shovel	$.12\frac{1}{2}$
Do Do	1 frying pan skillet	$.12\frac{1}{2}$
Do Do	1 Pot rack	.76
Do Do	1 Cotton Wheel	$.\ 6\frac{1}{4}$
Betsy Luallen	1 Cotton Wheel	$.37\frac{1}{2}$
Nancy Luallen	1 Griel wheel	$.\ 6\frac{1}{4}$
Do Do	1 Sifter & tray	.26
Do Do	1 Loom & apparatus	$7.07\frac{1}{4}$
Do Do	1 Coffee Mill	.26
Do Do	5 Chairs 2 smoothing irons 1 basket	1.25
Do Do	1 Hackle	$1.19\frac{3}{4}$
Jane Luallen	1 Chissel	$.31\frac{1}{4}$
Thomas Milicon	1 Cutting box & knife	1.00
Nancy Luallen	1 Oat stack	1.00
Do Do	1 Do Do	1.00
Sib Bailey	1 Oat Do	3.05
Betsy Luallen	1 Gray Mare	10.00

John Luallen	1 Iron Gray Horse	87.00
Nancy Luallen	1 Bag of flour	.25
John Severs	Empty Hogshead	.88¼
		131.38

(Pg 234)
Amount brought up

Nancy Luallen	1 Slop bucket & wash tub	000 . 6¼
Betsy Luallen	2 Blankets	. 6¼
Aron Slover	1 Shoe Hammer	.25
Betsy Luallen	1 Keg	. 6¼
Sib Bailey	1 Cow	9.53
Pleasant Hoover	1 Spotted Cow	10. 6¼
Hugh B Bowling	1 Heifer	3,56
Do Do	1 Bull	2.71
Nancy Luallen	1 Sow & two Pigs	.56¼
Betsy Luallen	9 Geese	.25
John Braddshow	1 Sow & 6 pigs	4.53
William Webb	3 Barrows 1st Choice	12.00
John Luallen	6 Stumped tailed hogs	7.00
Do Do	4 Shoats	3.25
		53.89¼

A list of Property of John Luallen dec.d Sold on the 6th
of September 1839

John Luallen	1 Sorrel Mare	$30.12½
Do Do	2 Chairs	. 6¼
Thomas Vowell	21 Saddle	5.00
John Luallen	1 blind bridle	1.37½
Sibstone Bayley	1 White Heifer	7.15
Nancy Luallen	1 Brass Candle Stick	6½
Do Do	1 Pot & Oven 1 pot	1.98¾
Elizabeth Luallen	Umbrella	. 6¼
Do Do	7 Plates 6¼¢	
	1 Bed 6¼¢	.12½
Nancy Luallen	1 Herring Black Girl	1.00
John K Keeney	1 Sow & 5 Pigs	2.56¼
John Luallen	1 Sandy Sow & Pigs	2.00
Charles Leinert	1 Sandy Sow	3.62½
Joseph Dagley	1 Spotted Sow	2.75
		$57.58¼

(Pg 235)
Amount Brought Over

Thomas Vowell	1 Sandy Sow & 6 Pigs	2.81¼
Joseph Dagley	1 Spotted Sow	2.87½
John Severs	5 head of Hogs	13.31¼
John L Keeney	5 head of Hogs	8.00
Joseph Dagley	7 Head of Hogs	9.06¼
Nancy Luallen	4 Head of Hogs	3.00
	Amount	
		$39.06¼

Recorded 11th Oct 1839

William Cross Clk
By his Deputy
        C Y Oliver

James Ross Administrator.
              The Estate of John Luallen Dec'd.

Last Will & Testament of J Butler dec'd.
    I Jacob Butler of the County of Anderson and State of Tennessee
planter do make and publish this my last Will and Testament hereby
revoking and making void all former wills by me at an former time
made and first I direct that my body be descently interedt in some
grave yard in said County in a manner Suited to my condition in life
and as to such wordly Estate as it hath pleased God to instrust me
with I dispose of the same as follows;
FIRST: I direct that all my debts and funeral expenses be paid as
              soon after my deceased as possible out of any moneys I may
die possessed of or may direct into the hands of my Executors
from my protion of my Estate real and personal
SECONDLY; I give and bequeath to my Dear wife Martha all my real
              Estate both land & Negroes during her natural life & at
the death of my Dear wife Martha that my servant Sharlot shall be
free & that an equal division of the rest of the Servants that may
remain at the death of my wife Martha to be equally divided in value
(Pg. 236) between each lawful Heirs & that all land belonging to my
estate be sold and equally divided between the Heirs an that my son
Thomas Buttlar shall pay out of his protion of my Estate to the Estate
five Hundred dollars & that my son Elias pay out of his Portion three
hundred to the Estate as that my son Richard pay out of his part
to the Estate four hundred dollars and that my Daughter Sally Spicer
pay out of her protion to the Estate the sum of one hundred and
eighty two dollars an also that my son Henry Buttlar pay out of his
part of the Estate the sum of one hundred and eighty dollars & that
the amount to paid in by my son Thomas Elias, Richard, Henry and my
daughter Sally be equally divided between the remaining Heirs & do
hereby make ordain and appoint my beloved Son Sons Jacob M. Buttler
Executors of this my last Will & Testament in witness whereof I
Jacob Butler the said testater have to this my will written on one
sheet of paper set my hand and seal this 16th day of October in the
year of our Lord one thousand eight hundred and thirty nine Signed
Sealed and published in the Presence os us who have Subscribed
in the presence of the testator of each other

                              A. Kirkpatrick
                              Sam Galbreath
                              Hardy F. Marshall
                                    her
                              Jacob   X Butler
                                    mark
                                             (Seal)

Pg. 237)
Last Will and Testament of Landon Rector Owing to the uncertainty of
life and the certainly of death and being weak of body but of sound
and disposing mind Landon Rector of the County of Anderson and
State of Tennessee do make and publish this my last will and Testament hereby revoking and making void all other wills by me at any

other time made first I direct that my funeral Expenses and all
My debts be paid as soon after my death as possible out of any
Moneys I may die possessed of or may come into the hands of my Ex-
ecutors

Secondly I give and bequeath to my beloved wife Elizabeth Rector
all my estate consisting personal Property for and during hir
natural life and to be disposed of at any time and in any manner
that she may think proper Lastly I do hereby nominate and appoint
my beloved wife Elizabeth Rector my Executors to this my last will
and Testament in witness whereof I do to this my last will set
My hand and seal this 19th day of September 1839

Signed   Sealed and Published in our presence and we have subscribed our names hereto in the presence and at the request of the
Testator

	his
Richard Oliver	Landon Rector
Polly Ann Hood	X
	mark (Seal)

(238)
Inventory of the Property of Beny R Harding dec.d property Oct.
1839

1 bed & Quilts(3)	1 sheet & quilts	parsell of wearing
2 hats 1 packet	1 coffee mill	clothes
1 Ten bucket	2 Meal bags	1 Coffee pot & cup
1 looking g	1 Set of knives &	
	forks	1 Tea Pot & sugar bowl
1 glass Tumbler	1 Shaving cup	5 plates 2 Saucers &
Tea cups	1 Milk Bowl	1 Salt Seller 3 spoons
1 pepper box	1 Gimblet	1 Bee stand
dried apples	1 Chopping ax	1 Mattock 3 Hoes
1 Bell	1 reap hook	1 Clevis 1 cream
1 iron wedge	1 pot rack	freezer
1 Drawing knife	1 pair of Gears	1 Table 2 rockers
2 Churns	1 slop pail	1 small pot
1 skillet 1 oven	1 pot one skillet	lid broken
1 pr Pot hooks	6 chairs	Bull Tongue Plow
1 stretcher	1 Shovel	6 shoats 1 cotton patch
1 Tobacco Patch	Quantity tobacco	9 bushels of wheat
1 pad lock	1 Cabbage patch	Parcel of beets
1 dresser	Some irish potatoes	3 old barrels

1 Crop of corn standing in the field Subject to rent
1 fire shovel   ½ bu onions   Old Basket
Sausage sifter
I Certify the following Inventory Contains all the property of
said Hackney as has come to my hands
                    John Jarnagin
                    Administrator & C
Recorded this 7th day of November 1839
                    William Cross Clk
                    by his Deputy
                         C Y Oliver

(239)
Amount of the property sold at the late residence of Benj R
Hackney deceased it being said Hackney viz To

William Burnet	1 Drawing knife	1 Scillet 42¢	0025	
	1 broken Scillet & lid 6¼	48¼	0.73¼	
John Farmer	1 Bell 38¢			
	6 Shoats	6.83		7.27
Benjamin T Hackney	1 Tea & Sugar Bowl	.25		
	1 Looking glass	.10	35	00.60
James Hicks	1 Set of knives & forks	.75		
	2 Bushels potatoes	.85		1.60
John Jarnagin	4 quantity of tobacco sold in 3 lots			13.00
Rice Levi	1 Bed & stid 3 quilts 1 sheet	9.00		
	2 bed quilts			
	1 pocket knife	.25	25	
	1 Sifter	.50		
	1 coffee mill & tin bucket	.50	1.00	
	1 Bushel dried apples	.50		
	2 rakes 2 churns & slop pail	.7¢		
	1 pot rack	.12½	19½	11.94½
Jane Levi	5 Plates 2 Saucers & Tea cups	.25	25	
	1 small pot	.77		
	1 Oven	.54	1.31	1.56
George W Hackney	Some wearing clothes and 2 hats	6.50		6.50
William McLean	1 pot	31		
	Parcel of beets	87½		2.18½
John Miller	1 iron wedge	28¢		
	1 pot rack	79¢	1.07	
	1 Cotton & tobacco patch	62⅔		
	3 bu wheat=80¢ 1 tobacco patch	1.66	2.46	
	Crop of corn subject to the rent	1.25		5.40½
Isaac Martin	1 fire shovel			
	¼ bu onions=old basket	.30		.50
Greif Talley	2 Meal bags	.37½		
	1 Coffe pot & Cup	.30		
	1 Chopping ax	.55		.85
	1 Mattock	.75		
	2 Hoes	.30		
	1 table	1.25		2.30
	1 Chair	11.00		
	1 Bull tongue plow	.51		2.13½
(240)				
	6 Bushel wheat	2.04		
	3 bells & dresser	.25	2.29	7.95
George Summers	1 Lot tobacco			.26
Willis W Talley	1 Bowl 1 salt seller			
	3 spoons 1 paper box	00.41		
	1 Hoe 26¢ 1 pr Gears .75	1.01		1.91½

Hiram Sharp   1 Shovel   49¢
                     1 Stretcher 49¢
                     1 Glass Tumbler & shaving cup   12½
                     1 reap hook Clevis Screw   8
                     frizia   25   00.37½
Sterling Smith   1 pair of pot hooks   6¼   6¼
                                                              _____
                                                              $61.80

I Certify the foregoing in the amt of sale of said Estate
sold at 6 months credit given under my hand 21st day Oct 1839
                    John Jarnagin
                    Admr s of the Estate of B R Hackney dec.d

Recorded 7th of November 1839
                    William Cross Clk
                    By his deputy C Y Oliver
Inventory of the Property of the Estate of Henry S Buttler deceased
1 Negro man named John 2 Head of cattle   1 yoke of Oxens
1 Mare & colt   1 Stack of Hay   2 Stacks of Oats
3 Stacks of fodder   Farming tools   2 feather beds & stead
1 feather bed & stead 1 Cupboard   1 Clock 2 tables
1 Loom 1 spinning wheel   Swifts Household &
kitchen furniture   Quantity of salt   1 Chest 1 trunk
Shoe bench   & tools last

                    Kesire Butlar
                    William G Butler
                              Administrator

(Pg 241)
Amount of the sale of the Estate of Samuel Tayler deceased
November 16th 1839
Breant Lewis   4 head of hogs $27.50
Chiles Henry   500 bundles of fodder per 100-75¢   3.50
Dome Williams   1 Cow & calf   14. 6¼
William Gallaher   1 drawing knife   .62½
10 head of sheep   14.62½
                     1 pair of half round   4.00
Gallaher George   1 Mowing scythe   0 0.50
10 head of sheep   12.87½
Bee stand   2.12½
John G Harden   two augers   15.50
1 bu keg   .87½
1 pair Hames   .92
1 Bellow & stake   7.42
1 Horn and tongs   00.89
1 Kag of beer   .75
1 Book Case   5.37½
1 Cotton Wheel   .62½
Harden Amos Jr   6.25
Hardin Joseph   Stack of Oats $2. 6¼
                     5 Oats Stacks   6.72½   8.79
                     500 bundles fodder
                     70¢   3.50

	2 Oats stack	1.62		5.12½
	1 wheaf fan	12.		
	1 bed & furniture	11.75		23.75
George Harden (G)	1 Sorrel Mare			55.50
	1 Bay horse			70.00
Benjamin Hagler	2 Ploughs	1.00		1.00
	1 Bull	9.50		9.50
Hall Austin	1 Cow & calf	12.37½		12.37½
John Jones	1 Colt	31.00		31.00
	1 bed stead & furniture	10.25		10.25
James M Kincade	1 Steer	$10.68¾		
	1 Grind stone	0 0.50		11.18¾
John Melton	1 Clock	9.38		9.38
James Nickle	1 Stear	7. 6¼		
	1 Blacksided heifer	4. 6¼		11.12½
Pitman John	1 Ax	1.52		
	1 mans saddle	10.19		11.71
Pitman William	1 Cross Cut saw	1.75		
	1 cutting Knife & Box	1.91½		3.66½
Shannon Henry	two Hogs	8.50		8.50
Shannon John	50 bushels corn per bu	.24		12.00
William Taylor (W)	1 hand saw	.50		
	1 ax	1.87½		
	1 log chain	2.00		
	1 double tree & chain	1.00		
	1 single tree & fork	3.75		
	2 weading hoes & spade	1.56¼		
Pg (242)	Hattack	1. 6¼	26¼	
	1 Half cut cross saw	2.87½		5.75
	1 pair Gears	2.87½		
	pair Gears	2.81¼		
	1 Barshear plough	5.87½		8.68¾
	1 Bull tongue plough	1.12½		
	1 Shovel P & C	2.12½		2.12½
	1 Oat Stack	2.87½		
	3 reap Hooks	.85¢		3.72
	1 Iron Square	.25		
	1 iron wedge	.43¾		.68¾
	1 Maul	.12½		.12½
Rebecca Taylor	10 head of sheep	10.00		
	1 cow	4.00		14.00
	9 shoats per hd.	1.25		15.25
	1 Cow & calf	8.00		
	1 yoke of oxen	20.00		28.00
	3 stacks Oats per stack	2.00		6.00
	100 bundles fodder per hdh	.50		3.00

****

	34 Head of Geese per head 12½			
	1 Side Sold Leth	5.00		9.25
	1 pair saddle Bags	.50		
	2 Beds & furniture	16.00		
	1 flax wheel	1.00		
	1 Dish	.50		
	1 Beuaro	5.00		6.50
	1 cupboard & ware	10.50		10.50
	8 chairs & Looking glass	1.50		1.50
	1 table & Loom & cotton wheel	2.75		2.75
	1 half bushel basket & table	2.00		2.00
	10 Pot vessels & 2 pans & iron	6.00		6.00
	1 Pot rack 1 Shovel & steel yards	1.25		
	2 smoothing irons	.50		
	1 Lot of sundry	1.50		2.00
	2 books	.50		.50
				122.90
John Taylor	1 Chissel & ax 1 cro bar	1.80		1.80
James Taylor	1 Heifer	5.50		
	1 Side sold L	15.20	50	15.70
	1 Bed stead & furniture	20.00		
	1 Chest	2.00		
	1 Flax wheel	3.00		43.00
Barbara Taylor	1 Chest	.50		
	1 feather bed	8.50		8.50
Terpin Martin	1 Sythe & Gradle	1.25		1.25
Winchester Jonathan	3 head of sheep	3.00		
	1 bed stead	2.62½		
	1 flax wheel	1.31¼		3.93¾
Joshua Christenberry	1 Ox Cart	15.00		15.00
Mellon John Jen r (pg 243)	1 Brown steer	5.50		5.50
				73.50
Cash on hand and notes on Solvent Men to the amt of				220.67
Joseph Harden for 2.90 Bushels of corn making a total amount of				$992.07½

George Gallaher
John Jones Admrs____
Recorded 5th December 1839
     William Gross Clk
     By his deputy
          C Y Oliver

The following is a list of the personal Property sold on 22nd day of November 1839 that belonged to Jacob Butler deceased at his late residence in Anderson County (to wit)

M Butler	1 falling ax	.25
	1 lot of irons	.87½
	Hoe Homes and collar	12⅓

	Three falling axes	.87½	
	1 beef hide	2.6¼	4.68¾
George Harden	1 small ax	.62½	
	1 foot add	.75	
	2nd lot Iron 8 per lb		
	77 lb	6.16	7.53½
Caleb Butler	1 Sprouting hoe	.25	
	2 Do Do	.25	
	2 reap hooks	.12½	
	2 Clevis & Pin	.25	
	4 Screws & gross	.18	
	3 wagon Hubbs	.25¢	
	1 pair Gears	4.62½	
	1 Grind stone 1 bucket	.43¾	
	1 drawing knife	.25	
	1 jar & jug	.31¼	
	1 stack of oats	1.00	
	7 Do Do	2.12½	
	2nd stack fodder per 100 Six	.51¢	
	3rd Hundred bundles	.51¢	
	1 farmer bench	.25¢	
	Cart Wheels	8.00	
	2 lot of tire iron 106 lbs 83¢	28.22¾	
John H. Butler	1 cutting knife 1.2.		
	1 wheel barrow	.27	
	1 Hand saw	00.80¢	2.09
(Pg. 244)			
William W Butler	1 lot sturrep Irons	.16¢	
	Stretchers and teners 100		
	1 Shovel	.50	
	1 red Cow & Bull	9.31½	
	1 Churn	1.00	
	10 bu of wheat @ 50¢ per bu	5.00	
	1 Sheep	1.00	17.97¼
John Keith	1 lot of farming tools	2.05	
	2nd stack oats	5.00	
	Cluring Stone	1.00	
Benjamin Hagler	1 bread tray	.31	
Joseph Black	1 handsaw	6¼	
Joseph Kail	2 Single trees	.31¼	
	1 Jack screw	.50	
	1 Red bull	2.75	
	1 yoke oxen	31.50	
	1 Black filly	18.00	33.06¼
Thomas Jones	1 White sow	3.56¼	
	1 Sorrel Colt	34.62½	
	Waggon box & froe	.62½¢	
	36 Lb wagon tire 6¼ per lb	2.34	
	1 plow	.31¼	
	2 Do	3. 7½	
	1 Hatl ? Chain	.43½	42.27½
Johnie Taylor	1 red shoat	1.00	1.00
William H Butler	1 spotted Sow	3.00	
	2 Sandy Boars	2.00	
	1 Bay Mare	63.00	
	1 pair of small steelyards	.62½	

	1 Shot gun	4.25	
	1 bag shot 12lbs @ 13½		
	per lb	1.57	
	1 Bull tongue plow		
	1 plow	@ 0.50¢	
John Smith	1 Spotted Sow	2.06¼	
William MaGill	1st Choice Shoats	16.00	16.00
William R Butlar	1 Sandy Boar	2.00	2.00
D L Bradley	1 Brown Horse	70.25	70.25
	1 Chain	.13	
	1 Set hind Gears	8.	79.44½
	2 Blind Bridles	1.06¼	
James Jones	1 Black Colt?	32.50	
	1 large oven & lid	.75	
	1 coffee Pailer	1.00	
	1 Sythe & cradle	1.75	
(Pg 245)	1 Hay stack	1.37½	
William Bennett	Roane Horse	30.00	30.00
Joseph Galbreath	1 log chain	2.00	
	4 Halter chains & collar	2.12½	4.12½
John Jones	wood works of wagon	27.00	
James Tiller	1 Bar & Male?	1.60¾	
	Hammer & Chain	1.93¾	3.62½
George Waller	1 Grind stone	1.56¼	
	Drawing chain	.81¼	
	1 candle stand	1.62½	
	2 pair of pot hooks	.37½	
	3rd Lot of hay	1.81¼	
	11Sorrel Mare	55.00	
	1 Halter chain	37.37½	
	4th Hay stack	2.31¼	
	9th Oat Stack	1.62½	65.49¾
Willis Pruitt?	1 5th chain	4.18¾	4.18¾
Joseph Seiber	1 Wheat Seive	2.06¼	2.06¼
Thomas Carnall	1 Pr steel yards	00.50	.50
William Davidson	1 turning steel	.62½	
Samuel Tunnelll	1st Clevis & Pin	.18¾	
	3rd	.18¾	
	1 Sandy Sow	4.62½	
	11 Shoats ¢ $1.00 each	11.00	16.62½
William Oliver	1 Spreader	.44	.44
Thomas Gallaher	2 Barrels & clover seed	.35	
	1 Vile	6.50	
	1st Lot Hay stack	1.18¾	
	1 blocking table	.50	8.53¼
L Moore	1 Red Cow & calf	15.03	
	1 Spotted Heifer	5.50	20.53
Solomon Lively	1 Cow & calf	10. 6¼	10. 6¼
Elias Butler	1 red calf	1.12½	
	1 White Do	1.06¼¢	
	1 Spotted Sow	3.75	
	1 Sorrel Horse	65.00	
	1 Saddle	1.75	
	1 Bed & furniture	10.87½	
	1 small Lot of iron	12½	
	1 pair of stretchers	.75	
	1 Spotted Sow	2.18¾	87.62½

(Pg.246)

Martha Butler	2 Bulls	8.00	
	1 Bay Mare	20.00	
	1 Lot Blacksmith tools	30.00	
	1 Lot of iron	.25¢	
	1 Table Bed & ½ doz chairs	2.00	
	1 Bed & furniture	1.00	
	1 Loom	5.00	
	2 Cotton wheels	.50	
	1 Cupboard & furniture	2.00	
	1 pair and irons	.25¢	
	6 sheep	2.00	7.25
John Nickle	1 Red Heifer	3.83	
	1 white Do	3.62½	
	4th chain blind bridle	.43¾	7.93¾
Beverly Freels	1 Spotted Sow	3.00	
Ambrose Copeland	Hammer & tracer	1.62½	
	1 Barshear Plow	.18¼	
	1 Coulter	.75	
	1 Beef hide 14¢ per lb 21	2.97¢	6.15¾
Elijah Cross	2nd pair chains	4.12½	
	1 iron rod	.25¢	
	1 mowing Syth	.62½	
	10 bu wheat @ 30¢ per bu	5.00	
John McKamey	3rd Choice blind bridle	1.01	
	1 Oven & lid	.75	
	1 pair of pot hooks	.25	
	1 Pot rack	2.00	
William Cross	1 Plow	.50¢	
William Freels	1 tray & pale		
Clark Freels	1 large pot	2.18¾	
J W Freels	1 small pot	1.87½	
William G Butler	1 Sythe and cradle	1.62½	
John Gennion	3rd Sythe & cradle		3.12½
William G Griffith	Mowing Sythe	.25	
Joseph R Robertson	10 bushels wheat @ 50¢ per bushel		5.00

(Pg.247)

Richard Oliver	3rd Stack of Oats	5.00	
	4th Stack Do	2.00	
	8th Do	2.37½	
	5th fodder stack ¢ 62 per hundred	2.22	
		1.79	
	9th Do 52 per hundred	1.83	
Azariah Russell	5th Stack of oats	2.06¼	
	6th Do ¢ 65	1.95	
A Kirkpatrick	4th Stack fodder ¢ 62½ per hundred		
	8th Do ¢ 22¢ per hundred 1.56		
	The 3rd Stacks making 900 bunds		
Elisha Pruvett	20 bushels corn ¢ 32½ per bushel		

```
                    20 bushels Do   ¢ @ 31½ per bushel
                     1 Barrel                            1.00
Alexander Galbreath  1 Wagon                            76.00      76.00
```

The foregoing is a full and perfect of the Sales of all the property
or the Estate of Jacob Butler deceased. directed by law to Sold   Notes
with good Security Due twelve Months after date were taken from the
perchasers the 22nd day of November 1839.   Sworn to in Open Court
                          William Cross Clk

                                    J M Butler &
                                    Caleb Butler
                                    Executors of
                                    Jacob Butler
                                              deceased

A list of Notes belonging to Jacob Butler deceased (to wit)
One Note on Elias Butler & Henry Butler Executors on the 28th of
November 1835
(Pg 248)   Due twelve Months after date good   for $38.91¼
One Note on George Fritts Due 15 Nov 1839 for good $300
One Note on Jacob Fritts Due 15 Nov 1839 for $600 good

In the name of God Amen   I Thomas Wilson of the County of Anderson
and state of Tennessee Frail of Body But of perfect Mind and Memory
do make and Ordain this My last Will and Testament revoking all
others viz
I will and bequeath unto my bloved Wife Elizabeth Wilson during hir
Natural life my black Girl Named Fanny
I further will & bequeath unto my wife Elizabeth the hire that will
be due for my black Man Stephen for the year 1839
I will and bequeath unto My John Wilson My land with the appertainances
and improvements thereunto belonging with the farming utentials wagon
Harness and Gear one log chain 1 young mare Callico Prince 1 rifle
gun and two beds bedstead & furniture
(Pg. 249)   I further will that funeral Expenses and all My Just debts
be paid and that any Moneys that may remain on hand together with what
may be due by notes of hand and book account also my Negroe my stock
of horses Cattles Hogs and sheep with my household and kitchen furniture with the Exception bequeath herein before made Should be Equally
divided between My son John Wilson and My daughter Ann D Boyd and
their Heirs   it is further My Will that the wheat corn hay and other
products of the farm with that Portion of the Hogs Now following viz-
Six head be considered as belonging to and bequeath with the farm and
further that my bloved wife Elizabeth shall have comfortable and Maintainance from and of the premesses during hir Natural life
I further will that My Old negro Woman Pleasent should not be con-
sidered in the division of the Negros between John Wilson and Ann D
Boyd but that she be priveliged to spend hir atternably and as near
Equally in the family of John Wilson and Thomas Boyd as Sircumstances
May it Convment to them and agreeable to hir throughs life
I further Constitute and appoint John Wilson and Thomas Boyd My last
Will and Testament and in ratification there of I do on this 9th day
of November in the year 1839
Signed Sealed and Acknowledged the same in the presence of subscribing
witnesses

Subscribing witnessess) Thomas Wilson
Ransom Haskin   )   (Seal)
                    Hardy F Marshall
  Pg   Mark Marshall
(250)
State of Tennessee   ) To the Worshipful County Court October
Anderson County   ) Session 1839

I Enoch Foster Guardian of the Minor Heirs of Richard Luallen de-
ceased do hereby report to your Worship an account Current of the
Propits and Disbursements of the Estate of Minors for the year ending
1st Monday of October 1839 Enoch Foster Guardian & C. to said Minor
Heirs Dr
To cash received of the Estate of Richard Luallen deceased
First report

		$
		$1110.18
To Cash received from administrater the 7th of November 1838		137.12½
To interest Due on the Amount up to the 12th September 1839 in		75.29
To Cash received for rent for the Martin and Seven places for 1838		64.80
To interest due on the amount of rent for 6 mounts up to the 15th of September 1839		1.94
		1389.33½

Disbursements viz
By the Amount paid

Clerk for Guardian Bond		550
By this amount paid Clerk for recording 1st report and exhibed of the amount of said Estate		.37½
By Amount paid Clerk for Settlement and recording the same		1.50
By Amount of four days Services to Knoxville in attending at the Chancery Court	1.50	6.00
By Seven days Services to the Bresiness of said Estate in the County	1.00	7.00
		15.37½

(Pg 251)

The whole amount with which I am Chargable is	$1389.33½	1389.33½
Total amount of Disbursement is		15.37½
		1373.96

This 9th day of October 1839 Sworn to and Subscribed before
Enoch Foster Guardian of Minor Heirs of the Estate of Richard
Luallen deceased this 9th day of October 1839

                        Enoch Foster
I do Certify that the above Settlement was made by me with Enoch
Foster Guardian of Minor Heirs of Richard Luallen dec.d and is now
offered to the Court for their Confirmation or rejection
                      William Cross Clk
Confirmed by the Court by his debts
                    C Y Oliver
And ordered to be recorded

                    Albst. William Cross Clk
                  By his deputy
                      C Y Oliver

State of Tennessee)   To the Worshipful County Court January
Anderson County   )   Sessions 1840

I John Jarnagin Guardian of Lindly Hill, James Hill, Lucy and
John Hill, Minor Heirs of Martin Hill deceased do hereby report to
your Worship and account Current of the profits disbursements of the
Estate of said Minor Heirs for the year ending 1st day of January
1840 John Jarnagin Guardian & C Dr to amount in Guardian hand 1st
January
(Pg 252)

1839	13.75
To interest on that some of 13.75 12 Mo	82
" rent for house and land adjoining Clinton	50.00
By Amount Paid Clerk for recording	64.75
Report and Settlement up to 1st Jany 1839	1.87½
By Amt Paid Bill Cents in the Circuit Court Butler vs Hansard admrs. & C	18.31¼
By Amount Paid Tax on land for 1839	1.85
By Amount Paid Clerk for recording report and settlement up to January 1st 1840	1.50
By Amount Paid J Jarnagin & C for Marchandise per James Hill	8.33
Do for Luck Hill	3.15½
Do for John Hill	8.26¼
Do given Miller as per recipt	5.15¼
Amt yet due Lindley Hill	13.75
	40.65½

Being his 1/5 Part due 18.38 & the whole amount with which   64.19½
said Guardian is Chargable for said Estate is   64.57   64.57
Whole Amount of disbursements   14.12½   14.12½
Balance due in Guardian hands to said Ward6___
Sworn to and Subscribed before me William Cross Clerk By my
Deputy   C Y Oliver
                         January 18th 1840
                                   John Jarnagin Guardian
of the Minor Heirs of Martin Hill deceased
The annexed Settlement was taken before me is now offered before
the Court for their Confirmation or rejection.
                    William Cross Clk
                    Confirmed By his Deputy
                         C Y Oliver

(Pg 253)
State of Tennessee   )   To the Worshipful County Court
Anderson County   )   March Sessions 1840

I Samuel Seiber Guardian of the Minor Heirs of Mocajph Chiles
deceased (to wit)
Polly Chiles Sally Chiles and William Chiles do hereby report to
your worshipful an account Current of the profits and disbursements
of said Estate of said Minors from the 31st of August 1838 up to the
1st day of January 1840
                    Samuel Seiber Guardian & C of sd Minor Dr
To Amount due on Settlement 31st of August 1838 $ 76.22½
To rent received for 1838

55 Bushels of Corn at 40¢ per Bushel   25.00
                                                                      102.22½
                             Disbursements
By Amount paid Widow of said Micajah Chiles deceased She having
not received hir Portion of said Estate say one fourth Part
                                                              $18.00
By widow Part of rent of 1838 Say   6.00
By Amount Paid removing about 200 panels of fence   2 00
Making 600 new rails and removing Laying olddrails
say 1300
By Amount for Clothing bearding and for educating
Miners for 5 years at   12.64½ per
year   63.22½
By Amount Paid Clerk for making Settlement and
recording the same Sworn to before me   1.50
                                                                   _____
                                                              $ 10222½

                        William Cross Clk
                        By his Deputy
                                        C Y Oliver

(Pg 254)

State of Tennessee)   I do Certify that Samuel Seiber ap-
Anderson County   )   peared before me at my office and made
the Settlement as per within Stated and the same is presented
to your worship ratification or rejection
                        William Cross Clk
Confirmed by the Court and by his Deputy C Y Oliver
Ordered to be recorded in the Estate book Attest
                        William Cross Clk
                        By his Deputy C Y Oliver

State of Tennessee)   To the worshipful County Court Febry
Anderson County   )   Sessions 1840

I John Gammon Guardian of Larcisa I Butler Minor heirs of
Thomas Butler Jr deceased do hereby report ton your Worship an
account Current of the profits and disbursements of said Estate
of said Minors for the year 1839 up to the 1st 18th August 1839
To the amount due on Settlement 18th August 1838
Is_____$866.77
To Interest on that Sum 12 Months   52.00 $918.77

Disbursements   918.77
By this Amount paid for Clerk   6.50
By this Amount paid for 1 dress   1.00
By Amount Paid Robert & McAmis as per Bill   2.65
By my Services for 12 Months   5.00
By this Amount Paid Clerk for Making Settlements Sworn
to me   1.00
Subscribed   16.15 $16.77
                        William Cross Clk
                        By his Deputy
                                    C Y Oliver
                        John Gammon   G R

(Pg 255)
The above Settlement was made with said Gammon Guardian as
above Stated upon as above Stated upon Oath I now offered
to the Court for their Confirmation or rejection
                              William Cross Clk Confirmed by the
Court by his dept C Y Oliver Attest
                              William Cross Clk
                         By his Dept C Y Oliver
An additional Amount of Sale of the Estate of John Luallen deceased made at the late residence of the said Luallen deceased in
Henderson County after having advertised according to Law on the
7th day of January 1840
1 Cow sold Nancy Luallen for Six dollars Sixty two and one half cents
on the 15th of February 1840
One negro Girl named Nancy to Betsy Luallen for five hundred and
fifty two dollars and one cent
The foregoing is a full and perfect amount of the sale of all the
property of John Luallen deceased dec.d
Notes with good Security due
The one for Six dollars 62½ Cents due the 24th of August.
The Other for five hundred dollars fifty two 1 ct. due twelve months
after date due 15th February 1841
This 15th day n of febry 1840
                              J Ross
                              administrator
Sworn to in Open Court

                              William Cross Clk of the Estate of
                              John Luallen deceased
(Pg 256)
An additional Amount of Sale of the property belonging to the Estate
of George Winton deceased
State of Tennessee)
Anderson County   )   An Inventory of some Property which has
come into our hands Sinne we made our last return to the Court together wh
with the sale and disposition We have made of the same viz
1 Lot of sale leather 2.34¼ lbs which we divided equally among
the legatus acupt William Winton whom lives in the state of
Missouri One lot of upper Leather divided by the Prices Market
by the Tanner Mr Warren (To wit)

James Winton	33½ Lbs	$8.00
Sam'l Montgomery	33½ Lbs	8.00
Wm Montgomery	33½ Lbs	8.00
J W Winton	33½ Lbs	8.00
Bobby Winton	33½ Lbs	8.00
John Grant	33½ Lbs	8.00
Whole Amount	2.42½	56.00

In addition to the above we find some cattle which have sold
as follows

2 Yearlings sold for	6.00
1 Heifer for	4.00
	10.00

The above we respectfully Submit to the Court February 3 1840
                              R Winton
                              J Grant Administrators

(Pg 257)
A return of the Amount of the Sales of the Estate of James Smith deceased at his last residence in Anderson County after having advertised according to Law

Ruby Smith	2 Hogs	12½ 00 12½	00 12½
Thomas Tirpin	1 Shovel Plow		00 31¼
Rubey Smith	1 Shovel Plow & Gun		50
William R Smith	1 Iron wedge		25
Rubey Smith	1 Tub & Pail		25
Andrew Smith	1 Pot		50
Rubey Smith	1 Oven lid & Pot Hooks		50
Do Do	1 Pot		25
Lewis Briant	1 Oven		.76
Andrew Smith	1 Pair drawing chains		.35
Ewing Thomas	1 HeelnScrew & Flax Cutter		.31¼
Rubey Smith	1 Tub		.25
William Bennett	2 Baskets		.12
Rueby Smith	1 Wheel & Card		1.00
Do Do	1 Bread tray & Seive		. 6¼
Do Do	1 Ax		12½
1 Piggin &	Churn		.25
Matthew Todd	1 Ax		.31¼
Rubeyb Smith	1 Bed stead	12½	
	4 Chairs	50	.62½
Do Do	1 Bed & furniture		4.12½
Do Do	1 Chest	12½	
	1 Lot of bacon	10.	10.12½
Do Do	1 Lot of hog lard		.50
Do Do	1 Table		.25
Thomas Turpin	1 Cow		7.06¼
Andrew Smith	1 Cow		7.00
Patience Walker	1 Heifer		4.00
Bloomer White	6 Small Hogs		4.18¾
Franciscis H Robertson	2 Hogs		6.49½
George Hardin	3 Hogs		5.32

(Pg 258)

Ruby Smith	1st Lot Cotton	.25
Do Do	2 Do Do	.50
Ewing Thomas	1 Mare	40.00
Jane Smith	1 Seddle	12.75
Rubey Smith	1 Bridle	.13
William N Smith	1 Loom	.41¼
Ruby Smith	1 Stack Fodder	1. 3¼
Spencer Keith	1 Stack fodder	2.19¼
James Shannon	1 Stack fodder	2.50
William Shannon	1 Stack Do	1.82¼
Do Do	Do Do	4.62½
John Pitman	50 bushels corn	13.50
John Shannon	25 bushels Do	6.75
Ruby Smith	25 bushels Do	3.75
Francis H Robertson	25 Do	6.37½
Ruby Smith	25 bushels Do	3.75
Do Do	25 Do Do	3.12½
William Shannon	8 bushels corn	2. 6¼
Jane Smith	Remainder of corn	3.43¾
Bloomer White	16 Bus. refused Corn	2.00

The foregoing is a full an Perfect Account of the Sale of all the
Property or the Estate of James Smith deceased directed by the Law
to be sold; Notes with good Security due twelve Months after date ta
taken from the Purchasers this 18th day of Feby 1840

                                Henry Shannon
                                    Admrs

Recorded the 15th day of April 1840

                              Ruby Smith
                              Admrx.
                 Attest   William Cross Clk
                              By his Dept
                                    C Y Oliver

(Pg 259)
The following is the Amount of the property sold at the sale of the
personal property of William McKamey deceased and Note Accounts
Moneys on hand and recept

Elizabeth McKamey	1 cupboard & furniture	$10.00	
	1 table	$1.	
	1 side saddle	5.	6.00
	1 Rifle gun apparatus	4	
	1 Chest	.75	
	1 Bed & furniture & Bed stead & 1 Do	10.00	
	1 Looking glass & state	1.00	
	1 Trunk	1.25	
	1 half bushel	.25	
	1 Wheel & Reel	2.25	
	5 Chairs	.75	
	1 Wheel	1.00	$36.10
John A McKamey	1 mans Saddle	2.00	
Robt McKamey	1 Mans saddle	1.00	
John A McKamey	1 Mattock	0.50	
Elizabeth McKamey	1 Mattock	0.37½	
Do Do	2 Sprouting Hoes	.50	
	8 weeding Hoes	2.00	$ 5.87½
John A	1 Shovel & Iron Pick	.37½	
Elizabeth McKamey	1 Cro bar 2 iron wedges	2.00	
John A McKamey	5 Mowing sythes	2.00	
Do Do	3 Axes	1.00	
John McKamey	1 Cast Mould board	.75	
Elizabeth McKamey	1 Cross Cut saw	2.00	6.12½
" "	1 Bull Tongue Plow & C	1.00	
John McKamey	1 Do Do	1.00	
William McKamey	1 Wagon	30.00	
Elizabeth McKamey	1 Sorrel Horse	40.00	
William McKamey	1 Gray horse	50.00	
John A McKamey	1 Roan Horse	50.00	
Elizabethn McKamey	1 Roan Mare	15.00	
Barton McKamey	1 Roan Horse	50.00	
John A McKamey	126½ Bushels of corn 25¢		272.27

(Pg 260)

Amount brought Up			$272.27
Barton McKamey	114 Bushels of corn	$22.80	
John A McKamey	15 bushels of wheat	5/25	
Barton McKamey	10 bushels Do	3.50	
Robert McKamey	10 bushels Do	3.50	
Do Do	17 bushels rye	3.20	
Do Do	50 bushels clover	15.87½	56.12½
John A McKamey	1 fodder stack	1.00	
Robt. McKamey	1 do do	1.00	
John A McKamey	1 Rye Do	2.00	
Do D o	1 Lot of fodder	.50	
	Oats	.25	75
	Hay in the stable loft	2.00	6.75
	1 cutting knife	.75	
Barton McKamey	1 Grind stone	.25	
Robt McKamey	1 Rye stack	3.00	
Barton McKamey	1 Do D o	2.50	
John A McKamey	Oat Stack	11.00	
Do Do	1 Do	1.00	8.60
Do D o	1 Do	1.50	
Robt McKamey	1 Oat stack	1.50	
John A McKamey	1 Pen of shucks	.25	
Robert McKamey	1 Horse	40.00	
Eoizabeth McKamey	1 Leg chain	3.00	
Do D o	1 wagon & Geers	90.00	135.25
John McKamey (A)	Blacksmith tools	45.00	
William McKamey	1 Shovel Mold	..75	
" "	1 Do Do	2.56¼	
William Smith	1 Shovel Mould	1.00	
William McKamey	1 Do Do	.93¾	
" "	1 Do Do	.81½	
Robert McKamey	3 Shovel Moulds	2.87½	
William Smith	1 Do Do	1.10	55. 3½
			$434.03
(Pg 261)			
William McKamey	1 Shovel Mould	$00.87½	
Barton McKamey	Bull Tongue Plow	1.00	
John McKamey	1 Shovel Plow	.75	
Robert McKamey	1 Plow & Share?	.50	
William Smith	1 Bar & Plow Mole	2.75	
Robert McKamey	1 Plow	3.50	
John A McKamey	1 Free	.25	9.62½
Elizabeth McKamey	hand saw & drawing knife	1.25	
Do D o	2 Augers & 2 chisels	.50	
Barton McKamey	1 Hoe & screw	.50	
William McKamey	Streacher chains	1.50	
John R McKamey	1 Lot of iron	2.00	
William McKamey	1 Bar of iron	1.00	
John A McKamey	1 Lot of horse shoes	.25	7.00
Robert McKamey	1 Bar Shear Plow	2.00	
Do Do	Do D o	1.50	
John A McKamey	1 Lot of plows	0.50	
E McKamey	1 Hoe	.25	
	1 Lot of hogs	20.00	20.25
Robt McKamey	1 Lot 2 Hogs	20.00	
Elizabeth McKamey	7 Calves	7.00	61.25

Robert McKamey	Oats Stacks	8.50	
John A McKamey	1 Do Do	3.00	
Robert McKamey	1 Log of hay	.50	
John A McKamey	1 Stack of Clover Hay	4.00	19.00
Peggy McKamey	1 Bay Mare & Colt	40.00	
John A McKamey	1 Lot of Hogs	43.00	
Do Do	1 Lot Do	33.50	
Do Do	Do Do	20.00	
Do Do	Do Do	18.00	
Do Do	Do Do	12.00	166.50
			$697.40½

(Pg 262)

	Amount Brot Up			696.40½
John A McKamey	1 Lot of Hogs 10	$10.00		
" "	1 Lot Do	$8.		
	1 n Do	7.	23.00	
" "	1 Lot Do	5.	5.	
Elizabeth McKamey	1 Horse Colt	15.00		
John A McKamey	1 Gray Colt	25.00		
Robt McKamey	1 Lot of fodder	4/01	82.00	
Elizabeth McKamey	1 Bull	10.00		
Barton McKamey	12 first choice of 32 Cattle	123.00		
Do Do	10 Choice of cattle	71.00		
John A McKamey	10 Cattle	41.00		
Do Do	1 Red Cow & Calf	8.50		
Do Do	1 Pided Cow & Calf	10.00		
Elizabeth McKamey	1 red one horn cow	10.50	274.00	
Do Do	1 red cow & calf		8.00	
Do Do	1 Pided cow & calf		7.50	
John A McKamey	Pided Cow & Calf		8.50	
Peggy McKamey	Red Cow & Calf		11.50	
Barton McKamey	White face cow & calf		8.25	
Elizabeth McKamey	1 Red cow & Calf	8.00	43.75	
James Willson	1 pited Cow & Calf	10.6½		
C S Lindsay	1 Brindle Cow	13.50½		
Patterson Robert	1 Black Cow	8.00		
C S Lindsay	1 Brindle Cow	6.10		
Barton McKamey	1 Red cow	12.00		
Elizabeth McKamey	1 Cream pale Horn Cow	7.00	56.56½	
Do Do	1 Pided Cow	8.50		
Robt McKamey	1 Red white faced cow	9.00		
Robert Patterson	1 Red Heifer	8.00		
Elizabeth McKamey	1 white faced cow	6.56½		
John A McKamey	1 White & red cow	9.00		
Elizabeth McKamey	1 white back cow	8.00	49.06¼	
			$1202.79¼	

(Pg 263)

Amount Brot Up			$1202.79¼
John A McKamey	1 red side Cow		8.00
Elizabeth McKamey	1 Brindle cow	7.00	
Do Do	1 red Heifer	6.06¼	

Do Do	1 Cow	8.50	
William McKamey	1 Lot 5 bushels of salt	7.50	
Robt McKamey	1 Lot 5 bushels salt	7.50	
Barton McKamey	1 Lot Do Do	7.50	
John A McKamey	1 Lot 3 3/4 bu Do	5.62½	
Do Do	1 Lot of bacon 100 lbs-	6.60	$64.38¾
Robert McKamey	1 Lot Do 100 lbs	7.07	
Elizabeth McKamey	3rd Lot Bacon 102½.	6 15	
Peggy McKamey	4th Lot Do 98Lbs	6.86	
Robert McKamey	5th Lot 107-	8.02½	
Barton McKamey	6th Lot Bacon 89lbs	7.12½	
Do Do	7 Lot Do 118 Lbs	9.44	
Isaac Breaden	8th Lot do 102 lbs	8.67½	53.34½
Robert McKamey	9th Lot do 95	8.07½	
John A McKamey	10th Lot do 150	9.75	
William McKamey	1 Lot of Iron	9.75½	70.47½
John A McKamey	2nd Lot Iron 211 lbs	14.77	
Robert McKamey	3rd Lot do 389 Lbs	29.45½	133.12½
Barton McKamey	4th Lot Do Do 93½-	6.78¼	
Elizabeth McKamey	1 foot addze	.25	
John H McKamey	1 Stake & Hammer	.25	
Elizabeth McKamey	1 Brand Iron	.12½	
" "	1 Bell & Collar 75¢ 1 Do 50¢	1.25	
Robt McKamey	1 Bell & Collar	1.00	
John A McKamey	Bell & Collar	3.00	
Do Do	Do Do	1.25	
Elizabeth McKamey	1 Bell & Collar	0.50	161. 6¾
Robert McKamey	1 Bell & Collar	1.75	
Pg (264)			
Amount Brought forward			2419.81¼
William McKamey	1 Bell & Collar	1.68¾	
John B McKamey	1 Bell & Collar	.87½	
William McKamey	1 Bell & Collar	.62½	
John A McKamey	1 Bell	.62½	
William McKamey	1 Bell	1.68¾	5.00
Do Do	2 Clevices & Pins	0.75	
John A McKamey	1 Plow	.50	
Do Do	1 Bull Tongue	.37½	
Do Do	2 reap Hooks	.31½	
Elizabeth McKamey	4 Collars & 5 chains	2.00	3.93¾
Barton McKamey	1 Clevis & Pin	.43¾	
John A McKamey	1 Bucket	.25	
Elizabeth McKamey	1 Jug	.50	
John A McKamey	1 Pot	.62½	
Elizabeth McKamey	1 Oven & lid	1.00	
Do Do	Do Do	.50	
" "	Kitchen furniture	.50	
	10 lbs of picked cotton	1.00	5.31¼
" "	Some flax	4.92	
" "	Seed Cotton	4.68	
	Kettle & Lid	2.	6.68
" "	1 Oven	.75	
Robt McKamey	1 Plow stock & Coulter	. 50	

Barton McKamey	1 Do Do	.25	
Elizabeth McKamey	9 Bu Gums	2.00	
" "	5 tubs	1.50	
Barton McKamey	1 Barrel	.50	
Elizabeth McKamey	1 Whiskey Barrel	.50	
Elizabeth McKamey	Plow Irons	.25	
John A McKamey	Plow Irons	1.00	$29.35

$2463.35½

(Pg 265)

	Amount Brot forward		2463.40
John A McKamey	Some Barrel Troughs & Tubs	4.25	
Elizabeth McKamey	4 beef Hides	9.25	
Barton McKamey	3 Head of sheep	4.50	
John A McKamey	1 knife	.37½	
Do Do	1 Lot of Irish potatoes	1.56¼	
Robt McKamey	2 Lots of irish potatoes 10 Bu	3.18¾	23. 17½
Elizabeth McKamey	1 Lot Do Buss	1.62½	
Barton McKamey	1 Lot Do 13 Do	4.22½	
Robt McKamey	1 Bridle	.43¾	
John A McKamey	1 Bull Tongue Plow	.35	
Do Do	1 Shovel Plow	.40	
Elizabeth McKamey	1 pair of steelyards	1.50	
John A McKamey	(1) Shovel Plow	1.50	
Elizabeth McKamey	Some tobacco	.50	
Do D o	1 pair saddle bags	.50	11.03¾
Do Do	1 Loom 1.00 1 Lot sheep 6.00	7.00	
John A McKamey	2nd Do	8.62½	
Barton McKamey	3rd Lot of Do 6	8.00	
Jacob McGhee	4th Lot do 5	6.61¼	
Do Do	1 Sythe & cradle	1.62½	
Barton McKamey	Some fodder & Hay	3.00	
John A McKamey	Some fodder on the floor	4.50	
Do Do	Some fodder on the loft	5.00	
Barton McKamey	Some Shucks	.50	
Do Do	Hay in stable loft	1.00	
Elizabeth McKamey	4 Calves	9.00	
John A McKamey	4 Calves	8.00	
Do Do	1 Sow & Pigs	3.00	
Barton McKamey	(1) lot of Hogs	20.00	
Andrew Breaden	1 Oat Stack	5.00	
Barton McKamey	Do Do	3.00	73.26½

$2576.87½

(Pg 266)

	Amount Brot Up		$2570.87½
Elizabeth McKamey	(1) Sorrel Colt	$ 2.00	
John A McKamey	1 Gray Colt	40.00	
Do Do	Ewe & Lambs	4.50	
William McKamey	Do Do	4.62½	
Elizabeth McKamey	2 Do Do	3.50	

****

William McKamey	2 Do Do	4.68¾	
Elizabeth McKamey	2 Do Do	3.00	
Jacob McGhee	2 Do Do	4.50	$84.80¼
William McKamey	2 Do Do	4.56½	
ElizabethMcKamey	2 Ewes2	2.50	
Barton McKamey	1 Sprouting Hoe	.50	
Do Do	Harness Collar & Bridle	2.50	
Do Do	1 Hay Stack	15.00	
Do Do	Some fodder	2.00	
Robt. McKamey	Shingles	.25	
John A McKamey	A Parcel of Hay Pin	.37½	27.68¾
Elizabeth McKamey	fire dogs Shovel & boxes	.50	
John A McKamey	Hams & Irons	.25	
Do Do	Hames	.33¼	
Elizabeth McKamey	1 Bridle	.12½	
John A McKamey	1 Chain 25¢ Beef 2.00	2.25	
" "	Saddle Collar & Sickle	1.00	
Robt McKamey	2 Big Coats	10.00	
Barton McKamey	1 Bed sted	2.00	
" "	Books	.50	
Robert McKamey	(1) Bed sted	.25	
John A McKamey	1 Piece of iron	.50	
Elizabeth McKamey	Counterpain & threads	5.00	
	Threads	5.00	
Robt McKamey	1 Record Book	2.00	
John A McKamey	Corn & fodder	3.00	
Robt. "	26½ Lb Iron	1.85½	29.56¼
(Pg 267)	(Amount Brot Up		$2712.92¾
			$2712.92¾
	Amount Brot Up		
Elizabeth McKamey	2 Boxes	00.25	
" "	Some Hogs Lard & Iron	.50	
" "	Soap 50¢ Hackle $1.50	2.00	
John A McKamey	1 Weading Hoe	.62½	
" "	4½ Bu rye		
	27 bushels Oats	5.87½	
" "	2½ B.Sweat Potatoes Seed	1.25	
Robt. McKamey	2 Bushels salt	3/00	
" "	1 Pack saddle	.12½	
Jacob McGhee	8 Bushels Rye	4.00	
John Webb	Sundrus	2.00	$2732.54¾
			$ 2732.54¼

One Note of Hand on Absolom Keith, Robert McKamey Samuel B. Young, William Freels and John Cross Due the 5th Nov. 1839
1.65

One Note on George Summers & James Summers recept in Interest Eleven dollars Eighty Six

and one fourth cents due 2nd day April 1836   .70.
One Note on Robert McKamey due 12 of April 1837   1.25
One Note on John McAdoo due 17th December 1836   .65
One Note on Joseph McAsher & Robert McKamey due 5th
December 1837   .90
One Note Elijah Adkins Due 12th of March 1839   441.66
One Note on William McKamey due the 6th of
October 1837
Credited for $ and fifty Cents the 16th
Nov 1838   31.50
One Note on Benjamin P Hackney due the 9th
December 1838   .20 $561.16

                                        3293.70½

                                    $3293.70½

One Note on Whistenn & McKamey due the 10th of April 1838
(Pg 268)   4.00
Two Notes on Robert McKamey due 25th of March 1827—182.21
A Note on John Severs due the 23rd April 1832   15.00
One Note on John Seiber due the 6th Sept 1832   20.
One Note on Matthew M Gammons, James Luttrell
and Martha Luttrell Due 26th of Febry 1837   10.00
One Note on Nancy Ann Buttler and Andrew
McKamey due 13th Oct   1838—261.06¼   261.06¼
One Note on Ross and Kirkpatrick due 19th
March 1839
for four hundred and Eighty dollars Credit on
the same for one hundred Dollars all the interest
paid up to the 12th May 1839   380.00
One Note on S Bogart & E W McEvils for 12
hundred dollars due the 11th of December 1833
Credit on the same for two hundred dollars
25th June 1839
Credit for Interest at different times for
four hundred and Two dollars   1000.
One Note on William B Smith due the 1st day of
January 1839   173.62½
One Note due on Moses Duncon due 14th of
January 1840— 30.
One Note on James McCampbell due 29th January—
1834— 18.28½

One Note on Joseph C Moore & Samuel due 7th March
1837.
Credit for   4.28 1/3   37.16 2/3

                                       6411.04½

(Pg 269)
Amount Bret Up   6411.04½

One Note on Joseph Cross due 10th Feby 1840 $50.
One Note on John Taylor and Price Wallace
due 24th Febry 1838 With the following Credits
thirty five dollars Sept 13th 1839 Also Eleven

Dollars. Ten Dollars 3rd of Febry   1840   44.00
One Note on Eli Rhea due 1st of June   1839   35.00
One Note on Philip Davis & Moses Duncon
due the 23rd of July   1839   12.50
One Note on James Kirkpatrick and Charles
Luallen due 2nd of Nov   1833
Recvd. Interest   20.00
                                                      100.00
One Note on Thomas due the 1st August   1830 for
two dollars   2.50
One Note on Thomas Heart due the 5th December
1839   18.00
One Note on John McAdoo due the 8th of May 1838   20.00
One Note on James Gray for   25.
One Note on A Burris   50.
One Note on Solomon Dougherty due the 10th
Nov.   1833   5.63¼
One Note on John Sevirs due the 20th Sept
1836   11.50
One Note on James Breaden due 15th March 1833   1.75
One Note on Jacob M Asherst due the 11th
June 1839 or interest paid up to that time   600.00
A receipt of John Armstrong for a Note of hand
due 19th Oct   1829   130.14¾
(270 Pg)
Amount Brot up   7441.82½
Certificate Barton & Southerland against
C McCormack for 13 days attendance @ 50¢ per day   6.50
Robert McKamey   1 Pack Saddle   25
                                                                7448.57½

                        Robert McKamey
                        Barton McKamey
                                Administrator
Recorded 16th April 1840
                        William Cross
                                Clk
                          By his Deputy
                                C Y Oliver

An additional Inventory of the affects belonging to the Estate
of Jacob Butler deceased returned to the County Court of
Anderson County at its May Term for 1840
the following accounts

To Mr. John C McErvin   Dr   17.34½
 "   "   John Smith   Dr   3.00
 "   "   George Pickel   Dr   2.00
 "   "   James Jones   Dr   2.00
 "   "   John H Briant   Dr   4.25
 "   "   John Hagler   Dr   5.00
 "   "   Edward Waller   Dr   3.00
 "   "   George Stubbs   Dr   4.00
 "   "   James Stubbs   Dr   4.00
 "   "   Evin E Duncon   Dr   5.00
Joseph Henry   Dr   1.37½

****

To Mr Thomas Jones	Dr	7.49
" Mary Walker	"	6.00
" " William Pitman	"	5.00
" " Jacob Peak	"	12.00
" Milly Hagler	"	4.00

$$85.96$$

(Pg 271)
Amount Brought up   85.96

To Mr. George Helomes	Dr	4.00
" " Jethra Monger	Dr	5.00
" " William R Butler	Dr	5.00
" " William G Griffith	Dr	2.50
" " Andrew McKamey	Dr	7.00
" " Drewry L Bradley	Dr	6.00
" " John Wiley	"	.37½
" " John C McKamey	"	8.37½
" " William McKamey	"	1.81½
" " Robert H McKamey	"	9.00
" " James Davis	"	1.06½

$$136.08¾$$

Sworn to in Open Court   J M Butler
                              Caleb Butler
                              Executors of Jacob Butler deceased
                              William Cross Clk

The following is an Inventory of the property belonging to the
Estate of Lucy Ross deceased returned to the County Court of
Anderson County at its June term for 1840 (To wit)

5 Beds Bed Steads & clothing	1 Set of blue plates	1 dish
1 pitcher 1 looking glass	1 spinning wheel	
1 pr of fire dogs	9 milk pans	1 large Bible
Some pot vessels	26 head of sheep	
	young and old	1 Chest
one clock one cow &one yearling		Shovels & tongs
1 Hatchet 1 Reel	1 Little wheel	

(272 Pg)
1 Sorrel Mare 2 saddles   1 Bridle 1 chest   at Rosses
1 trunk at Kirks
One **Note** on Charles Lamar for fifteen dollars 20¢ Due July 10 1837
Ballance on a Noteen Charles Lemar given July 23rd 1831
Five dollars & Sixty eight Cents   May 23rd 1840
One **Note** on Alijah Adkins for twelve dollars due Sept 25, 1839
A **Note** on J Jarnagin in &C
One pr $220 dollars being interest from May 16 1839
One for forty dollars due Sept 14 1839
A K on J Jarnagin for twenty dollars
Recorded 2nd June
                              James Ross
                              Administrator of Est. of Lucy Ross
                                        Dec.d
The following is an Inventory of the property belonging to the
Estate of John Rhea deceased returned to the County Court for Anderson

County at the July term of 1840 (To wit)

3 head of Horses	two yoke of oxen	2 milch cows &
Calves 1 Heifer	1 Cart 2 Shovel Plow &	Swingle & Clevices
2 Bull Tonga	1 Patent Plough	2 pair Geers
5 Axes 2 Mattocks	5 Hoes 1 log chain	8 sheep
7 head of hogs	6 Barrels	2 Bed steads

(Pg 273)

2 cupboards 1 Loom	3 Tables Iron 1 Syth	& Cradle
2 Syths 5 Chairs	1 Looking glass	1 clock
1 trunk 3 drawing knives	2Cfess for A Cooper	(1) hand saw
1 Adds 1 steelyard	1 pair of sheep shears	1 Kittle
1 Oven & Lid	1 Skillet & Lid	2 Pots
1 Cutting Knife & Box &	knife 1 spinning wheel	1 basket
1 half bushel Measure	1 frow 6 Augers	1 riddle

The foregoing is a true return of the property that has come to my
hands this 2nd day of June 1840

        James Moore
Recorded 7th July 1840 Administrator of Estate of John Rhea Dec.d
The following is an additional or second Sale of the property be-
longing to the Estate of Henry Butler decd. (to wit)

Douglas Oliver Jr.	1st Lot of corn	
1st Lot of Corn	10 bus 28 per bu	2.88
" "	2nd Lot corn 30¢ per bu	3.00
" "	3rd Lot " 31¢ " "	3.10
H C Winton	4th Lot " 31½¢ " "	3.15
" "	5th Lot " 33 " "	3.30
Douglass Oliver	6th Lot " 33½¢	3.30½
" "	7t Lot " 33½ " "	3.05
H C Winton	8th Lot " 35¢ " "	3.50
" "	10th Lot " 34¢ " "	3.40
Wm G Butler	1 Bee stand	1.31½
Wm S Butler	Bee Stand	1.00
Richard Oliver	1 Lot of salt 75 lbs	
	3½¢ per lb	1.46½
		35.88½ 35.88½

(Pg 274)

	Amt Brot up		35.88½
Wm M Butler	1 Briar Hook	.64	
Elijah Cross	1 Cow & Calf	1.26	
			$43.78½

We certify that the foregoing is a true amt of a second sale
of the personal Estate of Henry Butler deceased
        This 6th day of July 1840
        William G Butler
Recorded 7th of July 1840

        Kezeah Butler
        administrator and administratrix of
the Estate of Henry Butler deceased
The following is the return of a Sale of the property of the Estate
of Lucy Ross deceased as returned to the County Court at the July
Term for 1840 (To wit)

1 Cow & Earling	Bot by Rhoda Lemar	15.00
1 Ball Sorrell Mare	Do Do	60.00
26 head of sheep	Do " A Kirkpatrick	5/00

26 head of sheep	A Kirkpatrick	5.00	
1 Bead Bead Stead	& furniture	5.00	
1 Small trunk		.25	
1 Bed Bead stead &	furniture J Ross	4.00	
1 Chest	" "	1.00	
1 Bead Bed stead two			
pillows one Boulster &	Coverlid Rhoda Lamar	15.00	
1 Bed Bed stead &	furniture A Kirkpatrick	1.00	
1 Do "	" "	1.00	
5 plates	Rhoda Lamar	2.50	
1 pair of Irens	A Kirkpatrick	.50	
6 milk pans	" "	.75	$113.50
(Pg 275)			
1 Large Bible	Rhoda Lamar	3.00	
Some Pot vissels	A Kirkpatrick	3.00	
1 Chest	" "	1.00	
1 Clock	" "	4.50	
1 pr Shovel & Tongs	" "	.50	
1 Hackle	" "	1.00	
1 Real	" "	.25	
1 Flax wheel	" "	.50	
1 Side leather	" "	2.25	
1 Side "	" "	10.00	
1 Pot rack	" "	1.25	
1 Lot of Chains	Charles Lamar	2.00	

$142.75 $142.75

The foregoing is a full and perfect Account of the
sale of all the property of the Estate of Lucy Ross
decd. be sold for Cash the full amount taken from the
Purchasers this 12th day of June 1840
Recorded 7th July 1840   J Ross administrator of Lucy Ross dec.d
The following is the Amount of as Sale of the property of Henry
Butler Deceased as returned to the County Court at July Sessions
for 1840 (To wit)

Thomas Galbreath	1 Duck Oven	.75
Nancy McKamey	1 " "	.68¾
John Key	3 Falling	.25
A Kirkpatrick	1 Coulter	.50
Wm Griffith	1 Falling ax	.21
Eppy Lea	1 Shovel plough	.99
Wm Peak	1 Shovel Mould	.87
John C McKamey	1 Pull Tongue	.71
K Butler	1 Bar Shear Plough	2.00
Thomas Galaher	1 Small Hoe	.31¾
Isaac Duncan	1 Sythe Blade	..48
K Butler	Hames Chains & swingle	
	tree	.50
Thomas Gallaher	Sythe & Cradle	2.26
Wm R Butler	1 barrel of salt	7.92
George Waller	314 lbs " 1.37½ pr lb 8.63½	
John Key	300 lbs Salt 1.37½ "	8.25
George Waller	308 " Salt 1.37½	
	per 50 Lb	8.47½

The following is an Inventory of the property belonging to the Estate
of Henry Butler (To wit)

2 Oxens	3 fallowing Axes	1 Coulter
1 Shovel Plough	1 Shovel Mould	1 Bull Tongue
1 Bar Share Plough	1 Small Hoe 2 Sythes Blades	1 pr traces &
Harness	1 Swingle tree	9 bushels salt
1 Black Heifer	1 Black Earling	1 cupboard &
furniture	1 Clock 2 feather beds	& furniture
1 yoke oxen		

(Pg 276)

1 Stack hay 1 Mare	& Colt 1 Shoe makers bench	1 mans saddle
1 Loom 1 clock reel	1 table 2 Oat stacks	2 stacks fodder
1 Shove Plough		

Kiziah Butler
    administrator
Recorded 7th July 1840
of Henry Butler Dec.d

Moses C Winton	318 Salt	1.38 per 50 lbs	8.77½	
Do Do	300 "	"	8.28	
Do Do	288		7.94¾	
Do Do	278 "	1¼43½per 50 lbs	7.99½	
Do Do	288 "	" "	8.28	

$ 85 .07 $85.07

(Pg 277)

	The Amount brought forward	85.07
Elias Butler	1 Black Heifer	5.07
Douglas Oliver	1 Black Yearling	3.99
R Butler	1 cupboard & furniture	5.00
" "	1 Clock	5.18
" "	2 beds & furniture	8.00
" "	1 Yoke of Oxen	21.06¼
Wm Butler	1 Stack of Hay	4.06¼
X Butler	1 Mare & Colt	5.00
D Oliver	1 Shoe Makers bench	1.43
Elias Russell	1 Saddle	50
X Butler	1 Loom	1.000
" "	1 Check Reel 1 kitchen table	.50
Ric.d Oliver	1 Oat Stack	2.87½
D Oliver	1 Oat Stack	2.96
Elias Butler	1 Stack fodder	3.15½
D Oliver	1 Stack fodder	2.81½
Wm G Butler	1 Stack	1.90
Richard Oliver	1 Shovel Plough	.83

160.40½

Recorded 7th July 1840)
)

(Pg 278)
Last Will & Testament of William Brummett dec.d

I William Brummett do make and Publish this is my last Will and
Testament hereby revoking and making void all other wills by me at
any timme made first I direct that my funeral Expenses and all me
debts be paid as sworn after my death as possible Out of any money
Shall I die dispossed of or may first come into the hands of My Executors

Secondly I give and bequeath to my wife Patsey Brummett one gray

****

Mare and colt three caws and calves twenty head Hogs of her own
choosing. Thirteen head of sheep Thirty three head of geese One
big Pot One Small Pot One flat oven and lid One set of dog Irons
with all the household and kitchen furniture And also my wife Patsy
Brummett is to have the land I now live on her life time and after
hir death the land is to be sold at the highest bider for Cash on a
twelve Months Credit the the money Equally divided amongst all my Named
Children Elzira Payton Joab Ginary, Preston, Henry, George, John
William, Marget Calvin Lucy Aley Baner Hugh, Surreldy, and also the
ballance of the property to be sold at twelve Months credits and the
Money to be equally divided between the Ten first named Children. I do
hereby nominate and appoint Alexander Turner and My wife Patsy Brummett
My Executors in Witness Where of I do to this my Will Set my hand and
seal this 21st day of April 1840

                                        William Brummitt
                                                    (Seal)

Signed and Published in our Presents and we have Subscribed our names
here to in the Presence of the Testator This 21st day of April 1840.
(Pg 279)

                          Isaac Miller
                          John B Mitchell
Recorded the 7th day of August 1840 Attest
                                        William Cross Clk. of Anderson
                                                          County

I Joseph Overton do make and publish this is my last will and testament hereby revoking and making void all other wills by me at
any time made.
First   I direct that funeral Expenses and all my debts be paid as
soon after my death as possible out of any money that I may die possessed of or May first come into the hands of My Executers
Secondly I give and bequeath to my son Joseph Overton One tract of
land containing Sixty three acres adjoining the land of Daniel Foust
and Others also one large Chest, One Bed and furniture.
Thirdly I give and bequeath to my daughter Elmina one tract of land
containing thirty three acres and a third to be taken of the tract,
I now live on running square across the upper and also one third Part
of my ?   Also one bay horse Colt also one Dunn Cow and calf, also
one Bed and furniture
Fourthly I give and bequeath to my daughter Keziah & Ann the ballance
of the tract of land I now live on Also two thirds of my burca also
Two cows & Calves Also two side saddles
Fifthly I give and bequeath to my daughter Sally Davis one bed and
two sheats   (Pg 280)
Sixthly My daughter Kiziah 1 Horse called Tom Also to Ann one Colt
I do and bequeath to my three daughters Keziah, Ann & Elmina 1 Loom
cupboard and kitchen furniture also my chure? wheel & Cards All
the balance of my property Sold and equally divided between my
Children
Sixthly   I do hereby nominate and appoint John Overton and Charles
Davis Mu Executors in witness where of I do to this my will set my
hand and seal this Tenth day of August 1840   Attest
                                        James Moore
                                            John Overton
                          Sencain Mondom
                          Isaac Stokes
Signed   Sealed and Publish in our presence and we have Subscribed

Our names hereto in the presence of the Testator This the Tenth
day of August 1840.
Recorded this the 26th day of Sept 1840
                              Wm Cross   Clk

An Inventory of the Estate of E C Farmer received of Joseph Black
former Guardian
One Note of hand on Joseph Black & James Black $167.60
One Note of hand on George Winton   100.00
One Note of hand on John Chiles   100.00
One Note of hand on J C Alverson & John Chiles   61.60
One Note of hand on James Childress & Michael Clardy   23.78
One Note of hand on Margaret Litton & M Clardy   20.00
One Note of hand on Martin Hardin & Abraham Seiber   7.78
                                                          _____
                                                           479.76

Present date this 17th day of October 1839
Recorded 26 of Sept 1840
                         Henry Farmer

                              William Cross Clk
                              Guardian

(Pg 281)
Act Current with James H Nickle and Elizabeth Durrett admr. and
administratrix of the Estate of John G Durrett Deceases
To Amt of Sales returned to and received by the Court
Recorded 11th July 1836   3009.50½
An additional Inventory of the Amt found in the hands of
Richard Oliver admrs. of Mary Miller deceased
Recorded 13th July 1837   22.26¾
                                                          _____
                                                          $3031.79¼

By Amt paid Douglas Oliver as per proven Ak 30th April 1836   5.56½
By Amt paid James Galbreath as per Note on hand   23.87½
By Amt paid Luke Peak as per Note received on the 17th of
June 1837
By Amt paid Richard Oliver two Notes of hand   13.22½
By Amount paid Richard Oliver Auctioned at two Sale of the
Estate of John G Durrett   5.00
By Amt paid Sheriff McKamey Taxes for the year 1836   2.68
Do   Do   Do 1837   2.65
By Amt Jonathan Scarbrough as per proven   Ak seipt 28th June
                                                 1837   6.00
By Amt paid John H Crozier Atty for Canciel ?   and advice in
relation to the administrator of said Estate   2.50
By Amount paid William Cross Clerk his fees of Office 12th day
of April 1836   1.00
By Amt paid Douglas Oliver as per Note 19th June 1839   11.71¾
By Amt paid Collins Roberts as per proven A k 17th June 1837 10.25
Amt paid Collins Roberts 17th June 1837 as per Note   3.31¼
(Pg282)
By Amount paid Levi (To wit)
Attoy as per proven Account   2.50
Amt Paid Richard Oliver as per Note receipt 18th June 1837   1.72¾
Amt paid A Crozier & Son 20th of May 1837 as per proven receipt 24.63½
Amt paid Isaac Freels as per Note receipt   55.75
Amt   paid Collins Roberts as per proven Ak   8.62½

****

By Amt paid John Gammon 6th May 1837 as per note receipt	20.09-20.09
By Amt paid John Gammon as per Note receipt	36.64-36.64
Amt paid Douglas Oliver as per note	7.98
Amt paid Richard Oliver as per note	
Amt paid Moses White as per Note & Interest	11.36
By Amt paid Richard Oliver as per Note receipt June 1837	5.50
By Amt paid Do Do	26.85
By Compensation to administrators for the transaction of the bussiness of said Estate	90.00
Amt paid Clerk for making & recording this Settlement	2.50
	437.73½
A ballance in the hands of the admistrator due the Heirs of said Estate	259.73½
	3031.47

Recorded this 28th September 1840
                    William Cross Clk

(Pg 283)
Dr Account Current with Elijah Longmire administrator of the
Estate of Elijah Longmire deceased To Amount of Sale Made
18th of May 1836 and received by the Court as appears of record

Cr	268.39¾
By Amt Mahala Longmire widow of Elijah Longmire deceased on the 19th May 1837 per Voucher	45.00
Amt paid Peter Clear 4th May 1836 in part of the funeral expenses as per receipt	2.00
By Amt paid William Brummit 5th of May 1838 as per receipt	50.00
By Amt paid Mahala Longmire widow of said Elijah Longmire deceased as per receipt	55.00
By Amt paid Joshua H Gist 12th Oct 1839 for Longmire & disting? him & two witnesses	1.50
By Amt paid Dr M Tate 22nd March for attending on the dec.d Elijah Longmire as per receipt	2.50
By Amt paid William Weaver 19th of May 1836 as per receipt	37.50
Amt paid James Taylor 2nd July 1836 as per proven account	1.25
By Amt paid William Cross Clerk as per fees 28th November 1836 as per receipt	2.00
Making this Settlement & recording the same	2.50
	162 .12½
No fees To balance in the hands of administrator	106 .27½
	268. 39¾

Recorded 28th Sept 1840
                    William Cross Clk

(Pg 284)
Last Will & Testament of John Lay dec.d
I John Lay of the County of Anderson and State of Tennessee
being desirous to dispose of my wordly Substances as has
pleased God to Bless me with, so make this my Last Will &
Testament in the words following (to wit)
1st it is my will & desire that all my Just debts and funeral

Expenses be speedily paid

2nd

I give to my belovd wife one third of my Land and negro Girl Named
Kisey, and household and Kitchen furniture. One horse to have and
held during her life time. Also I give hir one part of my Hogs
Two cows and calves. One hundred bushel of corn

3rd

I give and bequeath to dNancy Weaver and John Weaver Children of my
Daughter Catherine Weaver dec.d that is to say one hundred dollars
to be the above Named Nancy Weaver an one hundred dollars to othe
above named John Weaver when they become of age or Marries

4th

I give and bequeath to Elisa Lay, Nancy Lay and John Lay, Children
of my Son John Lay (N) dec.d that is to say one hundred dollars
toElisa Lay as above and one hundred dollars to Nancy Lay as above
and one hundred dollars to John Lay as above when they become of age
or Marries.

5th

I further Will that all my other property Land, Negroes, Horses, Mules,
Cattle, Hogs and every Species of property be equally divided among
My under named Children Named as follows:
Jacob Lay, Sarah Lay, now Sarah Sharp, George Lay, William Lay,
Lewis Lay, Henry Lay Nancy Lay, Emanual Lay, Isaac Lay and Rachel Lay
Now it plainly understood that alln my Property be divided among my
above Named children Named in the 5th Article and the 6th I appoint
George Miller & Lewis Miller my Executors of this My last Will &
Testament revoking allother Testaments here to fore by me made in
witness here of I have hereunto set my hand and seal this 20th day
ofOctober 1840

                                                            his
                              William Lay   John X Lay
                              Henry Graves   mark

(Pg 285)   (Seal)
Recorded this 4th Nov 1840

                                        Will Cross Clk

In the name of God I John James of the County of Anderson and State
of Tennessee.
being weak in body but of sound Memory Blessed be God I do this day
February the 15th A D 1840 Make and Publish this My last Will and
Testament in the following Manner Viz
First I give to my bloved wife all my land goods and chattles to
have to hold as long as she remains my widow excepting the Land
from a Cross fence near where Winston Ballard now lives to the lower
end of the farm this I give to khe said Ballard my life time and my
wife he making no waste or distruction thereon and after the deter-
mination of his death the land and what ever remains to be sold and
equally divided among my children except my wifes Clothing and
beding. She can distribets as she pleases and make and Ordain hir
My said wife sole Executer of this my Will in trust for the interest
and purposes in this My will contained and make my friend Overseer
of this my will to see the same performed according to my intent
and meaning in witness
(Pg 286)
Where of I have to this my last will and Testament Set my rhand
Seal Signed Sealed and delivered in presence of
                                                    his
James S Fidden   John X James
                                                   mark

Recorded this 5th of Nov 1840

Will Cross Clerk

State of Tennessee   )   November the 2nd 1840
Anderson County   )   An Inventory of the Estate of Joseph
                           Worthington deceased

Amt of sale viz

Susanah Worthington	Chains	2.25	
	8 Chains	2.00	4.25
	1 cupboard & fur-niture	12.00	
	1 Bureau	6.00	18.00
	1 Bed stead & furniture	10.00	
	1 Do	12.00	
	1 Chest	2.00	24.00
	1 folding table	2.00	
	1 Looking glass	2.75	2.75
	1 Bed & furniture	7.00	
	1 Do Do	6.00	13.00
	1 flax wheel	2.00	
	1 Side saddle	10.00	12.00
	1 man saddle	6.00	
	1 Lot of Costons	7.50	13.50
	1 Pot & hooks	1.75	
	2 Cotton wheels	1.00	2.75
	1 Loom apparatus	1.50	
	1 table & apparatus	1.00	2.50
	1 Large Barshear plow & Clevis	1.25	1.25
	1 plough & swingle tree	.37½¢	
	1 do do	.25¢	.62½
	1 Set Smith Tools	2.50	
	1 Syth & cradle	.75	
	1 ax	1.00-	4.25
	1 Ax	.75	
	1 plough & double tree	.50	
	10 Hogs	6.00	7.25
	10 Hogs	5.	
	10 Do	4.50	
	10 Do	2.00	
	2 Do	2.50	15.00
Jesse Worthington	7 Hogs	17.50	17.50
Susanah Worthington	1 Cow	5.00	
	Do	5.00	10.00
	1 Do $3. 1 Do $2.		
	1 Do $1.50 1 Do		
	1 Do $4. 1 Do $4.	14.50	14.50
Ruben Russell	1 Bull	6.37½	6.37½
Limon Jackson	1 White stear	3.75	3.75
James England (Pg 287)	1 Heifer	4.93½	4.93½
Limon Jackson	1 Stear	$6.00	6.00
John Frazier	1 Red stear	4.93½	4.93½

Reuben Jackson	1 Stear		$6$32.37½
" "	3 Do		2.00
Susanah Worthington	66 Sheepe		3.00
	5 Do		2.00
	1 Gray Horse		25.00
Joseph Harden	1 Bay horse		62.00
Susanah Worthington	1 Bay Mare		45.00
" "	1 Bay? filly		20.00
" "	1 Sorrel Colt		15.00
" " "	1 Bay do		23.00
James Nickle	1 Gray Colt		10.87½
James England	1 yoke small stears		9.00
Susanah Worthington	1 Mans saddle		3.50
	1 Side Do		2.00
	3 Calves	1.50	1.50
	1 Addz Sickle 2 Angers & saw		4.25
Enos W Scarbrough	(1) pair steelyards		1.68¼
James England	1 Bed stead & furniture		20.75
Susanah Worthington	1 Lot pales Tins & C		.75
James Nickle	400 lbs flour	10.04	
	4 Do	10.04	20.08
Arthur Kirkpatrick	Lbs flour		10.04
David McKinis	400 lbs flour		10.04
Arthur Kirkpatrick	Remainder if any		2.50½
Susanah Worthington	50 bushels corn		9.00
	Do $9. Do $7.50 $ Do 8.50		25.00
Jesse Worthington	50 bushel of corn	11.50	11.50
	Do		11.50
Susanah Worhtington	1 Wagon		31.62½
1 pair of wagon Gears	& wagon & Bridle $2.		
	Do Do Do 1.50		3.50
	6 stacks fodder 12.		
	6 do Do 10.12½		22.12½
	1 pair saddle bags		.50
(Pg 288)			
Jess Worthington	1 Log chain Chain wedge and ax		3.50
John England	1 Barrel whiskey 33 Gal		14.35½
Abraham Justice	1 Barrel whiskey 35 Do		17.50
William Freman	1 barrel Do 3 Do		13.60
Douglas Oliver Jr	1 Barrel 32 Gallons		14.88
	Do 34 Do	$15.14¢	
	1 Do	15.51	
	12 gallons Do	5.82	36.47
Jess Worthington	1 Still & 8 tubs		26.50
	1 Hammer		.25
		Amount	$747.82½

An Inventory of the real Estate of Joseph Worthington deceased
viz.

four negroes Hannah age	32 years old	
Robert Nelson	age 12 years	
George Williams	" 9 years old	
Caroline "	" 14 years old	
Reuben Russell Note for $10.75 Due 27th Oct		18.41
Squire Justice Note "	33.10 Due 27th Oct 1841	
William Freeman Note "	15.84 Due 27th Oct 1841	

John Frazier Note   Note$ $.50 due 27th Oct 1841
Douglas Oliver   Note $1.86½ due 27th Oct 1841
James England   Note 34.88¼ due 27th Oct 1841
John England   Note 14.35½ due 27th Oct 1841
Joseph Harden   Note 62.   due 27th Oct 1841
Susanah Worthington   Note 340.37½ due Do   Do
Simon Jackson   Note 13.   Do   Do
Aurther Kirkpatrick   Note 10.04 Do   Do
David McAmis   Note 10.02 Do   Do
James Ross   Note 20.50¢ doubful Due oct 18th 1839
Interest on a Note $27.56½ due 27th Nov 1839
Interest in 465 Gallons whiskey
F H Robertson Note $10.60
Doubful Due Jan 8th 1840
(Pg 289)
A Judgment against James Tiller 15th August 1840 $17.00

                              Jess Worthington
                                 Administrator

State of Tennessee   )   To the Worshipful County Court
Anderson County   )   November Sessions 1840

I John Gammon Guardian of Louisa I Butler Minor Heir of Thomas
Butler dec.d Do report to your worship an account current of the
Profits and disbursements of the Estate of said Minor for the year
1840 up to the 18th of August 1840
To Amount due on Settlement 18th August 1840 is   902
To Interest due on that Some for 12 Months   34.12

                                               Cr   956.12
By Amount of Disbursements on last Settlement $ 16.75
 " Amt paid for Bonnett for said Minor   2.50
 " Amt ¼ yd Bunch Lawn   .12½
        (for 2½ Do Ribben   .93½
         for 1 Tuck Comb   12½
         1 pair stockings   50
         Amt paid for Lady Saddle & Blakit   22.50
         1 pair of Prunelle Shoes   1.00
         Amt of my Services for 1 Year Last Paid   5.00
         P Clerk for making and recording this   1.50

                                                       $ 48.95¾
                                                        907.16½

                  Balance due said Ward $907.16½
This Settlement made by me and now offered to m the Court for
Confirmation or rejection this 2nd day of Nov 1840
                              William Cross Clk
This Settlement is wrong $ 16.77¢
against the ward the 16.77cts Ough not be Credited to be
righten next time
(Pg 290)
A Settlement with Enoch Foster Guardian of the Miner Heirs of Richard
Luallen deceased mad on the 9th day of Oct 1840 (to wit)

State of Tennessee   )   To the Worshipful County Court of
Anderson County   )   December Term for 1840

I Enoch Foster Guardian of the Minor Heirs of Richard Luallen
dec.d do here by report to your worship an Account Current of the
Profits and disbursments for the Estate of said Minors for the year
ending the 9th day of October 1840 (to wit)
Whole Amount with which I am Chargable with Interest Including
is___ $1454.39½

To Cash received for rent of the Martin & Sworn Place for 1839-   33.00

                           Whole Amount   1487.39½

Credit by Amt of Disbursements
By this Amount paid Alexander G Luallen as per receipt   207.33½
By Amt paid for 4 days attendance at Chancery Court
at Knoxville at $1.50 per day $ 6.00
By 4 days attendance to the Business of said Estate @ 1.00 per
                                      day $ 4.00
By this Amt paid Clerk for the Exhibit of said Estate   37½
By Amt paid Clerk for making this Settlement   1.50
              Amt of Disbursements   219.21
              Summary Amt to me Charged Br $1487.39½
              Amt of Disbursements $ 219.21
              Ballance
                         1268.18½   1268.18½

In the hands of the Guardian this 9th day of October
1840 Sworn to and Subscribed before me this by Enoch
Foster Guardian of the Minor Heirs of Ric.d Luallen Dec.d
I do Certify that the above settlement was made by me with
Enoch Foster Guardian of the Minor Heirs of Rich.d Luallen dec.d
and is now offered to the Court for this Confirmation or rejection
                                       Wm Cross Clerk

                     Recorded 11th Dec 1840
(291 Pg)
An Inventory Account of sale made of the Personaly property of
the Estate of David Wyatt deceased at the residence of Martin
Turpins in Anderson County after having Advertised according
to Law

Isaac Ric.d	1 Plough Clivis & Swingle tree	1.25
Maryb Pitmen	1 Wash Pot	.25
W G Kincaid	1 pair Hames & Collar	.35½
Kiseah Wyatt	1 Umbrella	12½
Lydia Dunevan	1 Patent ax	1.75
John Patterson	1 hand ax	12½
Mastin Turpin	1 hand Saw	1.12½
" "	1 Auguor	.19
Wm Turpin	1 Iron wedge	.63
Mary Pitman	1 Umbrilla	.25
Iraah Rice	1 Key Saw	.12½
Iraah Rice	1 Cooper crow	.12½
David Turpin	1 Drawing knife	.35½
Kiseah Wyatt	1 Pot Skillet & Lid	.50
" "	1 Baker	.12½
Martin Turpin	1 Man Saddle	1.25
Kiseah Wyatt	1 Bed & furniture	1.50
" "	Plates & Dishes	.25
" "	2 Piggins	.12½

Lydia Danavan	1 Hoe	.15
Kisiah Wyatt	1 Chain	.25
Irash Rice	1 Cotton Wheel	.13½
Wm Taylor	1 Sow & Pigs	2.06½
David Turpin	3 Sheep	2.50
Lydia Dunevan	2 Sheep	1.25
Kisiah Wyatt	1 Cow & Calf	5.00
Do Do	1 Sorrell Mare	5.01
		$ 24.77½

(Pg 292)

The foregoing is a full and Perfect Account of the sale of the
property or Estate of David Wyatt dec.d directed by Law to be sold

                                          Martin Turpin
                                          Administrator of
Recorded 11th Dec 1840   David Wyatt

A true Inventory of the Estate of John Gibbs deceased, so far the
Sale has been Made and of Note on hand at the time of his deceased.

Enoch Foster	1 Lot of Hoes at	1.75
Wm Jones	1 dish of Scrap Iron	.26
" "	1 Box of Iron	.40
Isaac Fox	2 double trees	.15
" "	1 Broad Ax	.80
Wm Jones	1 hand "	.25
Enoch Foster	2 Plough	.50
John Robison	1 Ax	1.75
Elijah Longmore	1 "	1.50
Pleasant Rogers	1 "	.81¼
Wm McAdoo	2 Axes	.31¼
Wm H Gibbs	1 frow	.62½
Tho.t Landrum	1 Lot of iron	.32
Isaac Fox	Do Do	.37½
" "	1 Sythe Blade	.12½
Wm Jones	1 Cross Cut Saw	3.00
Henry Snodderly	1 Skillet	2.06¼
Tho Wallace	1 Oven & Lid	.12½
John Sharp	1 Sythe &Cradle	1.12½
James Diskes	1 Plow	.81¼
" "	" "	.87¼
Wm Foster	1 Large Do	1.62½
James Dikes	1 Pot full of Iron Scraps	.81¼
Simon Mandow	1 Cow	8.00
Obidiah Sharp	1 Cow	7.63
John McAdoo	1 Cow	10.25
Samuel Robins		5.50
Thomas Lamar	2 Steers	3.76
" "	" "	7.62½
James S Davis	1 Cow	6.25
Jos B Sharp	1 Horse	50.00
James Dikes	1 Horse	32.50
Elijah Longmire	1 Horse	40.00
Wm H Gibbs	1 Mare	45.00
(Pg 293)		
Wm H Gibbs	1 Colt	28.50

Levi Wallace	3 tubs	$1.68½
Nickolas Sharp	11 Wind Mill	15.20
Wm H Gibbs	3 tubs	50
A C Gibbs	1 Gun	10.00
Hezikiah Oaks	1 Yoke of steers	35.50
John McAdoo	3 Hides	2.50
A Carden	1 Cupboard	5.00
Henderone Sharp	1 Loom	2.87½
Solomonal Dmarcus	1 Bucket	.37½

Amt of Sale   464.81¼

One Note on Thomas Long for $35.00 Credit Credit 17.75 $17225
(Pg 294)

Wm G Gibbs	1 Lot of Smith tools	18.00
Levi Wallace	2 tubs	1.37½
John McAdoo	1 Table	.25
Wm H Gibbs	1 Bed stead	.50
Thos. Wallace	1 Co	2.25
A Carden	1 Do	2.30
Wm Reynolds	1 Little Wheel	2.06½
John McAdoo	1 Set weaven Harness	.68¾
Wm H Gibbs	1 Pick of Iron	.62½
Thomas Lundrum	1 Coopars adds	.75
" "	1 Lot of tools	1.00
James Hunter	1 Grind Stone	.80
Tho. Wallace	1 Do	.37½
Isaac Rutherfordl	1 Lot of Hogs	9.00
Wm H Gibbs	1 waggon	36.50
Isaac Rutherford	1 Lot of Hogs	3.62½
Wm Piles	1 Cart	5.35
Wm H. Gibbs	1 Tub	
" "	1 Lot of Hogs	6.50
" "	11 Do D o	12.00
" "	1 Do Do	21.00
" "	1 Do Do for 35 $	35.00
1 Do	on Abner Pose 113.20	113.20

Amt of Notes $165.45

(Division)

John Whistone	4 Slaves	$ 1416.00
John McAdoo	2 Slaves	850.00
Squire Williams	2 Slaves	50.00
Thomas Ingrum	2 Slaves	800.00
Ann E Gibbs	1 Slave	965.00
Wm Hibbs	2 Slaves	950.00

Amt Negroes
Amt Negroes $5561000

Aggregate
Amt of Sale $ 464.81¼
Amt of Notes   165.45
Amt of Negroes   5561.00

Total   6191.26¼

Recorded 12th Dec 1840

Wm H Gibbs)Adm &
Ann E Gibbs)Admtrix

(Pg 295)
Inventory of Property of John Lay Deceased Sold on the 1st day
December 1840

2 Ploughs	50¢	1 Do & Swingle tree 37½¢		$1.12½
1 Do	16	1 pr streachers & 3		
		swingle trees	1.00	1.25
35 lbs Iron	2.06½	1 Bunch of Iron	1.31¼	3.37½
2 Hoes 2 Do	31	1 Grubbing Hoe &		
		1 Hoe 2/3	2/3	1.00
1 Fifth Chain	3.06½	1 Oven & Lid	.56¼	3.62½
1 Oven & Lid	3/9	1 Do	4/6	1.37½
1 Do	.80	1 Anger	.50	
		1 Do & Sd	2/3	.87½
1 Do	.36¢	1 Do	.50	
		1 Do	.25¢	1.98½
1 Do	.40	1 Set blacksmith		
		tools	47.00	47.00
1 Beef Hide	2.25¢	2 Beef Hides	2 00	
		1 Do	1.62½	5.87½
1 pr Gears	1.25	4 Halter Chains	1.59	
		3 Pr chains	2.25	5.09
5 Blind Bridles	1.37½	1 Yoke oxenx	27.00	28.37½
1 waggon Line	.25¢	18 head Hogs	8.00	8.26
1 Spotted Cow	5.00	1 Bell Cow & bull	8.25	
		1 Muddy Heifer	3.00	16.50
1 Spotted Heifer	3.25	1 Crumbley Heifer	2.00	5.25
1 Brindle Cow	10.00	1 Brindle Steer	2.00	
		1 Heifer		14.00
1 Heifer	2.00	1 Horse Jim	27.00	
		1 Sorrell horse		
		(Buck)	45.00	71.00
1 Mule Jonny	44.50	Mule (Bill)	57.55	101.75
1 Mule	44.00	1 Mule Gry	41.25	
m		Sorrel Mule	5.	90.25
1 Shot Gun	8.50	100 Bs Corn	26.00	34.50
100 bs of corn	10.00	100 Do	13.00	23.00
100 Do	27.00	100 Do	29.25	
		100 Do	29.00	85.25
		100 Do	31.00	
		100 Do	30.50	
			30.00	91.50
100 Do		100 Do	30.50	60.75
100 Do	$ 30.25			

Amount   752.51½

(Pg 296)
Amount Brot forward   752.53½

50 Bs Corn	17.00	50 Do	$ 16.66½	33.66½
50 Do	17.00	50 Do	16.50	
		50 Do	15.25	48.75
50 Do	15.25	50 Do	16.00	
		50 Do	16.25	47.50
50 Do	15.00	50 Do	15.00	
		50 Do	14.62½	44.62½
50 Do	14.00	50 Do	15.00	29.00
45 Gallons	whiskey 42¾ ¢ pr Gal			19.23½

31 Do Do	332/3 per Gal				$10.66½
46 Do Do	32½ per Gal				14.95
1 Rest	1.37		1 Do	$1.25	
			1 Do	1.00	3.62½
1 Cutting Box & knife					1.00
1 Piece domestic	31 yds	20¼¢		6.27½	
1 Do Do	31 "	20¢		6.20	
1 Do Do	30 "	20½		6.12½	
1 Do Do	31 "	23½		7.27	
1 Do Do	30½ "	23¢		7.01	
1 Do Do	30 "	21½		6.45	
1 Do Do	31 "	20½		6.25½	
1 Do Do	30¼				
1 Do Do	30¾				
1 Do Do	31½				
1 Do Do	30				
	122 Yds 25¢			24.40	
				70.09½	70.09½
1 pr sock		26¢	1 do	3	
			1 do	.26	.82
1 piece domestic	28yds	18½¢			5.18
1 " "	28 yds	18½¢			
9 yds red flannel		40¢			3.60
20½ yds Bed Ticking		30½¢			6.30
16 Do Do Do		26½¢			4.24
1 Looking glass		26	1 do	.21	
			1 do	.21	
			1 do	.25	1.00
1 Do		25¢	1 do	.50	.75
23 yds Domestic		17¢			3.91
(Pg 297)					
46 yds Apron Check		12½¢			5.75
11¾ Marino		85¢			10.02
6 Tuck Combs		16¢	6 do	17¢	
			5 do	20¢	2.98
16 Hks Silk		6¼	2 Gross buttons	28½	1.28½
4 Spools thd.		5¢	4 paper pins	14¢	.76
4 Fine Combs		21¼¢	1 Bunch Thd	30	1.15
25 yds domestic		20¢	18 yds apron checks	18	8.94
1 Shaving Box		6¼	1 Do	10	
1 Do		7¢	1 Do	3¢	
			1 Do	3	.29¼
1 Do		6¼	4 Tuck Combs	18¾	
			7 Do	30	2.91¼
4 Tuck Combs			1 doz Do	18¾	3.05
8 Do		20¼¢	5 spool thd	5¢	
1 pr Spenders		11¢	1 Do	12½	2.10½
1 pr Suspenders		12½	1 Do	12½	
			1 dress	3 f	.75
4 Check H N T R		26½	1 Shovel	71½	
			4 Hn Fs	17¢	2.45½
4 Do 17 28 yds Calico		21¢			6.56
20 yds Calico		29¢	14 Do	27½	
			18 Do	26¢	12.77
11 Do		29¢	24 Do	27¢	
			11½ Do	17½¢	11.68

14 Do	26	13½ Do	27½		13.78
		11½ Do	17½		
1 Bucket		1 Bushel			
		Turkey red	4 25		5.00
22 Yds Domestic	26½	31 Do	25		13.62
9 Yds Ticking	26¾				2.38½
1 pen of Shucks			1.00		
1 pr Steelyards			1.00		2.42
6 papers needles			2.42		1.07
6 papers Nedles			.12½		
		4 Do	1.07		
1 Lot of Shucks	25	1 Lot of			
		Nubins	50	.56	.75
1 Bucket	54½	1 pen of			
		Shucks	.77		
		Nubins	.50	1.83	1.83
1 Bunch Nubins	25	1 pen of			
		shucksn	1.12½		1.37½
			1.37½		
1 pen Shux			1.18¼		
16 Geese			.25		
2 Ducks			..12½		1.56¼
1 Bund. fodder	20		1.00		
Do Do	20		1.00		
Do	20				.80
100 Do			.80		
100 Do			.91		
100 Do			.94		
100 Do			1.00		3.65
100 Do			.61		
100 Do			.61		
100 Do			.25		2.25
100 Do	6/ -	100 Do 6½			
		100 Do 6/			
100 Do	6/-	100 Do 93			4.93
100 Do	90	12½ Gals whiskey	46½		5.81¼
1 Saddle					5.00
					1240.64

(Pg 298)
Amount Brot forward $1240.64
We certify that above is all the personal Property Sold by
us that has come to our hands Except 8 Negroes Joseph, Rox
Sen. Rox Junr, Rachel, Charity, Seal, Elisha & James & Probdly
soem Come & Come Notes Accounts
                                Executors (Lewis Miller
                                          (George Miller

Inventory an Account of Sale of the Estate of Wm Brumet deceased
Sold on the 1st day of September 1840

1 Clock	$100	(1 Lot edge tools	3.50
1 Bible	3.00	(1 Sythe & Cradle	.25
farming tools	..50	(1 pr Gears	.25
2 flat irons	.75	(1 pr Streachers	.62½
		(	

1 Bar Shear Plough	1 25	1 Log Chain	.75
1 Mill Spindle	1.12½	1 Cross Cut Saw	6.25
1 Rifle Gun	5.06¼	1 Man Saddle	7.18¾
1 pair Saddle Bag	3.37½	1 foot adds	2.00
1 pr dog Irons	1.06¼	1 St Black Smith tools	19.13
1 Yoke Steers	22.00	1 Lot of Hogs	14.00
1 Flax Break& Hadget	.12½	1 Ax	.25
1 Ax	.25	1 Waggon	90.00
1 Horse	67.00	1 Bee Stand	.87½
1 Do	1.25	1 Grind Stone	.12½
1 Saddle	.06¼	1 Hammer	.06¼
1 Gimblet	.12½	1 Hog	1.56

Alexander Turner
Betty Brummett
Executors of
Wm Brummett
Deceased

Total Amt $204.75¼

(299)
Inventory and Amt of Sale the Property of John Rhea Deceased
Sold on the 23rd day of June 1840

1 Sythe & Cradle	1.62½	1 Do	.29
4 Hoes	1.15	1 hand saw	.06¼
2 Axes 1 Hoe	.50	1 Griter	.50
1 pr steelyards	1.00	1 Cog	.50
2 Bull tongue	1.00	1 Barrel	.18
1 frow	.40	1 Still tub	.63
1 Log Chain	.81½	Cittle	3.00
2 Mat axes	1.78	1 Still Tub	.70
1 Shovel Plow		2 Shoats	1.00
16 Singletrees		1 Do	.25
1 Chain	1.87½	1 half Bushel	.18¾
1 Sythe	.40	1 Tub	.06¼
1 Sythe	.18¾	1 riddle	.11
1 pr Sheep Shears	.85	1 Patent Plow	4.00
1 Grind Stone	.56¼	1 Shovel "	2.00
1 Cutting Knife	.25	1 pr Gears	.96
1 Hand Ax	1.00	1 Do	.06¼
2 drawing knives	.87½	1 Barrel	.38
1 Coopers addx	.25	1 Cutting Box	.46
3 Augers	.06¼	1 Bed & furniture	3.50
		1 Do	1.00
1 Chair	.12½	1 Cupboard	.62½
1 Table	.32½	1 Coffee Mill	.52½
1 Trunk	.12½	2 Pots	.75
1 Table	.05	1 Oven & Lid	.56¼
1 Iron	.12½	1 Table	.12½
1 cupboard & furniture	5.00	1 Shovel & tongues	1.37½
1 Clock	5.07½	1 basket	.26
1 Stale	.12½	(Pg-200)	
4 Chissels & looking		1 Pot & C	$ 1.18
glass	.87½	1 tub & trap	.62½
1 Loom	5.00	2 tubs	.25

2 reap hooks	.06¼	1 Spinning wheel	.25
1 Yoke Oxens	31.00	1 Cart	4.00
1 Do	13.00	1 Sorrel Mare	28.25
1 Cow & Calf	9.32½	1 Sorrel filly	40.26
1 Do	9.18¾	1 Colt	14.62½
1 Heifer	8.75	5 Hogs	6.00

The foregoing is a true return of the sale of the property of the
Estate of John Rhea   Dec.d
(Pg 300)   James Moore Administrator

An Additional Inventory of the Estate Efeects belonging to the
Estate of Jacob Butler Deceased returned to the County Court of
Anderson County at its February term for 1841 Season price of
News (to wit)

Dr Wm Kees	1 Mare	$7.00
Cas Peck	1 Mare Doublefeet	10.00
Pinkey Peck	1 More Doublefeet	6.00
Elia Fulks	1 Mare verry doublefeet	8.00
William Reuitt	To 30 days Hauling with waggon ¢ 2.00 per day	60.00
Nancy Ann Butler	1 Mare	8.00
Dr Moss	1 Mare Doublefeet	4.00
Christran ?	1 Mare " Do	4.00
Wm M Butler	doubt Verry	5.00
(Pg 301)		119.50

1841

Hugh Hallon	1 Mare	2.50
Willis Morris	2 Mares	3.00
Barry Dutson	$ 1 Verry Doubt	1.25
Isaac Freilds	Black Smith Tools	12.12½
Wm R Butler	Mare	5.
Elias Butler &		
Harry Butler	1 Note	8.13
Eli Harness	to Smith Work	.75
Carl Wallis	1 Mare	24.00
J M Butler	1 Negro Boy	801.00
Do Do	1 Negro woman & Child	323.00
		1284.59½

J M Butler
Caleb Butler Executors of
Jacob Butler Dec.d

March 1841
(X An additional Inventory of the Estate of John Lay Dec.d Sold
on the 12th day of June 1841 (To wit)

1 Negro Named Joseph sold to Jacob Lay	370.
1 Do Woman Rose Do Do Do	105.
1 Do Woman Rose sold to Alfred Sharp	485.
1 Do Named Rachel sold to Isaac Stuksberry	662.50
1 Do boy Elisha sold to Wm Lay Jr	581.
1 Do girl Charity sold to Nancy Lay	370.
1 Do Boy James sold to Henry Lay	353.75
1 Do Girl Seal Sold to Lewis Loy	361
	$ 3,288.25

Lewis Miller
George Miller Executors
(Pg 302)
A Credit to the Executors of John Loy Deceased Returned to the
County Court of Anderson at the March Term 1841   Viz

Jemmeah ? Romins	Bot 100 Bush 31 cts pr B	$31.00
James Baker	lacked 60 Bot 30 cts ps B	18.00
Allen McCoy	Bot 50 at 30½ cts got None	15.25
Lewis Miller	Bot 50 at 28¢ got None	14.00
		$ 78.25

March 1 1841

Lewis Miller)
George Miller) Executers

Additional Inventery of the Property Belonging to the Estate of
John Gibb dec.d sold on the 5th and the 27th of Feby. 1841 (to wit)

A E Gibbs	1 Lot of Hogs	$ 10.00
William Sharp	1 Keg	.18¾
Henry Tayler	2 Gimblets	.15
A Carden	1 Iron wedge	.18¾
Hiram Kirk	1 Do	.26
Wm H. Gibbs	1 Saddle	2.50
A E Gibbs	1 Drawing Knife	.37
Wm H Gibbs	1 pr Saddle bags	1 .18¾
Henry Tayler	1 Jointing Plan	.25
A E Gibbs	1 Still trap	1.00
A E Gibbs	1 pr Steel Yards	1.00
Silas Gentry	2 reap hooks	12½
James H Tayler	1 Ax	1.91
A E Gibbs	1 Cow	6.00
Wm H Gibbs	2 Books	.37½
A Carden	2 Books	.50
James H Tayler	1 Log Chain	2.25
A Carden	1 Syth	.25
		$ 28.12

(Pg 303)

Amt Brot Over		$ 28.12
Henderson Sharp	2 Augers	.15
James Hunter	25 Bu Corn	11.50
A Carden	25 Do	11.62½
A Carden	24 Do	11.04
A E Gibbs	1 Lot of Nubbins	6.90
Wm H Gibbs	1 Harrow	1.00
A E Gibbs	1 Lot of sheep	2.00
George Davis	1 Saw Blade	.12½
Robert Stooksbury	1 Piece of Leather	.91
Abraham Keith	1 Do	1.90
Wm York	1 Do	1.14
Wm Childres	1 Do	3.38
Wm Gwins	1 Do	1.46
John Sharp	1 Do	3.35
A E & Wm H Gibbs	1 Do	4.90
George Davis	1 Do	5.46

Wm H Gibbs	1 skin Do	.60

$94,56\frac{1}{2}$

Wm H Gibbs) Adm &
Ann E Gibbs) Admtrix
Inventory of the Estate Martin Carroll dec.d returned to the
March Court 1841 (To wit)

1 Yarling 1 Sow	4 pigs 1 plow & Hoe	1 Swingletree
1 Clevis	1 dresser 1 table	1 bed & bed stead
1 Oven 1 churn	2 water vessels	1 washing tub
1 Big Wheel	1 pr fire dogs	4 Chairs
1 rake doubletree		
debts on date	Allen McCoy	4.00
	Allen	$2.18\frac{1}{2}$

Oct. 11-18 36

(Pg 304)
1 Note on William Bowman for 7 Pounds Sugar bearing date 11 May
1837

1 Ack on Amos Wilson bearing date 1836				3.911/3
George Lay Dr to Act Not dated	3 Gals Whiskey			3.00
Wm Lay	Dr To 25 Cts			.25
A L Carden	Dr To 1 Gal & three Qts on date			
M Keys	2 Gal			
Jacob Vandergriff		1 Qt		
Enich Hukey	1 qt	Wm Henly	1 qt	
G A Hardin	75	Loftin Dykes Drforl gal		
Hardin & Carroll 1½ Whiskey			whiskey	1.00
				$ 1.50
John Wilson to 1 qt 25¢		George Lay	1 qt 25¢	.25
D Hardin ½ Gal	50cts	J Deis	1 qt 25¢	
1 Order on Lewis Adkins for $.00			Cr	$100
on the same July 25th 1841				
Lewis Harrill	Dr to Act			$ 200
T D Hardin	Dr 1 Act			1.00
A Ranse	1 Act	$.43\frac{3}{4}$		$43\frac{3}{4}$
Wm Graham	1 Act	.25		.25
A Pate		$1.62\frac{1}{2}$		$1.62\frac{1}{2}$
Lewisn Wakins		1.25	M Keys	5.00
A L Cardin		$11.43\frac{1}{2}$		

Wm Harbison   Adm-

Amount of Sale of the Property Belonging to the Estate of Joseph
Overton Deceased sold on the 29th day of Sept 1840
(To wit)

Kesiah Overton	1 plough $ .50	Sarah Davis-Gears	.90
Wm York	1 Do .32	Jas Overton 12	
Enoch Foster Jun	1 Ax $.12\frac{1}{2}$	Hogshead	.40
Enoch Foster	1 frow $.20\frac{1}{2}$	Thos J Lamar 1	
Alfred Overton	1 Hand Saw 1.72	kettle	3.27
Kesiah Overton	1 pr Gears .26	Jas Overton 1	
		Hogshead	.32

8.02

(Pg 305)

Amt Brot forward					$ 8.02
John Overton	1 drawing knife	.62½	James Moore	4 hogs 4.	
Ann Overton	1 Pot	1.76	Wm Brooks 3 Hogs		2.12½
Wm Brown	1 Mattock	.80	John York 4 Hogs		2.06¼
John Overton	1 Sythe &cradle	2.00	James Moore 1		
John Overton	4 Plains& Gents	.37½?	Buttress		.06¼
Wm York	1 Hoe	.22	John York 1 iron w		.26
Wm Brown	1 Burrough	6.25	Ezackeriah Hall 1		
John Overtton	1 Clock	4.00	Muley Heifer		8.00
Wm Brown	1 Bee Gum	2.75	Do 1 Heifer		7.00
Enoch Foster	1 Bee Gum	2.54	Do 1 Heifer		5.07
Enoch Foster	1 Bee Gum	2.35	James Kirk 5 sheep		5.12½
Wm Brown	1 Bee Gum	2.39	Stephen H Johnson		
Thos. J Lamar	Roane Mare	30.50	5 sheep		3.00
Moses Overton	1 Lot Hogs	3.06¼	James Overton 3		
Kisiah Overton	5 Choice Hogs	14.06¼	sheep		2.00
Wm Brown	4 Hogs	9.00	John York 1 Beef		
Thomas J Lamar	1 Anvil	1.00	Heifer		5.56½
John York	1 venigar barrel	.37½			
Kesiah Overton	2 Acres Land	5.00			
					$ 142.15

(Pg 306)

An Inventory & Amt of Sale of the Estate of Morton Carroll
deceased   22nd March 1841

Joseph Carroll	1(Yarling	.50	Sarah Carroll	1 bed stead	.12½
" "	11 Sow & Pigs	.50	" "	1 Oven	.06¼
" "	1 Plough & Hoe	.12½	" "	2 water vessels	12½
Wm H Harbin	11 swingletree & Clevis	.25	" "	1 churn	12½
Jos P Eaton	1 set of rake teeth	.12½	" "	1 washing tub	06¼
			" "	1 big wheel	06¼
Sarah Carroll	1 Dresser	.12½	" "	1 pr fire dogs	12½
" "	1 Table	.06¼	" "	1 tea Pot	
			" "	1 pr Pot Hooks	
			" "	6 ten cups	
				4 chairs	12½

13th April

$ 2.50

Wm H Harbison
                    Adm

Additional Inventory an Amount of Sale of the property ef the
Estate ef John Gibbs deceased April 5th 1841 (To wit)

1 Lot of castings (Rhine) of Ky	47.50
1 Horse	25.00
	72.50

rec.d 13th April 1841
A E Gibbs
Wm H Gibbs   Adm

(Pg 307)

A Settlement with Thomas Cole adm   of the Estate Hugh Murphy
dec.d

State of Tennessee)   To the Worshipful County Court of
Anderson County   )   Anderson County   April term 1841

****

I Thomas Cole Administrator of the Estate of Hugh Murphy deceased
present to your worship a Settlement Made with the Clerk of said
Court (to wit)

Dr To Amt of sale sold on the 20th of November 1838	$102.50½
Cr By Voucher No 1 Widow Murphy Receipt for her Years Support	63.41 2/2
By Services rendered and Money Expended by the Administrator No 2	
	37.40¼
By Voucher No 3 Shff McKamey receipt for town for the Year 1838	.87⅔
By Voucher No 4 Shff McKamey receipt for Tax for the year 1839	.37½
By Voucher No 5 This Sum per David Hall as pr Receipt	1.00
By Voucher No 6 This sum Pd Clerk Wm Cross as per receipt	1.50

Amt of Dibit	102.50½
Amt of Credit	106.82¼
Amt in favor at the	
	4.32

Thomas Cole Adm

(Pg 308)
A Settlement Made with The Ingram   and John Wilson Executors of
David Keisling deceased

State of Tennessee	)	To the Worshipful County Court
Anderson County	)	Feby Sessions January 30th 1841

A Settlement Made with John Wilson and Thomas Ingrum Executors of
the last Will and Testament of David Keisling dec.d (To wit)

Dr To this Amt pr Inventory	345.86
To Interest Rec.d on that Amt	5.19
Do To this amt for Note of hand Executors to David Keisling in his life time of Different dates with Interest on the sum	178.80
Dr To Second Inventory returned	4.50
Whole Amount with which said Executors is Chargable with------ --	530.35

By the following Voucher to Wit (N 1 To 13)

By this Amt pd David Hall Jr as pr receipt	1.50
By this amt Pd Francis Keisling as per receipt	50.00
By this Amt pd Parnell Ingrum as pr receipt & proven Act----------	3.75
By this Amt paid James Jackson as pr proven Act	2.13
By this Amt Pd Thomas Norman as pr receipt	.37½

(Pg 309)

By this Amt Pd Samuel M Chapman as pr receipt ------------------2.00	
By this Amt Pd David Hall Jr as pr redeipt ------------------4.29½	
By this Amt Pd S Cooper Jr. as pr receipt-------------------------4.25	
By this amt Pd J Childress as pr receipt----------------------------1.00	
By this Amt Pd Micijah Portwood as pr receipt-------------------- .75	
By this Amt Pd Recd. Oliver as pr receipt----------------------------2.55	
By this Amt Pd Eli Norman as pr receipt---------------------------- 9.75	
By this Amt Pd Samuel Galbreath as pr proven Act--------------- 6.00	
By this Amt Pd John Webb as per receipt--------------------------16.17	
By th s Amt Pd John C Alvison as per receipt------------------- 6.42	
By this Amt Pd M M Goins as pr proven Act-------------------- 11.58	
By this Pd Willie Young as pr receipt------------------------------ 14.00	
By this Amt Pd Daniel Yarnell as per receipt-------------------- 2.59	
By this Amt Pd Robt McKamey as pr receipt--------------------- 10.87½	
By this Amt Pd Richd Hall as pr receipt----------------------------- 59.49	

By this   Amt Pad J & H Butler as per dreceipt   30.00
(Pg 310)
By Amt Pd J Jarnagin & C as per receipt   10.92
By Amt Pd Thomas Wilson as per Note & receipt   43.26
By Amt Paid Clerk Cross for Letters & Bonds   1.50
By Amt Pd Richd. Oliver as pr receipt   7.34
By Amt Pd Whitson & McKamey as pr receipt   11.17½
By Amt Pd John Wilson as per proven Act   3.12½
By Amt Pd Elijah Carroll as pr proven Act   4.00
By Amt Pd A Gentry as per receipt   8.66 2/3
By Amt Pd Clerk Cross as recording Inventory   .75
By Amt Pd Clerk Cross for recording Inventory and Amt of Sale   1.50
By this Amt allowed the sd Executors of Said Estate   23.00

                                                                3591.21

                                                                 530.35

                              Whole Amt of Cr   359.21
                              Ballance   171.14
                              John Wilson
                               Thomas Jarnagin
                                 Executors

(Pg 311)
State of Tennessee)   To the Worshipful County Court
Anderson County   )   May Turm

A Settlement made with Susannah Moore Administratrix
Joseph C Moore Administrator of the Estate of James Moore deceased
(To wit)
Dr To this Amount which came into our hands as Administrator and
administratrix of Said Estate $4541.69¼
Cr By this following Voucher To wit
By Voucher No 1   481.75
By Voucher No 2   406.25
By Voucher No 3   300.00
By Voucher No 4   518.74
By Voucher No 5   300.00
By Voucher No 6   2.00
By Voucher No 7   12.12
By Voucher No 8   131.68
By Voucher No 9   6.67
By Voucher No 10   4.17
By Voucher No 11   6.46¾
By Voucher No 12   21.00
By Voucher No 13   34.73
By Voucher No 14   5.41
By Voucher No 15   5.88
By Voucher No 16   142.00
By Voucher No 17   23.00
By Voucher No 18   520.00
By Voucher No 19   123.21
By Voucher No 20   17.50
By Voucher No 21   61.00
By Voucher No 22   452.75

(Pg 312)
By Voucher No 23 Lewis & Mary Expended for   Od Estate $101.50

Amt of Cr	3,678.98¼
Compenison	
Amt of debit	4,541.69¼
Amt of Credit	3,678.98¼
Ballance	$$62862.71

in the hands of the adm- & C
Adm-) Joseph C Moore
Admtris) Susannah Moore

John McAdoo Guardian
Report of the amt. Put into my hands as Guardian for Martha Jane
Thompson Minor Heir of James Thompson Dec.d Nov 11th 1836 Viz.
One Note of hand on Spencer Keith & Rich.d Oliver , Executed the 31st
Oct 1838 Seven days after date for one on Richard Oliver &   200.99¼
Spencer Keith Executed 31st Oct 1838 one day after date for   161.19¾
Two Notes f hand on George Winton one for   121.54¼
the other for $54.75 $128.54½ both executed
the 20th Oct 1838 three days after   54.75 due
and One do on John Chiles Executed the 20th Oct 1838 three
days after due for   51.97½
John McAdoo Guardian
597.46

(Pg 313)

Additional Report John McAdoo Guardian & C To wit
State of Tennessee)   At the worshipful County Court
Anderson County   )   May Term 1840

I John McAdoo Guardian of Martha Jane Thompson Minor Orphan of
James Thompson Dec.d do hereby report to your worship an addition
Account fo the Estate of said Minor which has come into my hands
Since My last report to wit. a Note of hand on John Nail and
Thompson Gallaher for $ 152.13 cts
Executed 17th day of Sept
1839 due one day after date
John McAdoo
Guardian & C

Settlement with John McAdoo Guard
State of Tennessee)   To the worshipful County Court
Anderson County   )   August Term for 1841

I John McAdoo Guardian of Martha Jane Thompson Minor heir of James
Thompson dec.d do hereby report to your worship an Account Current
of the Profits and disbursements of the Estate of said Minor for the
year ending 11th November 1840
Dr John McAdoo Guard & C
To one Note on Spencer Keith and Richard Oliver   200 99¼
Interst on said Note   12.05¾
To one note on Richd. Oliver & Spencer Keith   161.19¾

Interest on said Note	9.67
To one Note on Geo Winton	128.54½
Interest	7.71

(Pg 314)

To one note on George Winton	$54.75
Interest	3.28½
To one note on John Chiles	51.97½
Interest	3.11¼
To one Note on John Nail and Thomas Gallaher	152.13
Interest	4.56
	$ 789.99

Cr By this Amt paid Clerk for taking Bond	50
By this sum paid for report	75
By this Sum paid for the Exhibit	37½
By this Sum paid for this Settlement	1.50
By this Amt for my Services for the Year 1840	5.00
Amt of Disbursements	8.12½

The Estate	789.99
Amt of Disbursements	8.12½
Amt due said ward	$781.86½

this 14th day of July1841
John McAdoo   Guard

Wm B Glovers Will

State of Tennessee)   December Dec.d
Anderson County   )   16th 1839

Know all persons to whom these presents shall come Greeting do
hereby make my last Will Testament tho sick and low in health in
proper sences and Mine and Knowing that there is a time appointed
for all Men to die
1st
I will and bequeath my Soulá to God who give it
(Pg 315)
2nd
I do will and bequeath to any bloved wife Martha M Glover all my
Property Cash Notes and Negroes and all Effects of mine to have
enjoy at his pleasure till my youngest child Mary M Glover come
oß the age so that the Effects of my Estate and property shall be
Kept together for the Maintainance of my children and the to be
Equally divided with my wife Martha M and my son Daniel A Glover
and my daughter Elizabeth M Glover and my son Joseph L Glover and
my youngest Daughter Mary M Glover
3rd
I appoint my wife Martha M Glover my Executors to attend to all the
Business of my Estate and to sell any of the property she may think
proper for the Support of hiß and the children as signed sealed
advised in the presence of me this 16th December in the year of our
Lord one Thousand Eight hundred and thirty nine
Attest   John H Kingston
Grigry Rector)   Wm B Glover
McWinton   )   (Seal)

Settlement withn John Jarnagin Guard &
State of Tennessee)   To the Worshipful County Court
Anderson County   )   July Sessions 1841

I John Jarnagin Guardian of Lindly James, Lucy, & John Hill Minor
Heirs of Martin Hilln ded.d d: hereby report to your worship and
account Current of the Profot and disbursments of the Estate of said
Minor for the year
(Pg 316)
ending the first day of January 1841
John Jarnagin Guardian & C Dr. To said Minores & Green Miller and
wife To one Note on James Weaver due Dec.d 1840
Which not was charged to me on last Settlement for Rent of home &
farm for the year 1840 $ 60.00
By this Amt Pad Atto J H Crozier for attending to law Suit
Cross vs Hill Heirs   12.50
Amt Paid Tax on Land   1.85
for 1840
Paid James Weaver for Rails & Repaifs onPlace   3.00
(AmtExpended and Serving Rendered attending Suit st Knoxville
and other Services as Guardian   5.00
paid Clerk for Settlement with me as Guardian up to 1841 1.50
                                                  28.85   36.15

Leaving thid ballance to be equally distributed to said
ward and Green Miller & wife who is entittled an Equail Shair
being heirs at Law Each is entittled 1/5 th Out after above
Amount Covered over
To Amt Book for Weaver   36.15
By Amt paid Green Miller & wife Martha   their i/5th part pr
                                            receipt   7.23
By Amt paid Mornroe Slaughter & wife Lucy
then 1/5th part for Receipt   7.23
By Amt paid for James Hill Shooling and Mrs Channin
Rect   7.23
By Amt Pd for John Hills Shooling & Mrs. Channer pr Ak & Rect 6/52½
(Pg 317)
                              To Amt Brot Over   36.15
By Amt Charged to Guardian   Bal due John Hill   7.01½
By Amt Charged to Guardian for AMT DUE Lindly Hill   7.23
for his 1/5 part of the rent of 1840
                  John Jarnagin Guardian Guardian Do
To Amt due John Nail on Settlement up to January 1st 1841   70. ½
To Amt due Lindly for his 1/5th part Rent of 1840   7.23
To Amt due Lindly Hill on Settlement 1st January 1840   13.75
            Interest on 13.75   12 Mo   83
                                                          _____
                                                             21.80
this Amt due John & Lindly   21.80
Hill --------------------------   22.50½
July 13th 1840 Land sold by Clerk and Master of the Chancery
Court at Knoxville for $850.00 To pay and satisfy debt & Cret
against said Martin Hill deceased leaving nothing in my hands of
said Minors Except the above Amount
The Court having the title Cut of said Minor
                                     John Jarnagin
Settlement made with James Ross Administrator of John Luallen dec.d

(To wit)
State of Tennessee)   To the Worshipful County Court
Anderson County   )   September Term 1841

A Settlement Made be the   Clerk of the County Court of the County
(Pg 318)
aforesaid with James Ross administrator of the Estate of John Luallen
dec.d to wit   John Ross Dr
To Amount as Appears of record $936.91¼
To Amt Received of Enoch Foster for rent   5.50
                         Whole amt of Debit   942.41½
                              Credit
By Voucher No 1   8.75
By Voucher No 2   174.20
By Voucher No #   5.93½
By Voucher No 4   3.30
By Voucher No 5   1.00
By Voucher No 6   9.00
By Voucher No 7   15.00
By Voucher No 8   4.25
By Voucher No 9   1.00
By Voucher No 10   .45
By Voucher No 11   .37½
By Voucher No 12   2.50
By Voucher No 13   .25
By Voucher No 14   83.32
By Voucher No 15   100.00
By Voucher No 16   79.12
By Voucher No 18   57.00
By Voucher No 19   81.84
By Voucher No 20   13.00
By Voucher No 21   29.68
By Vo ucher No 22   33.98
By Voucher No 23   31.16
                                                                    56.00

By this Amt paid Clerk for Settlement
(Pg 319)   2.50
By this Sum paid Clerk for Exhibit   .37¼
By this Amount allowed Adm for his Services in attending to said
Estate   49.00

                                        Amt of Credit $842.88
Amt of Debit Brot forward   942.41½
Additional Dr for one
Note on Charles Luallen   31.28
Whole Amount of Debit   Additional Credit $842.88   973.69½
By Voucher No   30   117.46

                                              690.34   690.34
Ballance in the hands of the   adm   13.35½
Credit
By Voucher No 24   2.67
By Voucher No 25   2.67
By Voucher No 26   2.67
By Voucher No 27   2.67
By Voucher No 28   2.67

                                        $ 13.35 $13.35

James Ross Administrator

Last Will & Settlement of William Keeney
I William Keeney of the County of Anderson and State of Tennessee
being afficted in body but sound of Mind and Memory blessed be
God for the same do make this last will & Testament in Manner &
form as follows:
First   I will that so much of my property Such as my wife thinks
(Pg 320) she can best Exepose of be sold and the Expenses of my burial
and all mu just debts be paid as soon May become. I will that the
Share of land become to one in a Joint due to Brother Joseph Keeney
and my self an which we now live yet in the an divided condition between U) be purchased by my Brother Joseph Keeney if he choses to
Purchase and if he My Brother Joseph Keeney should not chose to do so
for the land to be divided as the law directs and my share to be sold
to the best advantage at publick or Private sale and the price thereof used by My wife Fanny Keeney, and for his benefit to Purchase a form f
farm for his comfort. that she may have the means of Raising his *
farm Children for his to have and to hold as hir Right and possision
forever
Third   I will all my Little Stock that shall be Remaining My house
hold and kitchen furniture with my farming utensils to my beloved wife
Fanny Keeney for his proper use and Benefit for his to have and to
hold for everf and I hereby appoint my Brother Joseph Keeney the
Executor of this My Last will and Testament this eight day of March
1841
Signed with my hand and sealed with my seal this day o and the date
Just above written in the Presents of us
                              William Webb
                              Aron Slover Jr
                              Aron Slover Sr.
                                      William Keeney
                                            (Seal)

(Pg 321)
An Additional Inventory of the Effects of the Estate of Jacob
Butler dec.d the following property to wit.   One pare of Mill
stones on the clear fork of Cumberland in Morgan or Fentriss
County. Not knowing which) stones has not been sold because
we have no Knowlidged privison thethefsale andeMartin Watson to
five dollars for the season of the   one more Lina th the Sir Charles
                         (Jacob M Butler)
                         Caleb Butler
                         Executors of Jacob Butler dec.d

State of Tennessee) An Inventory of Money Nots & C which have
Anderson County) come into our hands and to our knowlidged belonging
to the Estate of George Winton deceased

Cash & Solvents Debst		Insolvents Notes	
Cash on hand	$47.90	John Golston	30.00
John Daniel	46.88	John Gussat	2.57
Lewis Frost	2.65	John Trimble	2.10
Wm Farmers	4.80	Arione Frild	9.86
Tho Bailey	7.75	J M H Lamar	60.00
C Lawson	10.01	Sterland Hackey	6.10
D Toter	30.00	John Martin	4.00
Calvin M Read	33.00	Charles McCopmal	11.50
In additional to		M Milicon &	75.00
the above we have		Daisa Vandergriff	

found and sold two Heifers for 10.00

$190.99

Elisha Vandergriff		Jess Farmer	30.00
Harman *	10.00	Jees Farmer	27.23

(Pg 322)

R M Dunnington	23.76	(A J Cox)	37.46
John Balie	8.00	James M Tucker	3.40
Jesse Ayers	40.00	E Cornell	3.48
James Moore	8.89		

Respectfully Submitted this the 6th day of Sept 1841

                                       B Winton
                                       J Grant
                                          Adms

A Settlement made By Wm Cross Clerk of the Count Court of Anderson
County with Jacob M Butler and Caleb Butler Executors of the last
will & Testament of Jacob Butler dec.d Mad on the 30th day of October 1841 which Settlement was Made and receiving in the following
words and figures (to wit) The whole Amount with which the Executors
are Chargable with as appears of records in the Estate book
                                                            $2302.33½

The said Executors are Chargable with as appears
The Said Executors produced the following vouchers (to wit)

paid Note to Reubin Walker	318.00
Paid Note to Reubin Walker	53.00
paid Judgment cost to Robert McKamey Sheriff	192.41
paid a Judgment Cost to R Oliver Sheriff for the use of	78.33
John Jenning paid a Judgment to R Galaher debt sheriff	
for the use J A Mabry	60.76

(Pg 323)

Paid Cost in a Suit between Jo Butler against J Butler to Sheriff McKamey	$ 315.54
Cash paid A Kirkpatrick on Promos Oct	37.16
By Account reported Suit brough Judgment against the Plaintiff	5.00
By Proven Account J M Butler	25.00
By Cash paid Clerk for fees	1.50
By Cash paid a proven account 8	3.00
By Note Paid to J Gammon	6.72
By Note Paid to W R Butler His attendance as witness J Butler vs J Butler	17.67
Paid R Walker proven Account	22.50
Cash paid F H Robertson pr receipt	2.00
Paid Wm Butler on Note	11.00
Cash Paid McCwins proven Account	1.48
By Cash paid Clerk for fees	2.00
paid Note to J Gammon	44.80
Cash Paid E Cross an proven Act.	7.00
paid Note to R Haskins	174.98
paid Swan & Alexander Atts. for Services in Suit J Butler Vs. J Butler	15.00
Paid W Friday Const as pr receipt	78.02

****

Paid J. H. Briant pr receipt	1.75
paid J. Hagler pr. receipt	1.17
paid Clerk for fees	2.44
paid Clerk and Master as pr receipt	229.89
paid Note to J. R. Nelson Atty	15.00
paid proven Account to J. M. Butler	48.00
paid Note to T. Jones	31.56
paid Proven Account to Wm. C. Griffith	3.00
paid J. Nail Cash pr receipt	1.00
(Pg. 324) Paid Wm. C. Griffith Cash pr receipt	1.00
paid Note to G. W. Churchwell Atty	123.78
paid proven Account to W. Swan Atty.	10.00
paid Judgement to W. Swan assigned of Aron Hardin	208.55
Paid to W. Swan Atty	123.78
Paid J. Nicnol Pr receipt	2.00
Paid Edward Freilds pr receipt	2.00
Paid Clerk Cash for Fees	.50
Paid A. Kirkpatrick pr receipt	24.86
Paid Proven Account to F. Hudson	10.00
Paid M. C. Weniter Proven Act	9.00
Paid Note to Wm. R Butler	5.26
Paid D. L. Bradly pr receipt	21.00
Paid Note to Richard White	47.55
Paid Account to Jm. Frields	1.82
Paid Note Thomas Scott	11.56
Paid A. Gw. Portwood pr receipt	1.00
Paid Joseph Alldrege pr receipt	3.00
Paid S. Galbreath Note	5.58
Paid Joseph Hardin Account	37.60
Paid Note Stephen Bradley	3.00
Paid McKamey Sheriff Judgement and cost in a Suit) Freilds vs. J. Butler)	38.00
Paid C. Y. Oliver pr Note	20.10
Paid Wm. C. Griffith per receipt	5.94
Paid Edward Freilds pr receipt	1.00
Paid Wm. C. Griffith Depy Sheriff pr receipt	.75
Paid R. Clough Cash pr receipt	1.63
Paid James Nail pr receipt	.60
Attendance By Clerk 4 pr Cent on debit	92.31
By Cash pd Clerk for Settlement & Recording	2.50

(Pg. 325)

Whole Amount of Vouchers	$ 2747.14
Whole Amt of Debit	2302.33
	444.87

The following is a list of debts belonging to the Estate of Jacob
Butler Decd in the hands of the said Executors of the last will &
Testament of Jacob Butler deceased which they had reported as Insolvant
and for which they Clair a credit Viz

One Note on Solomon Lively Absd	10.06¼
One Note on Bewely Freels Abcended	3.00
One Note on Geo. Waller doubts	55.00
one Note on Ezra Russell in	2.06¼
One Note on Elish Pruhit Abs	3.00
One Note on Pinkey Peak Ins.	6.00
One Note on Elias Fulks Abs.	8.00
an Act is Willis S. Print for 30 days hauling at $2. pr.day ins	60.00
One Do on Jess. Hope Ins	5.00
One Do on Benj. Hutson	1.25
One Do on Elias Butler doubt	4.34
Do Do Do	8.31
One Do Wm. Pillmore	5.00
	160.84½

Recapitulution

Whole Amt of Vouchers brot up	$ 2747.14
Amt of Credit	160.84½
whole amt of Debit	2907.98½
	2302.33
Ballance due the Executors	605.55½

(Pg. 326)
Inventory of the Notes and Acts belonging to the Estate of John
Lay decd

To wit

One Note on Isaac Miller for due 17th day of May 1836	92.50
One Note on Lewis Loy for due 16th decd 1839	3.87½
One Note on Henry Loy for due 16th Decd. 1839	1.62½
One Note on John Heatherly	4.06
One Note on Jacob Loy	2.00
One Note on Anderson Pate due 25th decd 1840	100.00
One Note on Jacob Miller due 9th June 1840	3.12½
One Note on Anderson Pate $25 Cr 4$ – due 25th Decd 1839	21.00
One Note on Anderson Pate due 25th decd. 1842	100.00
One Note on Anderson Pate due 25th Decd 1842	75.00
one Judgement on Nathaiel Rderson	4.02
One Note on Robetson Raily	1.60
One on John Kitchen	4.28
One on Henry Snotterly	3.75
One on Joseph Stuksberry	1.25
One Act on James Norton	.25

One Act on Robert Stuksberry Jr	$ 13.75
One Do William Dennis	1.30
One Note on Amos Wilson for	3.86
One Act on John Loy	
Old Man Canady	7.62½
Judgement on Cussnell White	1.31
	$ 46.18 1/6

(Pg.327)

One do on John Daniels	.75
An Act on Wm Pile pd in feathers 2/3 lbs	2.45
One Note on Wm Lôy Sen	500.00
due 25th day of Decr. 1838	

bearing date 14th April 1833 and said Note as
Above I as an Executor of the Estate of Jno Loy
decd filed a Bill in Chancery Court April 1841
returned. he not being alb to pay it

One Judgement on Haywood Gibert for	1.20
One " Wm Graham	.66
One Act on H. L. Carden for	10.71
One Act on Isaac Stuksbery	1.12½
O due 30 Decr 1840	
One Note on Jacob Lôy for	26.62
Due 30 decr 1840	
One Note on Alfred Sharp for	10.80
due 30th Dec 1840	
One Note on Wm Loy Jr. for	15.15
due 30 Dec 1840	
One Note on Gro. Ley for	20.35
due 30th Decr. 1840	
One Note on Hannah Nancy & Ana Stuksbery	1.62½
and Act on Wm Ley	26.07
One Do Geo. Miller	7.35
One Do John Mitchell	
One Note on Bnt. Rutherford	2.50
Acts	
Calvin Briant	4.37½
Robert Gilbert	3.41
Wm Bennett	2.56
(Pg.328) Nathaniel Robertson	
one Act of J. P. Eaton	3.77
one Do Amos Wilson	18.75
	21.00
One Do Docia Miller	.38

Indement & Doutful	
One Judgement on Pleasant Miller	6.66
One Do Do Do	.87½
One Note on Jno Loy	2.37½
One Note on Saml. & Geo. Pithbore	500.00
One Note on Alexander Wright	3.27½
due 22 Sept 1838	
One Act on Lewis Wadkins	1.30
One Note on Tho. Kith	1.25
due 22 Aug 1840	

One Note on Bradly Jenkins & Young Bridges (Ins)
    due 22 Mar. 1826   6.00
One Note on G. W. Loy Sen   20.00
Act 3rd 1805 due year after date on Judgement Alen McCoy   .74
One   Do   Do   6.25
One Judgement Wm. Martial   1.66
One Act on J. W. McKuan   .33
One Act on Martin Cornell   2.66
One Note on Jesse Cornell   4.56
One Judgement on John Fox   2.35

                      Lewis Miller)
                                  Executors
                      Geo Miller   )

(Pg. 329)
Inventory Report of John Lineart Guardian of Carlis Luallen Minor
Heir of John Luallen decd Showing the Amt of Property which has Come
into his hands as Such to wit

One Note of hand on Subrith Rich and John Luallen due 15th
    day of August 1841   60.00
One   do   on Pleasant Slover & Elisha Adkins   11.93¾
One   Do   on John Severs & B. Vowel   14.06¼
One   "   on John White & J. Vandergriff   10.00
One   "   on Thomas Vowel   Jun Milican   3.50
one   "   on John Luallen & S. Rich   3.00
                                      102.50

Also 40 acres of land 10 acres Clearing and about Second Quality
all of which is Respectfully Submitted this 1st day of November 1841
                                John Lineart
                                  Guard.

A Settlement Made by the Clerk with Jacob M. Butler and Caleb Butler
Executors and Lawful representatives of Jacob Butler deceased who was
Adm of William decd which Settlement Re   to the Estate of Wm.
Butler decd. stated as follows to wit

Amt with which said Jacob Butler is Chargable as appears
        of record   201.88¾
By Cash to Douglas Oliver Jr.   3.33
By Cash to Wm Butler   3.33
By Cash to Kiziah Butler   3.84
By Cash to Nancy Nail   2.20
By Cash to Nancy Monger   20.10
(Pg.330)
By Cash Pd. Shff Gilbreath   2.25
By Cash Pd. J. Rector   6.67
By Cash Pd. F. H. Robertson   2.00
By Cash Pd. Nancy Ann Butler   2.20
C ash Pd. John W. Butler   2.20
Cash Pd. Wm Butler   20.00
By Cash Pd. Clerk Fees   .40
By Cash to Wm R. Butler   2.20
By Cash to John Gammon   2.20

****

By Cash Pd. J. Bailey	2.20
By Cash Pd R. Oliver	2.75
By " " Do	7.68
By " " Jacob Butler	9.50
By Jacob Butler Disterbution Show	20.20
By Cash Pd. Wilson R. rector	40.00
	155.25
Executors Charged for Services	15.00
	170.25
By Cash pd Clerk for Making Settlement	2.50
	172.75

whole Amt of Debts	$201.88¾	
whole amt of Credit	172.75	
Ballance in the hands of Executors	$ 29.13¾	

(Pg. 331)

an Account Current Current of Jane Farmer Guardian of the Minor heirs of Luke Farmer decd. from the 12 day of August 1840 up to the 23 day of Oct 1841 to wit

One Note on John Courtney Richd Oliver & A Kirkpatrick with interest	158.74¼
One do on Saml C. Young	22.80
One Do on Elra Russell & A. Gilbreath	69.15
One Note on John Hoskins W. A. Hoskins J. Galbreath & H. Hoskins	22.10
One Do on H. Farmer	50.00
One Do F. England & A. McKamey	56.75
One Note on Thos Davis J. Duncan, Moses Duncan H. Hoskins. & J. Siber	35.31
One Note on Squire Justice and A. Justice	3.00
One Note. J. Justice & J. Justice	52.81¼
One Note on Robison & J. Seiber	21.10½
whole Amt of debt	$ 491.77

Disbursements

This Amt pd Wm Cross for Grand Bond	.50
For Exhibit	.37½
For Making this Settlement	1.50
Whole amt of Disbursment	2.37½

Amt of Debit	$491.77	
Amt of Credit	2.37½	
Said ward	$489.39½	

Jane Farmer
Guard.

(Pg.332)   Settlement with Jno Linart

State Tennessee   )
Anderson County   )   To the Worshipful County Court of
                        December Sessions 1841.

I John Leniart Guardian of Charles Lewallen one of the heirs of John
Lewallen decd do report to your Worship an Account Current of the
property and disbursments of said Estate this 9th Nov 1841 is Chargable
as appears of record in the Estate book Viz

One Note of hand on Sabrith Pick and John Luallen due 5th Aug 1841	$ 60.00
One Note on Pleasent Slover & Elisha Adkins due 5th of Aug. 1841	11.93¾
One on John Severs and Banister Vowel due 5th August 1841	14.06¼
One on J. White & J. Vandegriff due 5th Aug 1841	10.05
One on John Vowel & John Milican due 5th Aug 1841	2.50
One Note on John Luallen & Sabrith Rich due 5th Aug 1841	3.00
whole Amt with which said	$ 102.50
Whole Amt of Cr.	7.62½
Ballance due the Heirs	94.87½

                      John Linart G.n.d.

(Pg.333)   Inventory of the Effects of David Wallace decd

An Inventory of the personal Estate of David Wallace decd is as
follows To wit
Thirty head of Hogs. two head of Horses. ten head of Cattle
one Yoke Oxen. one waggon two stills and tubs eight hundred
Bushels of Corn more or Less, thirteen head of Sheep One Cuting
Knife and Box three whiskey Barrels, one Cross Cut Saw, one frow,
one Iron wedge and one set of Blacksmith Tools One Cupboard. and one
Table and one Chest. one Clock one Beauro one Bed and Clothing
five pare beadstead one set fire dogs and two Kittle and two Pots
One Oven and lid. One skilllt and one broken. and one trunk. five
Chairs and one big Spinning wheel and one Flax wheel and one Hackle.
twlve Sheaf Oats and to stack hay. and two Mans saddle and two Sythes
& Cradles two Mowing sythes and One Black woman About Eighty years of
Age an upwards and Augers and Three Chisels and One pare of steal
yards and two Mattock and Ten axes and Flax Sets of yearning and one
set of warping spools and one lock chain and five shovel Plows
Three Bulltonges three barchear Plows three Singletrees and four
Clevices and fore bridles and Seven Salt Barrels and One Broad Ax and
One foot addge and two Irons Sques and five and two plank Boxes
One Note on Silas A. Gentry for Six dollar and fifty Cents due 25th
(Pg.334)   Day of December 1841 One Note on James Wallace Jr for
two hundred dollars due 5th day of december 1841. One Note on James
Wallace Jr. due the 25th day of december 1842 One Note on J.F.Euton
and Wm G. Euston for thirteen dollars and fifty eight Cents due 17th
March 1841 one Note on Allen McCoy and Andrew Tate for Seventy Seven
dollars & thirty five Cents due the 25th of Dec 1841 Doubtful
One Note on Levi Burriss for four dollars due Nov 7th 1841

One receipt on James Davis for an Act the 2nd day of Oct 1841
one receipt on James Davis for fifty Cents received the 1st day of
Oct 1841   one Note on James Wallace Jr for Seventy three dollars
2nd day of Febuary 1841   James Wallace Dr for two bushels of Corn
at fifty Cents per bushel $1.00   five dollars and Seventy five
Cents in Cash $5.75

The Above is a Just and Perfect Inventory of the goods and Chattles
rights and Credits of the said David Wallace decd which has Come to
Our hands Possession or Knowledge or the hand of any person to the best
Our Knowledge and belief this 28th Nov 1841

                                    (James Wallace Jnr
                  Administrator   (Jas .Wallace Snr

(Pg.335)
State of Tennessee)
Anderson County   )   To the Worshipful C ounty Court of
                          December Sessions for 1841

I John Gammon Guardian of Louisa Jane Buttler a Minor Heire of Thomas
Buttler Jr Decd do report to your worships an account Current of the
profits and disbursements of the Estate of the said Minor for the
year ending the 18th August 1841

To Amount which said Guardian is Chargable as Appears
     of record is $ 907.16½
To Interest on that sum for 12 Months   54.42½
whole amt which said Guardian is Chargable $ 961.59

                          Cr
By Amt of Disbursements   To Cash Paid paid for Bridle $ 1.75
To Cash paid for Shoes   1.33 1/3
To Cash Paid for Bonnet   .75
To one yd Bonbasin   1.37½
To one do Ribbon   .6¼
Cr. by sum on last settlement
By Sirvises done for this 1st year   4.00
                                                              9.27½
Ending 18th of August 1841   5.00
                                                             14,27½
Paid the Clerk for this Settlement recording   1.50
                                                           $ 15.77½

Total Amt of debt $ 961.59
Whole amt of Cr.   15.77½
  due the ward $ 945,72½

(Pg.336)
State of Tennessee)
Anderson County)   I William Cross Clk of Anderson County Court
                   do Certify that the Foregoing Settlement was
Made by me with John Gammon Guardian as afore said and it is now Presented
to the Court for Confirmation or rejection
This the   of december 1841
                            Wm Cross   Clk

An Inventory of the Estate of Willie Gilbreath deceased

1	Note on John Russell due Jan 19. 1841	
	Doubtful F	.00
2	One Note on Samuel Current Bank Notes	
	due 20 Nov 1841	14.95
3	One Note on A. Manly and R. Oliver due July 27th	
	1839. Current Bank Notes	11.00
4	One Note on G. McPhearson John Butler	
	Current Bank Notes due July 27. 1839	14.62½
5	One Note on D A Peck	
	due 13tg Sept 1840 Doubtful	5.12½
6	One Note on Wm Scott	
	due June 27th 1840	9.00
7	One Note on J. B. Jones	
	due Feb 28. 1838. witn two Credits one of nine	
	dollars the 12th of Oct 1838 and one the 22nd	
	Sept 1841 for 5 dollars	20.00
8	One Note on R. Oliver due Feb. 24th 1838 with two	
	Credits one for 8 dollars and 25 Cents the	
	1st May 1838 and one five dollars the 23 day of	
	Sept 1839	20.50
		$ 102.20

(Pg.337) Amt brot forward		$ 102.20
9	One Note on R. Oliver	
	due 19th of Aug. 1837	40.00
10	one Note on Wm Scott due June 29th 1839	25.00
11	One Note on James Tilles due 1st Oct 1839 Very Doubtful	35.00
12	One Note on Wm. B. Butler due 19th June 1840	20.00
13	One Note on Squire Justice due first day of Sept	
	1838 with a Cr for 3 dollars No date	12.00
14	One Note on J. R. Gilbreath Due 26 March 1838	4.00
15	One Note on Wm Scott due the 4th Oct 1840	20.77
16	One Note on J. G. Gilbreath due March 26 1838	3.75
17	One Note on John Buttler Due April 16 1840	30.00
18	One Note on D. A. Peak due April 2nd 1839	10.00
19	One Note on Wm Right due Jan 17th 1838	8.37
20	One Note of Wm. G. Gilbreath due 22nd July 1838 with a	
	Dr. for 2 dollars June 1st 1839	5.00

21	One Note on John Butler due 29th July 1839	
	Current Bank Note	20.92
22	One Order on G. A. Gammah 22nd July 1841	3.37½
23	One Account J. J. Foster Doubtful	13.00
24	due Bill on John Taylor Jr.	.93¾
25	One Note on Wm Morris due August 1st 1841	25.80
		369.32¼

(Pg.338)

Amt brot Forward $ 369.32½

An Account of sales Made of the personal property of
the Estate of Miller D. Galbreath decd at this father
residence in Anderson County after having advertised
according to said Samuel G. Galbreath

43 lbs Iron 5½ per Lb.		2.58
John Willson 338 trer Iron 6¾ pr Lb.		24.19
Alexander Galbreath 1 Man Sadle		1.00
Do Do 1 Stallion		200.00
Do Do 1 pr Saddle Wallets		1.50
		608.50¼

The foregoing in a full and perfect account of sale of all the property
of the Estate of Miller D. Gilbreath decd directed by law to be sold
Notes with good Security due 12 Months after date was taken from the
purchases this 6th day of december 1841

                                        John Wilson
                                            Administrator
                                        of Miller D. Gilbreath
                                                Decd

Sworn to in Open Court.

State of Tennessee   )
Anderson County   )   To the worshipful County Court 1841

I. Hardy F. Martin Guardian of Clark Martin a legatee of the Estate
of Samuel Frost decd and a Minor do report to your worship an account
Current of the properties and Disbursements of the Estate of the said
Minor for the year ending 1st Jan 1840

to Amount with said Guardian

(Pg. 339) is Chargable in last Settlement	$ 22.65
Interest on that Sum of Twlve Months	1.35¾
	24.00¼

                    Cr

By Amount of Disbursments	
pd. Taxes for 1841	$ .37½
This Sum pd Clerk for This Settlement	
& recording	1.50
	$ 1.87½

```
whole Amt of Debt                        $  24.00
whole amt of Disbursment                    1.87½
Balance due the ward                       22.13
```

Last Will & Testament of Robt Galbreath decd.

I Robert Galbreath being of Sound Mind do Make and publish this My
last will & Testament hereby Making Void all Other Wills at any time Made
by Me   first I direct that funeral Expenses and all My debts be paid as
soon after My death as possible Out of My Monies that I May die possessed
of or May Come into the hands of Executors   Secondly I give and
bequeath to My Dear and beloved Wife Ann all my real Estate lands and
tenements and hereditament during her Natural life
Thirdly I give and bequeath to her My sorrel Mare and Colt   two Cows and
Three Calves to have
(Pg. 340) To have her Choice fifteen head of Hogs to Make her selection
of Ten head of Sheep and all My farming utensils My yoke of Oxens and
Cart all My house hold & Kitchen furniture at her death when ever it
shal be the will of Divine providances to Call her hence I want the
land sold or Divided as my Heirs May think fit or best To wit
my Son william and Robert and my DaughtersRosanah. Permelia and Zabella.
Fourthly all my goods and Chattles Not bequeathed to be sold at Publisk
sale or divided as the Heirs may Agree upon and the proceeds the from
be divided amongst my Heirs Afore.   lastly I do here by nominate and
Appoint my Son William and my wife Ann. my Executors
in witness where of I do to This My Will set My hand and seal This the
2nd day of Sept 1841

```
   Charles Y. Oliver    )            Robert Galbreath      (seal)
   D. C. McAmis         )
```

```
State of Tennessee       )
   Anderson County       )        To the Worshipful County Court for Anderson
                                  County    December Sessions 1841
```

I William G. Buttler Administrator of the Estate of Henry Buttler decd.
do hereby present to your Worships a Settlement made with the Clerk of
(Pg.   341)   your C ourt on the 18th day of Nov 1841. which Settlement
is in the following words and figures to wit

```
whole Amt. with which said Administrator is Chargeable
          as appears on record                              $  711.19
```

Credits

```
By this sum pd. H. England pr proven ak.                    35.65 1/3
 "  this Sum pd. J. Scarbro pr Note                          2.97¾
 "  this Sum pd. Collins Roberts pr receipt                 24.05½
 "  This Sum pd. Jos Galbreath  receipt                     74.41½
 "  This Sum pd. Jacob M. Buttler pr Note                   49.32
 "  This Sum pd. D. C. McAmis pr receipt                     4.23¼
```

By this Sum pd Roberts & McAmis	$	33.99
" this sum pd Miller D. Gilbreath pr receipt		4.53½
" this Sum pd Collins Roberts pr receipt		63.36½
" this Sum pd Wm Cross pr receipt		15.09
" this Sum pd Hardy F. Marshell pr receipt		10.00
" this Sum pd James Noel as pr Act		1.25
" this Sum pd W C. Griffith as per receipt		2.00
" this Sum pd Js Livley pr receipt		4.67
" this Sum pd John Key pr proven Act		1.50
" this Sum pd A. Kirkpatrick pr Note		25.44
" this Sum pd John England pr prov. Act		1.17½
" this Sum pd Jacob McGhee pr. prov act.		2.25
" this Sum pd Miller D . Galbreath pr receipt		6.45½
" this sum pd Alexander Galbreath pr receipt		25.18½
" this Sum pd Miller D. G albreath		
" this Sum pd Adm John G. Durrett pr receipt		144.01
" this Sum pd Ezra Russell pr receipt		6.21
" this Sum pd. Tho. C. Galaher pr Note		1.53
" this Sum pd. Richard Oliver pr Proven Ack		17.20
(Pg.342)		
" this sum pd Obediah Ashlock pr Note		2.00
" this Sum pd Miller D. Galbreath pr receipt		29.75
" this Sum pd Wm Cross Clk pr receipt		1.75
this Sum pd Wm. Cross Clk pr receipt		2.25
" this Sum pd Richard Oliver pr receipt		3.00
Amt. Vouchers	$	600.49¾

```
     recapitulation
Amt of Debt                              $    711.19
Amt of Credits                                600.49¾
Ballance in the hands of the Administrator  $  110.69¼
```

```
State of Tennessee   )
  Anderson County    )     I Wm Cross  Clerk of the County Court
                           for the County of Anderson do Certify that
the foregoing Settlement was made by me with Wm G. Buttler Adm. of
Henry Buttler decd. this 18th day of Nov. 1841
                              Wm Cross  Clk
                              By his Deputy
                              John Whitson
```

(Pg.343)   In the Name of God Amen.   I. Jacob Weaver Esquire a
Citizen of Anderson County & State of Tennessee Do Make Ordian and
declare this Instrument Subscribed with My Name to be My last will &
Testament. revoking all Others   all my debts which may Justly Owing
at the time of My deceased are to be punctually and Speedily paid
ITEM 1st   to My Daughter Elizabeth Hibbs I give and bequeath the
tract of land on Clinch river where on hir and hir Husband William
Hibbs Now live together with the Other property she has received
ITEM 2nd   to my son William Weaver I give and bequeath the tract of
land he now holds in possession Agreable the lines all ready run and

Marked togather with the propert he has Alread received to him and his
Hiers forever

ITEM 3rd   to My Son James Weaver I give and bequeath to the tract of
land where on she now lives Agreeable to the lines All ready run and
Marked together with the property he has all ready received to him and
his Hiers forever.

ITEM 4th   to My Son Benjamin Weaver I give and bequeath the tract of
land where on he Now lives agreeable to the lines Already run and Marked
together with the property he has Already received to him and his Heirs
forever

ITEM 5th   to My youngest son Lewis Weaver I give and bequeath the tract
of land where on I Now live Where on stands My dwelling House barn
Orchard &C Agreeable to the lines Alread run and Marked together with a
Negro Boy Named Addison   to him & his Hiers forever with the reason here
in after Named.

ITEM 6th   to My Well beloved
(Pg. 344)   wife Hannah Weaver I give and bequeath during hir Natural
life the dwelling house and all the furniture therein the Kitchen and
what is therein including the Negroes togather with hir Choice of One
Horse & three Cows all the Sheep and Hogs and that my said wife is to
hold possession of and have Cultivated as much of the land Out of Lewis
Part as will be Sufficient for hir Support during hir Natural life and
that she is to have the house hold furniture to hir and hir Heirs forever.

ITEM 7th   To my two grand sons Jacob & Henry Piles I give and bequeath
fifty dollars each to be paid at their grand Mothers deceased to them
and thire Heirs forever

ITEM 8th   to my Daughter Jenny Scott I give and bequeath Two hundred
dollars together with what she has received to hir and hir Heirs forever

ITEM 9th   to My youngest Daughter Rebecca Brown. I give and bequeath
One Negro Girl Named Eda togather with what she has all ready received
to hir and hir Heirs forever.

ITEM 10th   to My fore sons Already Named I give and bequeath all the
property which May remain Out of doors and Not Otherwise disposed of
to be equally divided between them at the deceased of My wife.

Lastly I do hereby Nominate and appoint William Weaver and James Weaver
Executors and Hannah Weaver Executor of this My last will and that be
required to give Security   in witness of all and each of
(Pg. 345)   of the things herein Contained I have here set my hand and
seal this Thirteenth day of March in the year of Our Lord 1833
                                     Jacob Weaver   (seal)
Attest
  Ro. Dew
Sloyd Rutherford

A. Codicil   I Jacob Weaver do Make. the following as an Alleration to
My last will Viz   The 5th Item 7th Item and 8th Item I revoke and
forever Make Void and in the time there of do give and bequeath as
follows to My Son Lewis Weaver in full for his Claim on My Estate I
have Paid to said Lewis twlve hundred & fifty dollars in hand as his
receipt dose show to him and his Heirs & in line of 7th Item after the
decease of My Wife I give and bequeath unto Jacob Piles & Henry Piles
Jointly that Part of the tract of land whereon I live which lyes Northwest
of the Creek. Including a Spring in the southeast Bank of said Creek
to them and their Hiers forever   as Above reserved in the line of the
8th Item after the decease of My Wife I give and bequeath to My Daughter

Jane Lett that Part of said home tract lying southeast of the Creek
Including the Mansion House Orchard & Other buildings to hir and hir
Hiers forever
in witness of all and each of the foregoing bequeath I have hereunto set
My hand and seal this 25th of June 1839.

                                        Jacob. Weaver   (seal)

Attest
Ro Dew
Henderson Longmire

(Pg.346)
State of Tennessee)
Anderson County   )   To The worshipful County Court
                            January Sessions 1842.

I Enoch Foster Guardian of the Minor Heirs of Richard Luallen deceased
do hereby report to your Worship an Account Current of the profits and
Disbursments of said Estate from the first Monday in december 1840 Up
to the 1st December 1841.

To Amount which said Guardian is Chargeable
        on the last Settlement $ 1268.18½
To Interest on that Sum 12 Months   76.09
To tnis Sum received on sales of land sold by
        the Clerk and Master with Interest   572.94
                    Cr $ 1917.21½

        By amount of disbursments
Paid Nancy Luallen as pr receipt   68,22
Paid To I R oss
Amount for Merchandise   5.22
Paid Amount to I. Ross for Merchandise
as pr receipt for Nancy Luallen   62.18
Paid J. H. Crozier Attorney as pr receipt   20.00
Paid A. G. Luallen as pr receipt   238.31
Paid Charles Luallen Admrs &c. as pr recpt   66.83
Paid Clerk for this Settlement   1.50
By this Sum Allowed Guardian for his Services 1 year   13.00
                                                     $ 475.21

whole amount of debt   1917.21½
whole amt Vouchers   475.26
Balance due the Wards $ 1441.95

I Enoch Foster Guardian &c do Certify that the foregoing report by
me Made
(Pg.347)   Is Just and true   This 11th December 1841.
                                        Enoch Foster

State Tennessee   )
 Anderson County   )   I William Cross Clerk of Anderson County do
                            Certify the foregoing Settlement was Made by Me
with Enoch Foster Guardian as aforesaid which Settlement is Presented
to the Court for Confirmation or rejection   This 11th day of december
1841.
                              Wm. Cross Clk.

recorded this 5th January 1842.

                              Wm. Cross Clk
                              By Deputy C. Y. Oliver

The Amount of Sale & Property Specifically as Sold of the Estate of
Robert G albreath deceased & Assets so fare as Come to Our Knowlidge
which are as follows (to wit)

Samuel Tinnell	red Cow	3.25
Richard Oliver	red Stear	3.25
Do Do	Black C ow	5.99½
S am Tunnell	red Heifer Calf	1.00
Do Do	4 Choice Sheep	3.00
Do D o	3 Sheep	1.50
Robert A. Galbreath	Sow & Pigs	2.00
George Galbreath	Do Do	2.00
Robert Oliver	1 blue Sow	1.26
Robert A. McKamey	1 Sorrel Filly	20.75
		$ 44.01½

ANDERSON COUNTY

WILLS AND SETTLEMENTS

1830 - 1842

INDEX

NOTE: Page numbers in this index refer to those of the original
volume from which this copy is made. These numbers are carried
throughout the copy within parenthese.
Index made by Rebecca Colyer, Russellsville, Tenn. Sept. 1937.